CHRISTIANS ACTIVE IN THE WORLD

Yves Congar OP

CHRISTIANS ACTIVE IN THE WORLD

Translated by P. J. Hepburne-Scott

HERDER AND HERDER

1968
HERDER AND HERDER NEW YORK
232 Madison Avenue, New York 10016

Original edition:
Sacerdoce et Laïcat, second half,
Paris, Les Editions du Cerf.

Nihil obstat: John M. T. Barton S.T.D., L.S.S., censor. Imprimatur: ✠ Patrick Casey, Vic. Gen. Westminster, 28th November 1966.

Library of Congress Catalog Card Number: 67-14142

Printed in the United States

CONTENTS

CONTENTS

ABBREVIATIONS

AAS	*Acta Apostolicae Sedis* (Rome, from 1909)
CIC	Codex Iuris Canonici (1918)
CSEL	*Corpus Scriptorum Ecclesiasticorum Latinorum* (Vienna, from 1866)
DACL	*Dictionnaire d'Archéologie chrétienne et de Liturgie*, ed. Cabrol and Leclercq (15 vols., 1907–53)
Denz. Bann.	H. Denziger, *Enchiridion Symbolorum et Definitionum*, etc., 28th edition, after that of C. Bannwart and others, Freiburg, 1952
Dict. Bibl.	*Dictionnaire de la Bible*, ed. Vigouroux (5 vols., 1895–1912)
Dict. Sp.	*Dictionnaire de Spiritualité*, ed. M. Villier and others (from 1937)
DTC	*Dictionnaire de Théologie Catholique*, ed. Vacant, Mangenot and Amann (15 vols., 1903–50)
Doc. cath.	*La Documentation catholique*, Paris
EC	*Enciclopedia Cattolica* (12 vols., 1949–54)
EL	*Ephemerides Liturgicae* (Rome, from 1887)
JTS	*Journal of Theological Studies*
Lay People	Congar, *Lay People in the Church*, London and Westminster, Md., 1957, translated by Donald Attwater
L. Th. K.	*Lexikon für Theologie und Kirche*, ed. Burchberger, (10 vols., 1930–38)
Mansi	J. D. Mansi, *Sacrorum Conciliorum Nova et Amplissima Collectio* (31 vols., Florence, 1759–98)
NRT	*Nouvelle Revue Théologique*
PG	*Patrologia Graeca*, ed. J. P. Migne (162 vols., Paris, 1857–66)
PL	*Patrologia Latina*, *ibid.* (221 vols., 1844–64)
QLP	*Questions Liturgiques et Paroissiales* (Louvain)
Rech. S.R.	*Recherches de Science Religieuse* (Paris, from 1911)

R. Bibl.	*Revue Biblique* (Paris, from 1892)
RHPR	*Revue d'Histoire et de Philosophie religieuses* (Paris, from 1950)
RSPT	*Revue des Sciences Philosophiques et Théologiques* (Paris, from 1953)
Rev. S.R.	*Revue des Sciences Religieuses* (Strasbourg, from 1925)
RTP	*Revue Théologique et Philosophique*
Sum. Theol.	St Thomas Aquinas, *Summa Theologica*
TWB z. NT	*Theologisches Wörterbuch zum Neuen Testament* (ed. Kittel from 1933)
Vie Int.	*La Vie Intellectuelle*
Vie Sp.	*La Vie Spirituelle*
ZKT	*Zeitschrift für katholische Theologie* (Vienna, from 1947)

CHRISTIANS ACTIVE IN THE WORLD

CHAPTER ONE

Respect for the Apostolate of of the Laity among Priests and Religious[1]

THE OBJECT OF THESE PAGES IS NOT TO STUDY the many, immediately practical problems of a genuine lay apostolate, but to illuminate these problems as a whole by considering them more radically, in the light of theology and history. History will not here be traced for its own sake, but invoked because it is indispensable in helping us to a correct diagnosis of the present situation. That is true for our first step, which consists in enquiring *how, in what context, and therefore why, initiative on the part of the laity has sometimes been neglected and even unknown.*

It was not so in the first centuries of Christianity, including not only those marked by the constant threat of persecutions, but those which immediately followed the peace of Constantine, which are those of the Fathers and the great councils (fourth and fifth centuries). There were warnings, certainly, to respect order, like that of Gregory of Nazianzus: 'Sheep, do not tend your shepherds, do not judge your judges, do not make laws for your lawmakers;'[2] or that of Pope Celestine: 'The people must be taught, not followed.'[3] But only very exceptionally could one then find derogatory terms or statements of the kind we shall quote from the next period.

The fact was that early Christianity lived, and knew that it lived, in a world which had all its weight and toughness as an earthly world. That world was opposed to it, sometimes with great violence. But even when it had become officially favourable, that world possessed, by its culture inherited from the pagan era, by its political and juridical organisation, by its traditions and prestige, a solidity and visibility which did not allow it to be unaware of Christianity as an equal, and so as a rival, even when it had become an ally. While living in that world, the Christians stood, as it were confronting it: Christianity appeared to them as *something else*, as a life connected with another kingdom, one that is eschatological. Under these conditions clergy and laity, despite the strongly marked inequality of their positions, were more readily aware that they formed the people of God, on the march to its true country, the goal of its pilgrimage.

From the patristic age, however, we find a tendency to express the opposition between the two worlds on the moral level and in terms of ascetic life, as a difference in the quality of Christian life. The historical consideration of a present and a future world certainly did not disappear; but another notion was often superimposed upon it, that of two moral worlds co-existing in this life: a world from above and a world from below, regarded as a world of the spirit and a world of the senses, in a climate of thought where a platonic view of things was not unfamiliar. It contained the germ of a certain depreciation of the earthly life, a germ which was developed in later ages, so steeped in the monastic spirit.

Yet another cause of the depreciation of the laity began to appear in the classical age of the Fathers. Since the conversion of Constantine, the Church had enjoyed the favour of authority. This favour took the form, among others, of granting privileges to the clergy: bishops, priests and monks obtained important immunities.[4] A whole series of enactments resulted in distinguishing the priests from the laity, by the type of life (celibacy),[5] the wearing of a special dress copied from the monks (latter part of the fifth century),[6] and so on. The clergy thus stood aloof from the ordinary Christians, whose life was considered more carnal.

Another process was soon to operate in the same direction, perhaps even more strongly: the general lowering of culture, the disappearance, total or partial, of schools in the West, subject to the barbarian invasions. The Church, as the only institution to keep its place, vested with the prestige of religion and of Rome, became the sphere where learning and the knowledge of letters survived. Culture became a sort of monopoly of the clergy and the monks. From the late Middle Ages down to the Renaissance, *litteratus* ('one who knows letters', that is, Latin), was synonymous with 'cleric', whereas the synonym for 'layman' was *illiteratus* or *idiota* (a simple person, one who cannot explain things).[7]

It is not surprising, therefore, to find in the Middle Ages certain signs of what might well be a depreciation of the laity and of their ability to carry out the Church's tasks, signs which have their full meaning in the circumstances we have just mentioned. There is, for example, the distinction between *majores* and *minores*, that is, between those who by their state had more powers and responsibilities and those who had less: the people of above and the people of below (without, in the case of the latter, any pre-Marxist consciousness of frustration).[8] This distinction (while justifiable on practical grounds in the existing conditions of education) tended to give the laity a state of inferiority or tutelage, sometimes accompanied with some contempt and even mistrust with regard to their capacities. The absurd philology which derived *laicus* from *lapis*, on the ground that the laity had minds as hard as stone, did not meet with much success,[9] but innumerable were the texts which likened the laity to the obscure or mean term, in comparisons where the glorious or noble term was applied to the clergy. The clergy were the day, the laity the night;[10] the clergy were the heavens, the laity the earth, or again, the soul and the body respectively;[11] the clergy were like angels or gods, the laity like beasts of burden, *jumenta*,[12] *laicorum genus bestiale*.[13] Texts were quoted from Scripture, such as Job 1:14: 'the oxen were ploughing, and the asses feeding beside them,' the *asinae* were the *simplices*, the laity. . . .[14] Or Num 22:22: 'Balaam was riding on his ass': Balaam represents the clergy and his ass the laity.[15] Or Deut 22:10: 'You shall not plough with an ox and an ass together:' this text was sometimes applied to laity and clergy, who should not be put to work together.[16] It is true that this was on the subject of definite judicial functions, but the quotation, in connection with others, is still characteristic, especially when compared with the formulas of today, strongly favouring the association of ox and ass,—if that is what they are. It is also true that in the atmosphere of the ideal of organic unity which inspired the Middle Ages, all these comparisons did not have the scornful and insulting sense they would have today: they then signified participation in one whole rather than opposition.[17] Nonetheless they stand as a proof that the laity were allotted a place of minority.

This is all the more true since these comparisons belong to a whole context of ideas and values, from which we can only select the most important for our subject: a scale of values of very monastic inspiration: a strictly gradated society: a clergy amply endowed with generally recognised privileges: a society subject, or meaning to be subject, to 'Holy Church', that is, to the priesthood; and finally, in harmony with all this, a priesthood or 'Holy Church' regarding itself very largely as *authority*.

In a Christian society, all of which has become the Church, there is no longer true tension between a Church purely the Church and a world truly the world. Tensions exist, of course: they are everywhere, but they are to do with the interior of the Church. From the end of the eighth century till the time of Gregory VII, the name *ecclesia* was regularly given, in the West, to the whole Christian society, which was both temporal and spiritual, almost without distinction. Even after the Gregorian reaction, which was aimed at escaping from this confusion, the whole Cistercian current of thought, and many authors of more or less theocratic tendency, accepted the identity of the Church and Christian society, in their theory of a Church composed of different *ordines*. Then the tensions were transferred to the interior of this *ecclesia*-cum-Christian society. There was the tension between the clerics and laymen, culminating in the incredible statement of Boniface VIII, calmly announced as if it were self-evident: 'That the laity have always been extremely hostile to the clergy is what we learn from antiquity, and what the experience of the present time makes abundantly evident. . . .'[18] Then there was the tension between the power of the kings and the authority of the priests, between the secular and regular clergy, even between different Orders among the regulars. These tensions fill the whole history of the Middle Ages, each one representing a paragraph in the chapter of each century's history.

The condition of the laity was to change with the birth of the modern world, of a world, that is, which was really a world, and therefore lay. Up to then, ever since the conversion of the princes, who had inaugurated and founded the régime of Christendom, the princes had been practically the only laymen to be active in the Church's service. They were trained to piety in order that they might make laws in accordance with the demands of religion, and in this way a world was maintained in existence which was subject to the commandments of the faith and the directions of the priesthood, or rather, for high and low alike, to its authority. But when the age of criticism began, that is, when men seized their independence in the various fields of politics, science, reflection and research, judgement and criticism, the organisation of life and, in short, of the City, a real world was found—or refound—outside the Church and face to face with her. Laymen rose up to take their part in the Church's fight, in the various fields where it was waged. There were lay missionaries, like M. de Renty († 1649), lay apologists, like Pascal. This new phenomenon greatly increased in extent when the nineteenth century, following on the French Revolution and its aftermath, so steeped in the spirit of the eighteenth, brought the Church face to face with a world which was vigorously independent and enterprising, profoundly alien and hostile to the Church's traditional positions. Then lay people were seen to engage in the defence and apologetical exposition of the faith (Chateaubriand, Joseph de Maistre, Goerres, Donoso Cortès, Auguste Nicolas . . .), in political action for the cause of religion (Daniel O'Connell, Montalembert, Windthorst, Lueger, A. de Mun), in influencing public opinion through the press (Baron d'Eckstein, Louis Veuillot), in charitable and missionary work (Ozanam, Pauline Jaricot, etc.).

Hostile reactions were not lacking. Most of those I have named had to overcome bitter criticism from the clergy, springing from old habits which some, perhaps, took for Tradition. I have quoted a certain number elsewhere,[19] but I may recall two or three. There was the archbishop of Rouen, criticising the action of Montalembert, (who was defended and praised, however, by Mgr Parisis, Bishop of Langres): 'The best thing they can do is to pray!' Or Mgr Talbot, writing in a letter of 25th April 1867: 'What is the province of the laity? To hunt, to shoot, to entertain! These matters they understand, but to meddle with ecclesiastical matters they have no right at all.' He was reacting against Newman, who thought quite differently about the laity, and wrote soon after this: 'As far as I can see, there are ecclesiastics all over Europe, whose policy is to keep the laity at a distance, with the result that the laity are disgusted and have lost the faith.'[20] But even Cardinal Wiseman, who cannot be compared with the rather mediocre Talbot, had written on the subject of the staff of *The Rambler*, that he 'could not agree to laymen taking the initiative in questions concerning the defence of the Church: their true place', he thought, 'was in politics, business, the army or the navy, science or the arts'.[21]

Such reactions may now be seen as ancient history. The declarations of popes, bishops, pastors and theologians, calling on the laity to take their part in the Church's work, and not only on the temporal side are so numerous, so emphatic and so fresh in men's minds that there is no need to quote any. Confirmed by so many facts, they have removed all the force from Loisy's words in 1908, when he spoke of 'a Church for whose progress the laity have no right to work'.[22]

What has happened? Quite simply, that there is now a world—and what a world!—which is truly a world, *and that we know it*. For it is not enough for a world to exist: we must know it as such and reckon with it. It could easily be shown that even today, wherever the Church is not faced with such a world, or does not realise that she is, traces are still to be found of those internal tensions, sometimes both futile and petty, which were so evident in the ages of faith. The lesson of history, some episodes of which we have just recalled, is very clear. It will dominate all that we have to say here. History shows that the apostolate of the laity is only taken seriously when a real 'world' exists to confront the Church, and the Church is aware of it. Then the tension is felt for what it is, a tension between the Church, seed and sacrament of the kingdom of God, and the world. In those conditions priests and laity feel themselves to be called and yoked to the same task: the laity are no longer mere passengers in a ship navigated by the clergy alone: they are, in their own place, part of the ship's company.

But even today there is still to be found among certain clerics something of the mistrust, low opinion or reserve which was often shown by their seniors towards the initiatives or activities of the laity. The laity, at least, feel it to be so and complain of it. They say they feel that they are not taken seriously when they take part in certain Church matters or merely give their opinions about them. I have received several proofs of this feeling, and I venture to reproduce two of them, at least in their essentials. The first comes from a married couple, both teachers, who had undertaken some Christian action, primarily liturgical, in the framework of the parish, and had interviewed the bishop about the problems facing them:

> This interview, like others with other bishops, was both comforting and disappointing. The bishop heard us with much attention and kindness, but would only refer us to the authority of the Church. 'The bishop has not to invent the liturgy but only to receive it himself from the Church (. . .). My pastoral letter about the school simply repeats the papal teaching!' But we did not have the impression that he recognised the existence of any problem. Our real trouble was certainly the impression that the questions which were important for us seemed so secondary to the bishop that he did not even have to tell us in what respect they were so (. . .). Each time, we came away comforted by the paternal attitude of the bishop and the cardinal, but disappointed that we had been treated like children who had not reached the age of reason: 'the bishop has everything to give, nothing to receive'.

This document clearly shows what it is that prevents the two points of view from coinciding: the laity do not always allow for what they are challenging on the side of tradition, while the priests do not always see the urgency of what is at stake in the way of needs and problems. They have charge of a larger whole and have to preserve its difficult balance. Now we turn to the evidence of a layman who has long been engaged in international Catholic affairs and is always in the thick of the movement of Church life:

> I have very rarely met ecclesiastics who 'played ball' with the laity. They declare that they expect things from them, but in fact they expect practically nothing, or else they expect them to deputise or supply services. Electing a responsible office-holder for a movement, at whatever level it may be, often means meekly voting for someone who has already been ap-

pointed. How can one escape the impression of a farce? The result is known in advance. A layman is always more or less a subordinate agent, or else a 'good boy' . . . How often have I heard priests or bishops speak of 'our laymen'. The higher one goes in the scale of ecclesiastical duties, the stronger grows the impression that *in practice* the laity hardly count. The latest illustration of this is surely the preparation for the Council, typically clerical. Behind the most sympathetic declarations, and in spite of remarkable (and remarked) exceptions, an unconscious clericalism is widespread, the product not so much of bad intentions as of bad customs.

The illustration he quotes is perfectly true. Lay people sent suggestions to the 'Commission on the Laity', but they were not represented on it. A layman sat on the 'Commission on Seminary Studies', but he is a member of a secular institute, which means that anthropologically speaking he is not a real layman. It is true that laymen were not invited to take a real part in the preparation for the Second Vatican Council. They have often been told that the whole Church, including them, must put herself in a 'state of council'. But how? Is it, as the Archbishop of Rouen said, speaking of Montalembert, by praying? Certainly, and that is no small thing. But what else? It is true that tradition has never granted the laity a place as deliberating members in the actual Councils. The laity, in so far as they assisted at the Councils, played their part by advice, witness, consent and publication of the conclusions adopted.[23] But before the Council there was its preparation: that was the work of the professionals and experts, most of whom were not bishops. There was nothing to prevent laymen having a place among these experts, at least in the capacity of consultors. Now practically nothing of this sort happened: once again, the exception only serves to prove the rule. Is not this, again, a sign of the existence in many churchmen of certain attitudes or views, which imply an inadequate appreciation of the action of the laity? Attitudes of caste, *esprit de corps*, habits of wielding a sacred authority.

Let us admit that this has in fact been the case. We shall try to analyse the reasons or find out the roots of this deficiency. Even if it has not been general, we must admit that it exists here or there, and that it represents a danger. Our analysis will at least hold good for those cases. In any case, it will enable us, by a simple and easy transposition from the negative to the positive, or from criticism to a programme of the ideal, to form an idea of the conditions in which respect for the apostolate of the laity may become a fact among priests and religious.

I believe we can discover, at the root of all depreciation of the laity, a deficiency in ecclesiology and a deficiency in anthropology.

An Ecclesiological and Pastoral Deficiency

This is bound up with our admirable and holy Catholic objectivity: the most insidious temptations are not the common, blatant ones, but those that are noble and concealed. Now with us, belief is guaranteed in objectively defined dogma, in the infallible statements of the catechism, the encyclicals, our manuals, our Denzigers. The conduct to be followed in almost any circumstances is determined in a whole system of jurisprudence and casuistry: we have only to consult a good author or *L'Ami du Clergé*. Worship is regulated by precise rites and rubrics: the prayer I am obliged to offer is ruled by an *ordo* printed eighteen months in advance: the administration of the sacraments is prescribed and defined, not only in its liturgical and ritual aspect but as a pastoral action, which derives in turn from a known system of casuistry and jurisprudence.

The grandeur of all this is the objectivity of the order of salvation and the structures of the covenant: it is not for me to make them, I have simply to enter into them, somewhat as in the Scriptures I am invited to 'enter into' the kingdom. They are indeed the means, offered to me, of sharing in a redemption and a unity of holy life. The fundamental meaning of that objectivity, like the meaning of that often wrongly interpreted principle, *ex opere operato*, depends on the absolute primacy of the *action of Christ*, who is, of course, sovereign and free, but has freely bound himself to certain essential structures of the Covenant, which are also those of the Church: dogma, sacraments, decisive acts of the apostolic ministries. . . . It is what Augustine so magnificently vindicated against the Donatists. This Catholic objectivity of faith, ministries and worship is the source of a great and joyful freedom, for instead of being enslaved by the necessity of undergoing the human effort of creation in doctrine or liturgy, I can unite myself very freely and flexibly to what is there, offered and given from the beginning, as a spiritual home awaiting me. Yes, in that Catholic objectivity there is all the assurance of a home.

But there is a great and by no means imaginary danger that the assurance of the system may let us out of performing, in all this, a spiritual, personal act. We run the risk of treating the faith and worship, and even the ministerial acts for which the faithful resort to us, as ready-made 'things', of which we are hardly more than mechanical transmitters. We risk seeking to maintain a ready-made system, not committing ourselves by a spiritual, personal act. Many priests, especially those who were trained before the last world war, have got into a deeply-engrained habit of serving in the first place 'the Church', her greatness, her influence, her prestige. In all good faith on their part, this sometimes obscures in their eyes the primacy of persons. They come to see 'the Church' herself as the first thing to be served, instead of as the constant recipient from God of all she needs for the service of men. And so they handle 'things', which are self-contained and dispense them from looking for the event of a personal encounter with God, with Christ, with the gospel and its claims, with grace, with prayer.

It is God who brings about that event, or rather, the event is simply his coming. So it is free, and can be brought about even through the 'things'. In itself, however, the event belongs to the order of personal relations. Inasmuch as it falls to us to prepare its ways[24] it requires an intense effort from us, to ensure that each of our pastoral acts, whether in the conduct of worship, or preaching, or the various relations with men as priests of the Gospel, may represent so many real *spiritual acts*. By 'spiritual act' I mean an act in which I commit myself laboriously, as a spiritual man, offering myself for the action which the Holy Spirit is carrying out, perhaps through me, for the good of other men, and which is the right one for encountering them, challenging them, in the sight of God, in the name of the gospel. This presumes that I commit myself as a religious man, living by the grace of God and under the call of the Gospel.

Reading St Paul one is struck by the number of times when he intervenes, quite explicitly, not as using his authority, but as a spiritual man. He might appeal to his authority; he knows it and says so, and sometimes, in fact, he orders or prescribes.[25] But most frequently, and in the same matters, he appeals to his experience, to his grace.[26] He prefers to appeal to the gifts he has received, rather than to his authority, as he shows in his earliest epistle.[27]

Do we priests often speak like that? Yet we find similar language in the Christianity before Christendom. Here, for instance, is Pseudo-Barnabas: 'For my part, it is not as a teacher, it is as one of yourselves, that I offer you some small counsels which can give you joy in your present circumstances.'[28] 'I beseech you once again, I who am one of you, and love you all with a special love, more than my life.'[29]

From the point of view of ecclesiology, what demands such an attitude is the experienced conviction, formulated by an age-old tradition, that it is not the walls, but the faithful, that make the Church;[30] not a system, but men touched by Christ and engaged in personal encounter with the God of the gospel. If our pastoral work is directed in practice (whatever our intentions may be) to the application, the service and the reinforcement of a ready-made system, the faithful can only be treated as objects or 'patients' of our action, or as material for the power of the Church. If our pastoral work aims at producing real spiritual acts, and ensuring that something really happens spiritually, then the faithful are personally involved, and called to commit themselves; they can *do* something with us: not only when they are the beneficiaries of our ministry, but as members of the ship's company, jointly responsible with us for the voyage, co-operating in the whole pastoral work, for which the priest, under the authority of the bishop, is obviously the one chiefly responsible and the leader, or, to keep to our metaphor, the ship's captain.

It is only on the basis of an ecclesiology which is spiritual, not thing-centred (*chosiste*), and a concept of the Church as made of the faithful, not of walls, that we can understand and restore the patristic idea of spiritual motherhood as the function of the whole Church. The texts of the Fathers on this subject are extraordinarily numerous and forcible.[31] To them we must add the witness of the liturgy: we can never comprehend Lent as the liturgy understands it unless we see the work of conversion, which is its aim, as the undertaking of the whole *ecclesia*. In the eyes of the Fathers and the liturgy, as soon as a Christian has been engendered by faith and grace, he engenders others in his turn: and not only by his witness but by his whole Christian life, which is prayer, penitence and charity. Once again, it is a matter of administering 'things', the priest is adequate and he can do it alone: he is, alas, the 'medicine-man'. But if it is a matter of engendering souls to Christ, leading them to God, helping to produce a personal encounter with him, then the laity exercise that spiritual motherhood personally, and the whole Christian community exercises it collectively. The rôle of the priest is, then, to 'organise the saints (all the faithful) for the work of the ministry'.[32]

There is a very simple, infallible way to find, in practice, the true attitude. It is connected with the concept of the Church as made chiefly of Christians, for it follows from that, that Christianity has precedence in the Church over whatever is simply system or 'things'. Augustine constantly repeated to his flock, in this form or some other, *Vobis sum episcopus, vobiscum Christius*: 'For you I am a bishop, (but first of all) I am a Christian with you.'[33] Or again, disciple with you, servant with you,[34] sinner with you, beating my breast with you. . . .[35] In the Liturgy of St John Chrysostom the priest often places himself as it were with the faithful, praying as one of them to receive grace and asking to be forgiven for his unworthiness. Often, even in the Middle Ages, the priest, conscious of his own defects, asked the faithful, before beginning his sermon, to pray for him and with him by reciting the Lord's Prayer, for example.[36] The feeling expressed in all this is one which was developed in the French spirituality of the seventeenth century, by those wonderful educators of the priestly spirit, Condren and Olier whose thought was borrowed and adapted by Abbé Huvelin.[37]

A Deficiency of Anthropology

And so with cosmology: if priests have too little faith in the laity, it is no doubt because they have too little faith in man; at least those, once again, who had their training before the last war. Let us get this clear: it is not a matter of substituting faith in man for faith in God: there must be a high esteem of man and man's work, an esteem whose deepest foundation, I am convinced, is precisely a true theology, that is, a fully scriptural knowledge of the living God, for 'the Bible is not a theology for man, but an anthropology for God'.[38] Say, rather, that it is both, or better still, that it is the unity of both.

There are many lay people who accuse us of not having enough faith in man. We often give them the impression that we are carrying out a rôle, a programme of obligations, rather than being at their service, to help them practise, in their actual life, that anthropology for God of which we spoke.[39] It would be very interesting to make a critical study of the anthropology professed and the anthropology implicit in the documents of the teaching authority, and even in the more or less classic authors used in the training of the clergy and the religious orders since the Council of Trent. This study has just been briefly outlined for religious, at least for those of the American teaching congregations, by Justus George Lawlor.[40] He has inquired what, exactly, are the roots of what we here call a deficiency of anthropology, and which we could also call a deficiency of humanism (provided we do not confine ourselves to the literary connotation of the word), in the education given by so many religious. He believes these roots are to be found in the spirituality of the great French writers of the seventeenth century, who placed all their emphasis on the nothingness of man and his abasement before the majesty of God, with the consequence, for every serious Christian, of an attitude of opposition to the world, and a pessimistic judgement on the world, without sufficient distinction between the world as the domain of the evil one, and the world as cosmos.[41]

It is true that the bible, and all other Christian tradition, contrast the 'All' of God with the nothingness of man. But there is more than one way of conceiving and practising the contrast. The biblical way is wholly theological and theonomic: it does not involve any depreciation of man, who, being placed in a relation of faith to God, is invited, on the contrary, to action in the world. His 'anthropology for God' implies that. The way of the 'religion' followed, as I see it, by the classics of the period after 1660, is not the way of 'Faith': it has not that dynamism, it stops short at the presentation of the pure nothingness of man before the majesty of God. And that 'majesty' of God is itself something other than the Absolute of the Living God, of the 'who is, and who was, and who is to come'.[42] The 'Religion' certainly has its theological and theocentric grandeur, which we can measure in a man like Berulle. But it led to what Péguy calls the party of the *dévots*, which he characterises, not by an excess of the theological, but by a lack of humanism.

> In order to rise into the category of grace it is not enough to abase nature . . . Because they have not the strength (and the grace) to belong to nature, they think they belong to grace. Because they have not the courage of this world, they think they have begun to penetrate the eternal. Because they have not the courage to belong to this world, they think they belong to God. Because they have not the courage to belong to one of the parties of men, they think they belong to God's party. Because they do not belong to man, they think they belong to God. Because they love no one, they think they love God.[43]

Certain priests, again among those who were trained before the last world war, practically never get near the sort of men who are fully engaged in the stern competition of the world. They would rather avoid them. They are in contact with some men and women (and children, of course) who belong in some degree to the world of the devout: much religion, not much man. The devout world makes a sort of halo round them which isolates them from the real world of men. They run the risk of never meeting any but people of their own religious world, people like themselves: whereas the real world is very different, very separate from our world, and is becoming increasingly so. In fact our pastoral ministry is very largely one of like to like. In a country like France, at least, where *up till now* practically all the children have been baptised, been through the catechism and even made their first (often last!) communion, our pastoral ministry has been largely a ministry of recovery, if only *in extremis*, of those who had belonged and still virtually belong to our religious world. A ministry of like to like.

But the world becomes more and more apart and even foreign. It was the realisation of this fact that impelled Cardinal Suhard to write in his *Carnets*, during the war: 'I observe a fact: that our population as a whole no longer think themselves Christian: between them and the Christian community there is a gulf fixed, which means that in order to reach them we must *go out from our own ground and enter theirs. That is the real problem.* So far our efforts have been almost without result: even our ordinary Catholic Action admits it is helpless: it is an action of Catholic milieux, Catholic at least in belief, it is not Catholic action on pagan milieux.' It is clear that this statement of the facts commits us to a pastoral ministry of full witness to the faith in a world which we confront with no safety margin, as one confronts the open sea.[44] Clearly, in this pastoral situation, the relation between priest and lay people can only be one of full collaboration, of apostolic and missionary action in common. But it also presupposes that the clergy have convictions about man and the world, anthropology and cosmology, which flow from a scriptural faith in the living God!

This collaboration between priests and laity has often been described by the names of 'team' (or 'crew')[45] or even 'the priesthood-laity *couple*'.[46] I like this expression for its mental associations, and also for its accuracy. The couple is both a community and a hierarchy, a friendship and a legal structure, a diversity and a mutual completion. It is on this last aspect that we should like to dwell for a moment, to show in positive fashion the advantages and fruits which the activity of the laity contribute to the Church's apostolate.

That the action of the laity is complementary to that of the clergy is verified in several ways. Here we shall consider three: the object, the mode of action, and the human quality.

1. *The Object.* There is only one mission of the Church, entrusted to the whole *ecclesia*, priests and faithful, to each one according to what he is and the place he occupies. This mission includes a primary object, to make disciples of all nations, and a second, which is to teach them to keep the commandments of Christ, not only in each man's personal life but also in the life of society as such, which must strive to order itself according to God and towards God. The first task is one of evangelism, of pure witness to the faith and charity of Christ; it aims at converting men to the Gospel. The second is to influence the temporal sphere, that is, all the work of the earthly city of men, so that it may be as little unfavourable as possible, and even as favourable

as possible, as fully conformed as possible, to the order of God and the Christian life.

The faithful are responsible, on their level, for evangelisation and witness, and they exercise it no less effectively than the priests. But strictly speaking, the clergy (here including the religious sisters) could be sufficient to cope with the task, if not entirely, at least in its essentials.

In their own sphere, the priests have the task of influencing the temporal. They perform it, as it is right that they should, by proclaiming its necessity, by teaching a doctrine about it, by forming consciences and by giving spiritual support to men engaged in temporal work. But normally the clergy themselves have not formally temporal responsibilities: they are not even in a position to have direct responsibilities, apart from those which fall on even the least qualified citizens. Normally the cleric cannot accept a political mandate nor practise a profession which counts in the national economy. Even scientific speculation, in the field of the secular sciences or techniques, can only be for him an exception, justified by considerations of the common good (of the Church, more often than of society). The priest, then, is not inside that temporal sphere which he has to guide according to God and towards God. Who can do that, on the plane of effective action, if not the Christian layman, the real mediator between God and the world? He belongs to both worlds. It is by him and in him that they effectively touch each other. It is therefore by him and in him that this part of the Church's mission is effectively carried out, and in such a way that *without him it would not be* carried out. The speech of Pius XII has often been quoted, in which he said that the laity not only belong to the Church, but *are* the Church, inasmuch as she must be, for the sake of the Kingdom of God and by a process of influence, the soul of human society.

2. *The Kind of Action.* Many problems can be clarified when we bear in mind the fact that the Church, before having a mission in and for the world, is, in view of that mission, a certain order of realities apart. This is true dogmatically. It is also true juridically, sociologically, and even, up to a point, economically. As an order apart in the world, the institution called the 'Church' is upheld and represented chiefly by the clergy. Embodied in a

particular group of men, she becomes a reality apart, both on the anthropological and on the cultural level, in actions, habits and attitudes, in an *ethos* and even in a particular language.

Whatever we may do, all our apostolic action is marked by the specific character of the Church as a sacred reality apart. Everything done in our churches, in Catholic activities, under the direct control of the clergy, bears this mark, which is both venerable and slightly repellent. Everything touched by the priests tends to be drawn into that particular world of the Church, into which many men never enter and where—perhaps even more serious—a certain type of man will never be at home.

The laity do not carry out the Church's activity, as the priests do, by the *public* methods and in the public frameworks of the Church herself; liturgy, preaching, etc. They do this sometimes in some Church works, and thereby run the risk of being drawn into the sociological and anthropological world of the clergy (see what I said before about the halo of clericalised women which forms around priests). But for their proper field of action they have the immense domain of the natural structures of the world or society: the framework of family life, cultural and leisure activities, social relationships undertaken on the plane of human life and in the ordinary vocabulary of men, etc. Their Christian witness and influence follow, in a way, the design of men's life. This gives their action a character which is 'private' (ecclesiologically speaking), even when, by fame, talent or popularity, it is widely publicised. One thinks of the great literary and philosophical works of men like Etienne Gilson and Jacques Maritain. To employ a distinction we used lately, which may claim the authority of Aquinas,[47] their activity is then Christian not *ex officio*, but *ex spiritu*.

There is a kind of action of outstanding value, which characterises the apostolic action of the laity; the action of witness in the actual categories and the actual speech of men, action by influence, with no pretence to authority. Whatever is thus expressed and becomes part of the human truth and familiar background of the natural human structures, which are distinguished only by their greater human authenticity, has unrivalled efficacy and importance for men. The Catechism taught by the mother of a family in her own language, in the familiar setting of her home, has an unequalled value, all the more that it is not her 'job' (*ex officio*): if she does it, it is because she believes in it (*ex spiritu*).

3. *The Human Quality*. This already follows from what has been said: the quality of the Christian action of the laity is bound up with the mode of that action: but there is ground for developing a particular aspect of it. By giving their Christianity its full *human* quality, the laity give it the fullness of its *truth*. This strikes me most clearly as it concerns the training of children and the problems of adults.

As to the children, the laity's action is the condition of the efficacy of our own. We priests have all experienced it: our catechism, our instruction on the use of the sacraments, and even on prayer, have serious results only where they find roots, and those roots are planted not by us but by the family. Where there is no Christian family, our efforts are nearly always stillborn: where there is one, they have a future. In short, it is not we who make Christians, it is the parents. We seldom achieve much by working on the children: we achieve everything almost certainly when we work on the parents.

And for the adults, they have their problems in life. But we disappoint them whenever we offer them a solution drawn from our theological and moral bookcase. On the other hand, when we first listen to them, when we talk with them, above all when we try, in a fraternal group, to seek with them the attitude or the answer called for by the facts, then we feel we are reaching a fullness, a genuineness, a truth, compared with which the ready-made products of our bookcase seem so shabby that we nearly begin to doubt whether the bookcase contains anything good at all—in which we should be wrong, in spite of all.

We have the same experience when, in the same conditions, we try to discover the genuineness and truth of the Church's actions themselves: not just of our attitudes and answers, but of the ceremonies, the worship and our priestly message. As the things and the actions of the Church, belonging to that sacred order *apart* of which we spoke, these run the risk of being outside life and being ritualised, in the bad sense of the word. Looked at afresh, with lay people who are new to them, who live the life of men in the conditions of the world, they are set free from their facile ritualism and as it were forced back to become evangelical and Christian. Yes, it is just that: the world, whose fresh air is brought in by non-clericalised laity, forces us to be Christians. There is an element of truth in this remark of a Communist, whatever concrete connotations he may personally have given it: 'Anticlericalism drew from the Church only an embittered riposte of clericalism; socialism and communism have drawn from it something almost forgotten: Christians. From Lamennais until, shall we say, Martin-Chauffier, the democratic and revolutionary movement aroused in a handful of Catholics a *nostalgia* for Christianity.'[48]

The questions put to us by the laity, for which no rubric is provided, no answer prepared in the shelves of our theological bookcase, are an irreplaceable source of fertility for us. Fertility comes to the mind from questions, as it comes to the earth from seeds. As early as the middle of the third century, Origen wrote that the mind must be wounded for the blood and water of truth to flow from it, as from the wound in the side of Christ.[49] I have already quoted a very fine passage from Paul Claudel in the same sense.[50] Answers which do not come from a mind fertilised by a real question are answers which literally answer nothing. Unfortunately there are 'rites' of language as there are rites of worship, and they are equally without real vitality. They are part of that world of the 'ready-made', which is like an attribute with no living subject in which to inhere. We priests run the risk of our words being like that if they are not drawn from us by the laborious but blessed necessity of answering men's real questions. Laborious, because it makes us bleed. Blessed, for in it we attain to the genuineness and realism of what we shall thus have drawn, in co-operation with research, from the treasury of the gospel.

In conclusion I should like to define briefly the foundation of ecclesiological truth which is the source, when it is ignored, of the abuses revealed by history and, when it is honoured, of the fruits and advantages revealed by experience and analysis. This foundation may be summed up in the three following points:

First, in giving the word 'Church' its proper meaning. Having devoted myself since 1929 to the study of ecclesiology, I have made it my practice always to substitute mentally, for the word

'Church', its real meaning in the context, and similarly in the texts I read. The experience is perhaps disappointing, but instructive. In the majority of cases, and especially in modern official documents, the real meaning of the word is the hierarchy, the government of the Church, the pope and the Roman curia. On the contrary, in the writings of the Fathers and the liturgy, it is hardly ever wrong to substitute, for *ecclesia*, 'the Christian community'. The Fathers and the liturgy are also full of the idea, outlined above, of the spiritual motherhood which pertains to all the faithful with their priest. The work of the ministry is carried out by all the 'saints'; the priests have to 'organise' it.[51] Their character as 'mediators', on which much emphasis is laid, is very real. It is not exhausted by the hierarchical sense of the expression. Far from it: it comprises also, and decisively on the level of pastoral reality, the function of being the centre in which the unity of the faithful is bound together, in the parish or the diocese. St Basil writing a letter of consolation to the Church of Ancyra on the loss of its bishop, compares him to the soul which binds together all the members of the body in one single communion.[52] This first point is summed up in a few words, but its consequences are infinite.

In the second place, all that pertains to the juridical structure of the Church really belongs, and should be seen as belonging, to the heart of the reality of the Christian life, or of Christianity. This is the case, in particular, with the relation of superiority or subordination implied in the fact of authority. We must not posit authority *first* and *in itself*, and then say that it is wielded over Christians for spiritual ends, and must be used impartially, in a spirit of service. Christianity must be posited first, and then the fact of authority in it. In this way, it is qualified as Christian from its very roots; it *is* service, because the Christian life *is* service.[53] We must first lay down the *vobiscum Christianus*, and then, included in it, *vobis sum episcopus*. To do this is to establish, from the outset, healthy relations between persons in authority and those who are subordinate.

As for concrete expressions or interpretations of this healthiness, they can easily be imagined. Nowadays, thank God, we no longer lack good books expounding the subject, though they are not numerous.[54]

Third, and last: the most comprehensive law of a healthy Christianity is that the Church should be the Church, that the world should be the world, and that both should be recognised for what they are, alike in their distinction, their opposition and their necessary connection. It has sometimes happened that the world has been to some extent the Church, in the symbiosis of Christendom, when *ecclesia* denoted the Christian society. In those conditions, however, not only did the Church tend to adopt the ways of the world, but the tensions were readily transferred from without to within and were set up between the clergy and laity, or between distinct categories of clergy. When there is not really a world, there is not really a laity. If the world is not taken seriously, neither is the laity. When the Church is confronted with a world which is really a world, she is aware of herself, both as being *something else*, eschatological, and as having a mission to the world, and the responsibility for the world, for the sake of Jesus Christ and his kingdom. She is aware of being so in her entirety as community of the people called to the kingdom. She is structured, of course, but first she is living. In the Fathers, and for the liturgy, the Church is first of all baptism, by which a man exists in his state as Christian, member of the holy people, that is, *ipso facto*, in the state of witness for the world.[55] 'At the day and hour when anyone comes to the faith, it is also required of him that he set his hand to the work of the vine.'[56] That is the Catholic tradition. It is also an ecumenical truth. So I may be permitted to close this paper with a quotation from one of the founders of the Church of South India: 'To be a layman in the Church means to be part of the mission of God in the world.'[57]

NOTES

1. Translation of an article published in German in *Lebendige Seelsorge heute. Erfahrungen, Ueberlegungen, Anregungen*, edited by C. Pohlmann, O.F.M. and S. Richter, O.F.M.
2. *Orat.*, XIX, 10; *PG*, 35, 1053.
3. Labbé-Cossart, *Concilia*, vol. II, col. 1622. But Celestine also wrote: 'Let not a bishop be imposed on a people without its consent.'
4. See J. Gaudemet, *L'Église dans l'Empire romain (IVth–Vth cents.)*. (*Hist. du Droit et des Inst. de l'Égl. en Occ.*, III), Paris, 1958, pp. 240f (biblio.).
5. Gaudemet, *op. cit.*, p. 156; Hinschius, *Kirchenrecht*, vol. I, pp. 144f.
6. In 428 Celestine I rebuked Honoratus, abbot of Lérins, who had become bishop of Arles, for introducing a special dress, the tunic fastened with a girdle, which was the monastic habit. It was an innovation. Compare his letter to the bishops of the Narbonne country, *Epist.*, IV, 1. 2 (*PL*, 50, 431). See L. Cristiani, 'Essai sur les origines du costume ecclésiastique' in *Miscell. Guil. de Jerphanion* (*Or. Christ. Per.*, XIII, 1947), pp. 69–80.
7. See documentation and bibliography in my study 'Laicus = Sans lettres', in *Études de l'Hist. de l'Ecclésiologie* (to be published).
8. A theological history of this implicit doctrine of faith is found in G. Hoffmann, *Die Lehre v. d. Fides implicita*, 3 vols., 1903–9; but preferably, as regards scholasticism, in R. M. Schultes, *Fides Implicita. Gesch. d. Lehre v. der fid. impl. u. expl. in d. kathol. Theologie*, Ratisbon, vol. I, 1920.

In 1311 a woman accused chaplains and religious of not explaining Holy Scripture clearly to the people, so as to preserve their superiority, and hence their domination: Limborch, *Liber Inquisitionis Tolosanae*, 1692, p. 377 (quoted by F. Kropatschek, *Das Schriftprinzip* . . ., vol. 1, p. 23, n. 4).

9. Guy de Baisio ascribes this derivation to Huguccio: . . . *Populus, alibi laos, lapis interpretatur; inde laicus, id est popularis vel lapideus respectu clerici* (*Rosarium*, in C. XII, q. 1, c. 7, s.v. *Aliud*). At about the same period (1286) John Balbi of Genoa wrote in his famous *Catholicon*: . . . *Vel potius a* laos, *lapis. Inde laicus, i.e. lapideus, quia durus est et extraneus a scientia litterarum.*
10. In Caesarius of Heisterbach, at the end of the twelfth century: *Homil. Festivae*: Dom. 2 Adv. Edit. Coppenstein, Cologne, 1615, vol. III, pp. 172–3.
11. In Humbert of Romans (1286), in a passage I shall quote, because it is one of the most synthetic and representative, and emanates from a man of an open and realistic mentality: *Notandum quod sicut in mundo quaedam pars est superior, scilicet coelum, et quaedam inferior, scilicet terra; et in homine quaedam pars magis comprehensibilis, scilicet anima, et quaedam minus, scilicet corpus; et in tabernaculo quaedam pars sancta et quaedam pars sanctior, quae dicebatur sancta sanctorum; ita et inter fideles Christi sunt duo genera hominum, scilicet clerici, qui sunt superiores dignitate et magis intelligentes per scientiam et sanctiores habent esse, quam laici, qui in his minus abundant. Ad notandum autem istam distinctionem sunt in ecclesiis Christianorum duae partes, scilicet chorus, qui ad clerum pertinet, et navis, quae ad laicos. Notandum autem circa laicos, quod ipsi non debent ascendere ad scrutandum*

secreta fidei, quam tenent clerici, sed adhaerere implicite juxta illud Iob (I, 14), Et boves arabant et asinae pascebantur juxta eos; *quod exponit Gregorius dicens quod asinae, id est simplices, debent esse contenti doctrina suorum maiorum . . .* (*De Eruditione Praedicatorum*, lib. II. *De modo prompte cudendi sermones . . .*, tr. 1, c. 71 (*Sermo ad omnes laicos*), in *Max. Bibl. Vet. Patrum*, vol. XXV, Lyons, 1677, 491 CD).

There was also the idea of the two sides of the body, see my *Lay People*, p. 11.

12. See, e.g., Robert Grosseteste, mid-thirteenth cent., *Epistolae*, ed. Luard, London, 1861, p. 219.

13. See E. Curtius, *La littérature européenne et le Moyen Age latin*, trans. Bréjoux, Paris, 1956, p. 261.

14. Hugh of St Victor, *De Sacramentis*, I, part 10, c. 3 (*PL*, 176, 332): the context shows that nothing derogatory to the laity is intended. The origin of the application is Gregory, *Moral.*, II, 30, 49 and 45, 72 (*PL*, 75, 578 and 589). Humbert of Romans quotes this from it (*loc. cit.*, n. 3): *Notandum autem circa laicos quod ipsi non debent ascendere ad scrutandum secreta fidei quam tenent clerici, sed adhaerere implicite juxta illud Iob: . . .*

15. Thus Gratian, *Dictum post* C. 42, C. 2, qu. 1 (Friedberg, col. 496); Innocent III, letter to the Church of Metz, included in the Decretals, Bk V, tit. 7, de haer., c. 12 (Friedberg, col. 786); Blessed Jordan of Saxony, sermon for St Martin's day, Oxford, 11th Nov. 1229: *Balaam super asinam sedebat, et isti* (*sc.*, the priests who use their position in a carnal manner) *super populum simplicem, ei dominantes* (see A. G. Little and L. Douie, 'Three sermons of Friar Jordan of Saxony, the successor of St Dominic, preached in England, A.D. 1229', in the *English Historical Review*, 54 (1939), pp. 1–9: p. 11).

16. Second Council of Seville, 619 (Bruns, vol. II, p. 72), quoted in C. XVI, qu. 7, C. 22 (Friedberg, 806) and the *Glossa Ordinaria* of John the Teuton, *in loc.*; see R. J. Cox, *A Study of the Juridic Status of Laymen in the writings of the Medieval Canonists*, Washington, 1959, pp. 62 and 63. Then by the University statutes of Paris, 1254 (Denifle-Chatelain, *Chartular.*, I, no. 230, p. 257), and by St Thomas, *C. Impugnantes*, c. 3 (ed. Lethellieux, *Opusc.*, IV, p. 21; ed. Spiazzi, p. 48.

17. See L. Guelluy, 'La place des théologiens dans l'Église et la société médiévales', in *Miscellanea Historica A. De Meyer*, Louvain, 1946, vol. I, pp. 571–89.

18. Bull *Clericis laicos*, 25th Feb. 1296, in P. Du Puy, *Hist. du différend d'entre le pape Boniface VIII et Philippe le Bel . . .*, Paris, 1655, Actes et Preuves, p. 14; *Sexte*, c. 3 *de immunitate* 3, 23 (Friedberg, col. 1062).

19. See *Lay People*, pp. 231 and 343. Other references, not reproduced here, will be found there.

20. Letter of 10th Dec. 1873.

21. See his brochure *Words of Peace and Justice*, 1848; see R. Aubert, *Le pontificat de Pie IX*, Paris, 1952, p. 242.

22. *Simples réflexions*, p. 234.

23. See *Lay People*, pp. 234–8.

24. *Et tu, puer, propheta altissimi vocaberis, praeibis enim ante faciem Domini parare vias ejus.*

25. See 1 Cor 7:10, 17.

26. *Ibid.*, 25, 40.

27. 1 Thess 2:7–12, 'though we might have made demands on you, as apostles of Christ'; comp. 2 Cor 10:7–8; 11:23f; 12:1f, 11f; Phil 8–10, 'though I am bold enough in Christ to command you to do what is required, yet for love's sake I

prefer to appeal to you—I, Paul, an ambassador [*marg.*, an old man] and now a prisoner also for Christ Jesus . . .'.
28. 1:8.
29. 4:9.
30. See next chapter.
31. See K. Delahaye, 'Mater Ecclesia, Beitrag des Frühchristlichen Bewusstseins zum Aufbau einer Theologie der Seelsorge', in *Wiss. u. Weisheit*, 16 (1953), pp. 161–70; *Idem, Erneuerung der Seelsorgsformen aus der Sicht der Frühen Patristik*, Freiburg, 1958. Also many texts (though not developed in this sense) in A. Müller, *Ecclesia-Maria. Die Einheit Marias und der Kirche*, Freiburg, 1951. For the biblical outlook, see K. H. Schelkle, *Discipleship and Priesthood*, New York, 1964, pp. 108ff. For St Augustine, J. Hofmann, *Der Kirchenbegriff d. hl. Augustinus*, Munich, 1933, pp. 263–75. Compare, though much less precise, 'Doctrine et pastorale du sacrement de pénitence', in *NRT*, 1953, pp. 449–70.
32. Eph 4:12.
33. See *Sermo* 340, 1 (*PL*, 38, 1485); *En. in Ps.* 126, 3 (37, 1669); *De gestis cum Emer.*, 7 (43, 702); *Serm. Denys.* 17, 8 (*Miscellanea Agost.*, I, p. 88). Or again, 'Christiani propter nos, praepositi propter vos': *Sermo* 46, 2 (38, 271); 91, 5 (569); comp. *C. Crescon.*, II, 11, 13–14 (43, 474). And see M. Jourjon, 'L'évêque et le peuple de Dieu selon S. Augustin', in *Augustin parmi nous*, Le Puy-Paris, 1954, pp. 149–97; 'L'évêque comme membre du peuple de Dieu selon S. Aug.', in *Bull. des Facultés catholiques de Lyon*, N.S. 11 (1952), pp. 21–41.
34. Christians, all *servi*, *discipuli*, Augustine their bishop, *condiscipulus*, *conservus*: *Sermo* 340, 1 (*PL* 38, 1483); *En. in Ps.* 126, 3 (37, 1669); see *sermo* 179, 7 (38, 970); 23, 2 (38, 155); 292, 1 (1320); *Guelferb.* 32, 4 (*Miscell. Agost.*, I, p. 566).
35. *Sermo* 56, 11 and 135, 7 (*PL*, 38, 383 and 749).
36. See A. M. Landgraf, 'Weisungen der Mystik in den Werken der Frühscholastik', in *Collectanea Franciscana*, 27 (1957), pp. 196–205 (see pp. 202–5: texts).
37. *Some Spiritual Directors of the Seventeenth Century*, London, 1927. See my *A Gospel Priesthood*, p. 102. Herder & Herder, New York, 1967.
38. Abraham Heintschel.
39. Complaints in this respect, for example, in Dr Jouvenroux, *Témoignages sur la spiritualité moderne*, Paris, 1946, pp. 46–7, 79, 82; *Esprit*, 1946, nos. 8–9, pp. 213, 245.
40. *The Christian Imagination*, Westminster (Md.), 1955, pp. 38f; *The Catholic Dimension in Higher Education*, *Ibid.*, 1959, pp. 54f. See also the reflections of 'Un Directeur de Séminaire', in *Vie Sp.*, 73 (Dec. 1945), pp. 541–55 and 74 (Jan. 1946), pp. 59–68, which denounces possible seeds of defects much earlier than the seventeenth century. Some indications can also be found in B. Groethuysen, *Origines de l'esprit bourgeois en France. I. L'Église et la Bourgeoisie*, 2nd ed., Paris, 1922. It is worth studying the many manuals of priestly spirituality and conduct published in the seventeenth, eighteenth and nineteenth centuries. Fairly representative of the attitude in question is *Pratique du zèle ecclésiastique ou Moyens, pour tout prêtre, de rendre son ministère honorable et fructueux . . .*, by M. l'Abbé H. Dubois, 2nd ed., Lecoffre, 1853.
41. The theme we have indicated should be studied by following a method like that employed by Henri Bremond. Some indications are given in Daniel-Rops, *L'Église des temps classiques*, Paris, 1958. He suggests that a distinction should be made between religion before and religion after 1660. The great French directors of the earlier part of the century are men of action, who have a religion of charity: St Francis de Sales, St Vincent de Paul. The religion of the 'classics' is

rather a worship paid to the (kingly) majesty of God, with the corollary of the abasement of man. A similar view will be found in Péguy's analysis of Corneille and his *Polyeucte*, on the one hand, and of the religion of the *dévots* on the other. See note 43.

An outline for such a study (but the case is peculiar, being that of a former Trappist) will be found in S. Bonnet and P. Santini, 'Le Magasin sprituel de René Adam', in *Mémoires de la Société d'Agriculture de Chalons-s.-Marne*, 1960, pp. 130f.

42. Rev 1:4.

43. 'Note conjointe sur M. Descartes', pp. 174–5, in *Oeuvres compl.*, N.R.F., vol. IX, pp. 180f.

44. The notion of 'confronting' is here very apt. E. Mounier, who wrote *La petite peur du XXe siècle*, also wrote *L'affrontement chrétien*, perhaps his best message.

45. *Équipe* (= team or crew) comes from *équipage*, *équiper*, which are derived through *esquif* from a root which means a boat in almost all European languages; 'ship', Spanish and Portuguese *esquife*, Italian *schifo*, Old High German *skif*, (Gothic 'ship'). Here we link up with our earlier comparison of a ship's company (*équipage*).

46. See *Lay People*, pp. 271, 358.

47. See, for example, *Quodl. XII*, qu. 28: *ex officio, sua sponte.*

48. G. Mounin, in *Esprit*, Aug.–Sept. 1946 (Monde chrétien et monde moderne), p. 214.

49. *In Levit.*, hom. 16, 9 (G.C.S., *Origenes Werke*, VII, p. 152); see H. Urs von Balthasar, *Parole et Mystère chez Origène*, Paris, 1957, p. 130, n. 25.

50. In his reply to his welcome as a new member of the French Academy: 'That many-sided affair, the Dreyfus case, the protests it aroused, and its repercussions, had in common, however, a double character: it was spontaneous, and it took place, moreover, outside the Church, even when it was not in contradiction or in violent opposition to her. But, as our Mother seems to say in the words of St Paul, "Who asks a question and I am not questioned?" It is not only to her new though unconscious friends, who come from all points of the horizon to her who was called desolate, it is to her enemies that God's Church cries: "I was expecting you, and here I am! And all I have to say is: Blessed is he who comes to me in the name of the Lord! If you knock at me, it is because you need me. Knock, and it will be opened to you! Knock, and you will not be disappointed! I can never have too many of all these questions, under all their forms, the most insidious and the most blunt, to bring forth from me what of mine belongs to you, what I guarded in me of the word of God, which was for you; that word in me, appropriate to each one of you, which was indispensable to you" ' (*Doc. cath.*, 30th March 1947, col. 441).

51. Eph 4:12.

52. *Epist.* 29: *PG*, 32, 312.

53. On all this, see 'La hiérarchie comme service selon le N.T. et les documents de la Tradition', in *L'épiscopat et l'Église universelle* (*Unam Sanctam*), Paris, 1962, pp. 67–99.

54. See the works of Abbé Michonneau; Archbishop T. D. Roberts, *Black Popes*, London, 1954; P. L. Laberthonnière, *La notion chrétienne de l'autorité* (published by L. Canet, Paris, 1955).

55. See 1 Pet 2:9–10.

56. St Gregory of Nazianzus, Orat. XL, 20 (*PG*, 36, 386 A). See John Chrysostom, in the collection of baptismal catecheses published by A. Wenger,

(*Sources chrét.*, 50, Paris, 1958), and S. Tromp, 'De Corpore Christi mystico et Actione catholica ad mentem S. Ioannis Chrysostomi', in *Gregorianum*, 13 (1932), pp. 177–210, 321–72.

57. Bp. Leslie Newbigin, *The World Mission of the Church*, London.

CHAPTER TWO

'Not the Walls but the Faithful are the Church'

ONCE THE WORD 'EKKLESIA', 'CHURCH', HAD been applied to the places where the faithful met for worship,[1] it was natural to give frequent reminders that the same word *ekklesia* meant, in the first place, the actual company of the faithful. If there is one idea which is familiar to the Fathers, it is certainly this, that the Church consists of men: it is made up of the faithful, the sanctified.[2] This idea is often expressed in terms of a temple; the true temple of God is the believing soul or, rather, the community and unity of the faithful. Or again, and this is equally in conformity with the letter of the New Testament, the faithful are the living stones of this spiritual building.[3]

At the beginning of the second century St Hippolytus of Rome writes: 'What we call "church" is not a place, nor a house made of stones and earth: we cannot even describe a man, considered in himself, as "church", for a house is subject to destruction, and man to death. What, then, is the Church? It is the holy company of those who live in righteousness.'[4] This is echoed by Clement of Alexandria: 'It is not the place, it is the assembly of the elect which I call the Church. . . .'[5] In the literary sense we come nearer to the classical form of the *topos* with Lactantius, who wrote between 305 and 310: *Et domus quam aedificavit* (Salomon) *non est fidem consecuta, sicut Ecclesia, quae est verum templum Dei, qui non ex parietibus, sed in corde ac fide hominum, qui credunt in eum, ac vocantur fideles.*[6]

Hilary of Poitiers composed his book against Auxentius, the

Arian bishop of Milan, in 364. He issues a solemn warning to those who dare not face the trials of exile for the sake of loyalty to the true faith. 'Beware of Antichrist: you do very ill to be so attached to the walls, you do very ill to place your veneration for the Church of God in roofs and buildings.'[7] Ambrose, Auxentius' successor in the see of Milan, was well aware that the Church is spiritual and its walls are formed of the faithful.[8] It is not precisely our *topos*, since St Ambrose does not so much contrast the faithful and the walls as equate them, but it is the same thought in another form. John Chrysostom, on the other hand, proudly proclaimed, as he went into exile: 'The Church is not constituted by her encircling walls: she exists in the number of her members (. . .). Is it the walls which make the Church? No, it is the society of the faithful.'[9] Chrysostom actually followed Hilary's warning; far above all attachment to walls he ranked his freedom of speech and his loyalty to his faith: for their sake he accepted exile in a desert land.

St Jerome was fond of our *topos*. *Ecclesia non in parietibus, consistit, sed in dogmatum veritate. Ecclesia ibi est ubi fides vera est.*[10] *Parietes non faciunt Christianos.*[11] Augustine relates the case of Victorinus, converted by reading the scriptures, who considered himself a Christian by that fact alone, although he had never been baptised. When Simplicianus said that he could not regard him as one, because he was not to be seen among the faithful in the church, Victorianus had replied ironically: 'Is it the walls, then, which make Christians?'[12] Augustine himself applied an analogous principle to the actual city of Rome and what it stood for, when it fell to the barbarians' assault: *Civitas in civibus est, non in parietibus*, he wrote,[13] and he repeated: *Forte Roma non perit si Romani non pereant. . . . Roma enim quid est, nisi Romani? Non enim de lapidibus et lignis agitur, de excelsis insulis et amplissimis moenibus. . . .*[14]

A text of St Cyril of Alexandria is sometimes quoted, but I have not been able to check its accuracy. *Cum dicimus Ecclesiam, non circuitu murorum vim hujus dictionis accommodamus, sed piorum potius in ea sanctissimam multitudinem significamus.*[15] I conclude this series of patristic texts, as is only right, with St Gregory the Great. He lamented the fact that of those who fill the walls (*parietes*) of the Church on a great festival, not all belong to the flock of God's elect.[16]

Gregory, like his contemporary Isidore, stands at the meeting-point of antiquity and the early medieval world. The latter was evidently familiar with the apparent tension between the church as material building and the Church as society of the faithful. Witness Rabanus Maurus († 856),[17] for example, while about the end of the ninth century an anti-Roman poem, the *Versus Romae*, played on the words *mores* and *muri*.[18] We have Attonius of Vercelli († 961?, in any case after 940), who wrote: *Haec itaque domus, non ex parietibus manufactis, sed ex vivis et electis lapidibus, id est sanctorum coetibus elegantissime constat*. . . .[19] And there is the Council of Arras in 1025, the text of which is so significant and instructive, taking up the theme that the Church consists of the faithful rather than of the walls.[20]

From this time onwards, our *topos* was used in ways which were influenced by a certain juridical sense of the word *ecclesia*. The origin of this sense is to be found in the measures taken to assure the clergy of the normal means of support. There existed a law of Justinian on this point, forbidding clerics to be ordained unless they were assured of a living.[21] These measures emphasised the link between ordination and means of support, between a cleric and a *titulus* or an *ecclesia*, in this new sense of not simply a given community of men—which was their original meaning—but of certain means of support, a combination of property and rights. The increasing use of this sense of the word *ecclesia* was favoured in the West by the system of 'private churches', which was developed though not created under German influence. From the ninth century, and still more from the tenth, *ecclesia* often means the building for worship and its appurtenances in rights (tithes, etc.) and temporal possessions.[22] In the collation of a benefice by its patron there was an 'investiture', with the phrase *Accipe ecclesiam*. . . .[23] We may note that in the same climate of feudal institutions and language *parietes*, one of the terms of our *topos*, meant the feudal homage or the revenues of a fief:[24] a detail to be borne in mind if we are to appreciate all the connotations of certain texts. On the one hand, the church was thus made over, as to all its material existence, to the lay lords: the reform initiated by St Leo IX and St Gregory VII aimed, not unsuccessfully, at delivering it from this situation. From another point of view, the Church was thus powerfully endowed, privileged, committed to the weight of the temporal: a whole series of spiritual movements from the end of the eleventh century, aimed at criticising this state of affairs and breaking with it, by denouncing in it whatever was irreconcilable with the gospel.

It is this situation and this use of the word *ecclesia* which govern the two great groups of texts we have now to consider, groups which correspond to two great periods in the use of our *topos*: first, in connection with the anti-ecclesiastical movements or sects of the twelfth century, and then among the canonists or in dependence on them.

1. *Spiritual movements or anti-ecclesiastical sects of the twelfth century.* These aimed at restoring a Church, weighed down by the temporal, to her true spiritual state. This was the less disinterested aim of the unknown author of the tracts contained in the Cambridge MS (Corpus Christi College, no. 415), sometimes called the 'Anonymous of York' or the 'Norman Anonymous'. He wished to establish a full sovereignty of the royal power even over the Church on earth. He was fond of contrasting the true temple, made of living men, with the material Church,[25] the incorporeal heaven with the corporeal.[26] Of the spiritual movements, the chief is that of Peter de Bruys (the Petrobusians), who criticised a Church far too weighed down by the earthly and the temporal, in the name of the principle *quod nomen ecclesiae, non structuram parietum, sed congregationem fidelium signaret.*[27] On which grounds, they proceeded to destroy churches! Peter the Venerable, who has told us of this movement, accepts the spiritual definition of the Church: *Dicitur Ecclesia, ut ipsi dixistis, congregatio. . . . Ecclesia, hoc est in Christum credentium congregatio*[28] *cum Ecclesia Dei non constat multitudine sibi coherentium lapidum, sed unitate congregatorum fidelium. . . .*[29] The same theme is found, at the end of the twelfth century, in Alain of Lille, writing against the Waldensians and the Cathars, who on this point at least were united in criticism of the existing Church and all external forms of religion,[30] or again, in 1242, from the pen of Moneta of Cremona: *Ecclesia dicitur dupliciter. Vel congregatio fidelium constans ad minus ex episcopo, presbytero, diacono et subdiacono, vel domus materialis. . . .*[31]

A reply to the spiritual movements, neither apologetic nor critical, was given by men who were truly spiritual: St Bernard, who knew that the walls of the Church often have to be rebuilt with the mortar of charity, by men who must ever be overcoming the carnal mind;[32] by Hugh of St Victor and others, who proclaimed the traditional theme of the true temple, whose stones and walls are formed of the faithful, united by charity.[33] But the final Catholic reply was given by Francis of Assisi. The vision attributed to Innocent III, of men (Francis or Dominic) propping up the cracked and tottering walls of his Lateran cathedral, is perhaps a legend. But the legend is a fair expression of the facts. It is a fact, at any rate, that Francis of Assisi, who carried detachment from material conditions and temporal goods to its highest pitch, had the greatest possible veneration for the Blessed Sacrament, for priests and for the actual church buildings. Did he not begin by restoring San Damiano and by repairing or cleaning many other little country churches round Assisi?[34]

The ideas of the twelfth-century sects were resumed in the seventeenth by George Fox, for whom the material church, which he affected to call the 'steeple-house', symbolised a whole concept of Christianity which he rejected. 'What is it you call a church?', he once asked an Anglican clergyman, 'the building, or this multitude?'[35] Clearly, he thought he was propounding a dilemma, which is not one at all.

2. *Canon Law.* The canonists constructed, in their own fashion, a union of the two ideas. They did so in reply to the question: to whom do the Church's goods belong? The second half of the twelfth century and the beginning of the thirteenth basked in the corporative ideas which have been analysed, in particular, by B. Tierney (*Foundations of the Conciliar Theory. The Contribution of the Medieval Canonists from Gratian to the Great Schism*, Cambridge, 1955). Men were trying to define the respective positions of the prelate and of the community over which he presided, with regard to the ownership of property. The true owner was the community: *illa bona competunt ecclesiae catholicorum, non enim parietibus, sed congregationi fidelium*, declared Uguccio, who was Innocent III's teacher at Bologna.[36] This juridical position was not shared by all the Decretists,[37] but by a fair number, and those the most important, of the Decretists or Decretalists.[38] As is often the case with the medieval canonists, the choice on this particular point, which might be thought secondary, is pregnant with a

choice on the most general and important questions. Here it is a question, ultimately, of the very notion of *ecclesia* and of the place held in that notion by the community, as such, of the faithful.

The positions adopted by the canonists are found in many theologians of the late thirteenth and early fourteenth centuries, in terms which are of interest to our enquiry. We shall conclude this by quoting some significant passages from these theologians.

First there is Humbert of Romans († 1279), who notes, in precisely the manner of the canonists, that the Church means the souls belonging to the churches, not their fields or vineyards, that is, their possessions.[39] Then there is Geoffrey of Fontaines, who classifies and summarises the accepted meanings of the word *ecclesia*. *Per ecclesiam possumus intelligere primo domum materialem, scilicet templum lapideum vel ligneum in quo principaliter Deus extrinsecus colitur corporaliter. Secundo, domum spiritualem, scilicet fideles, in quibus Deus colitur spiritualiter per virtutes theologicas, scilicet per fidem, spem et caritatem, qui corporaliter colunt Deum in ecclesia praedicta materiali. Item bona exteriora temporalia, scilicet redditus et possessiones et hujusmodi, quibus ministri Ecclesiae corporaliter sustentantur.*[40] A perfect explanation, but hardly new. Analogous distinctions are found in William Durandus the Speculator,[41] and a profession similar to that of Humbert of Romans in Agostino Trionfo of Ancona, who went so far as to say: 'If by the Church we mean the walls, towns and temporal goods, we cannot say that Christ died for the Church.'[42] Here we can detect a reaction against a purely external point of view which may well be that of the canonists. There is the same reaction, in 1312, in the works of John of Mont Saint-Eloi.[43] Finally, some twenty years later, we have the Franciscan Alvaro Pelayo, who writes: *Item Ecclesia, quae est corpus Christi mysticum, et quae collectio catholicorum . . . non est ambitus murorum,*[44] or again, *Non est Ecclesia parietum vel murorum, sed collectio catholicorum.*[45]

NOTES

1. The article by F. J. Dölger (*Ant. u. Christ.*, 6, 1941, pp. 161–95) gives nothing on the word *ecclesia.* See H. Leclercq in *DACL, s.v.* 'Église', vol. IV, col. 2221; *ekklesia* (*eccl.*) is found, denoting the local church, as early as Clement of Alexandria (*Strom.*, VII, 5: quoted in n. 5, below) and in Lactantius (see *Vigil. christ.*, 1948, p. 169).

2. Besides the passages from Hippolytus, Ambrose and Jerome quoted later, see, e.g., Origen, *De princ.*, II, 8, 5 (*PG*, 11, 225: *Quia multitudo credentium corpus illius dicitur*); *In Isaiam*, hom. 2, n. 1 (ed. Baehrens, p. 250: *Nos sumus Ecclesia Dei*); *In Cant.*, 1 and 3 (Baehrens, pp. 90 and 232, 1. 21–2); St Cyprian, *Epist.* 33, 1, *Ecclesia in episcopo et clero et in omnibus stantibus . . . constituta*; Augustine, *Serm. Guelferbyt.*, I, 8 (*Miscell. Agost.*, I, p. 447: *Sancta Eccl. nos sumus . . .*); etc.

3. See C. J. Plumpe, '*Vivum saxum, vivi lapides.* The concept of "living stone" in Classical and Christian Antiquity', in *Traditio*, 1 (1943), pp. 1–14. For the theme of a spiritual temple in the Fathers, a complete monograph is lacking, but see P. Ternant in *Proche Orient chrét.*, 2 (1952), pp. 319–32; D. Sanchis, 'Le symbolisme communautaire du Temple chez S. Augustin', in *Rev. Ascét. Myst.*, 37 (1961), pp. 3–30 and J. Gaillard, art. 'Domus Dei' in *Dict. Sp.*, vol. III, col. 1551–67.

4. *In Daniel.*, 1, 17, 6–7 (*GCS*, *Hippol.-Werke*, I-1, p. 28, 1:20–4).

5. *Strom.*, VII, c. 5 (*PG*, 9, 437 C; Stählin, III, p. 21).

6. *Inst.*, IV, 13 (26); *PL*, 6, 486–7.

7. *C. Auxent.*, 12 (*PL*, 10, 616): *Cavete antichristum: male enim vos parietum amor cepit, male Ecclesiam Dei in tectis aedificiisque veneramini . . .*

8. Ambrose, *Apologia David*, 16, 83 (*PL*, 14, 922): *Muri itaque Jerusalem fidei propugnacula, disputationum munimenta, virtutum culmina sunt; muri Jerusalem ecclesiarum conventus sunt toto orbe fundati, Ecclesia enim dicit: 'Ego murus et ubera mea turris'* (Cant. 8. 18). *Et bene muri Jerusalem ecclesiarum conventicula sunt; quoniam quisquis bona fide atque opere ingreditur Ecclesiam fit supernae illius civis et incola civitatis quae descendit de coelo. Hos muros lapidum aedificat structura vivorum.*

9. *Hom. ante exsilium*, n. 2 and 3 (*PG*, 52, 429 and 430). See *In Eutropium* hom. 2, n. 1: 'Thou art Peter, and upon this rock I will build my Church, and the gates of hell shall not prevail against it. I say the Church! And by that I understand, not the building, but a faith, a rule of life. Not the material walls, but its laws. When you take refuge in the Church, do not ask a place for refuge, but your own heart. The Church, in fact, is not the wall and the roof, but the faith and the conduct of life . . .' (*PG*, 52, 397). He said again: 'It is not for the walls that the deacon cries: "Let us pray for the catechumens . . ." ' (In 2 Cor hom. 2: *PG*, 61, 404).

10. *In Ps.* 133 (*PL*, 26, 1223 A).

11. *Tract. in Psalm.* 123 (ed. G. Morin, *Anal. Maredsol.*, III–2, p. 292). Jerome also expounds the theme *vera ecclesia, verum templum*: *Tract. in Ps.* 86 (*ed. cit.*,

p. 104), *Vera Ecclesia, verum templum Christi non est nisi anima humana*; *Epist.* 58, 7 (*PL*, 22, 584), *Verum Christi templum anima credentis est. . . . Quae utilitas est parietes fulgere gemmis et Christum in paupere fame periclitari?*

12. *Confess.*, VIII, 2, 4; *PL*, 32, 750.

13. *Sermo de Urbis excidio*, 6: *PL*, 40, 721. The formula was to become classical, for we find it in Isidore, *Etym.*, XV, c. 2, n. 1: Civitas *est hominum multitudo societatis vinculo adunata, dicta a civibus, id est ab ipsis incolis urbis. . . . Nam* urbs *ipsa moenia sunt,* civitas *autem non saxa, sed habitatores vocantur* (*PL*, 82, 536 BC). See St Bernard, *Video et alios* (*quod non sine dolore videri debet*), *post agressam Christi militiam, rursus cupiditatibus terrenis immergi: cum magna cura erigere muros, et negligere mores . . .* (Hom. 4 super *Missus est*, 10: *PL*, 183, 85 B). Yet I have found nothing of this kind in the classical authors: nor do Forcellini or Otto (*Sprichwörter u. Sprichwörtlichen Redensarten der Römer*, Leipzig, 1890) indicate anything resembling, or even concerning, our *topos*.

14. *Sermo* 81, 9: *PL*, 38, 505.

15. Quoted by J. Launoi, *Opera*, vol. V–2, p. 671, giving as reference *Orat. IV sup. Isaiam.*

16. *Hom. in Evang.* 19, 5: *PL*, 76, 1157.

17. *En. in Epist. Pauli, lib. XXIII, in epist. i ad Tim.*, c. 3 (*PL*, 112, 607 B): *Id vero cognoscendum, quoniam domum Dei Ecclesiam, non domum orationis dicit, secundum plurimorum opinionem, sed fidelium congregationem.*

18. *Moribus et muris, Roma vetusta, cadis*: quoted by E. H. Kantorowicz, *The King's Two Bodies*, Princeton, 1957, p. 82, n. 99.

19. *Libell. de pressuris Ecclesiae*, I (*PL*, 134, 53 C).

20. Can. 3: Mansi, XIX, 437 C.

21. On this point and what follows, see V. Fuchs, *Der Ordinationstitel von seiner Entstehung bis auf Innocens III . . .* (*Kan. St. u. Texte*, 4), Bonn, 1930, pp. 138–95.

22. P. Hinschius, 'Zur Gesch. der Incorporation u. des Patronatsrecht' in *Festgaben Heffter*, Berlin, 1873, pp. 1f; P. Thomas, *Les droits de propriété des laïcs sur les églises et le patronage laique au moyen âge*, Paris, 1906, pp. 17f; 76f; V. Fuchs, *op. et loc. cit.*

23. See A. Hauck, *Kirchengeschichte Deutschlands*, vol. III, pp. 52–69; P. Imbart de la Tour, *Les élections épiscopales dans l'Église de France du IXe au XIIe siècle*, Paris, 1891, pp. 74f.

24. *Parietes* = *Pariae*. See Du Cange, s.v., with quotation from a charter of 845.

25. For example, Tract. II: *Libelli de Lite*, vol. III, p. 653.

26. See Tract. XXIX, in H. Böhmer, *Kirche und Staat in England und in der Normandie im 11. u. 12. Jahrh.*, Leipzig, 1899, p. 479.

27. Peter the Venerable, *Contra Petrobusianos*: *PL*, 189, 738 A.

28. *Ibid.*, col. 738 B and D.

29. *Op. cit.*, col. 762.

30. *De fide catholica contra haereticos*, Bk I, c. 69: *Non desunt qui dicunt locum materialem non esse Ecclesiam, sed conventum fidelium tantum . . .* (*PL*, 210, 571); he replies to this, c. 70; c. 71, col. 573: *Quod locus materialis dicatur domus Dei ad quam conveniunt fideles ut orent, variis probatur auctoritatibus. . . . Sciendum ergo quod tam locus materialis quam conventus fidelium dicitur Ecclesia Dei. . . .*

31. *Summa adversos Catharos et Valdenses*, Bk IV, c. 8, 3; ed. Richini, Rome, 1743, p. 456. Moneta replies to the objections of the Cathars, who did not admit the existence of material temples (sec. I, p. 454) or that they are called 'churches' (sec. III, p. 455).

32. *In festo S. Michaelis sermo 2*, n. 2 (*PL*, 183, 452).

33. Hugh of St Victor, *Sermo 3. In dedic. eccles.* (*PL*, 177, 905): *Jerusalem civitas*

sancta et civitas Sancti, Ecclesia est . . . Habet haec civitas sancta, id est Ecclesia, lapides suos, murum suum, turres suas, aedificia sua, portas suas. Habet lapides, scilicet fideles, qui sicut per caementum lapis jungitur lapidi, sic per charitatem junguntur sibi. This kind of passage was frequent at that time: see J. Sauer, *Symbolik der Kirchengebaudes*, Freiburg, 1924, p. 104; F. Heer, *Die Tragödie des hl. Reiches*, Vienna and Zurich, 1952, p. 193, with corresponding notes.

34. In his *Testament* Francis said precisely: 'And God gave me such faith in the churches . . .' See J. Jörgensen, *Saint François d'Assise*, pp. 52f; Kaj. Esser, 'Die religiösen Bewegungen des Hochmittalters und Franziskus v. Assisi', in *Glaube und Geschichte. Festg. J. Lortz*, Baden-Baden, 1958, vol. II, pp. 287–315.

35. *Journal of George Fox.*

36. In P. Gillet, *La personnalité juridique en droit canonique*, Malines, 1927, p. 101; B. Tierney, *op. cit.*, p. 118.

37. So by the *Glossa Ordinaria*, the *Glossa Palatina*: Tierney, *op. cit.*, p. 118. The legists similarly accentuated the preponderant position of the *clergy* in relation to the community: see O. v. Gierke, *Das Deutsche Genossenschaftrecht*, vol. III, p. 360, especially n. 22.

38. See B. Tierney, *op. cit.*, pp. 118–19. Also p. 140 (Innocent IV); later, John of Paris (in Gierke, *op. cit.*, p. 255, n. 33).

39. Model sermon *Ad studentes in jure canonico*, in his *De Eruditione Praedicat.*; in *Max. Bibl. Vet. Patrum*, vol. XXV, Lyons, 1677, p. 490.

40. *Quodl.* X, qu. 18: in 1293.

41. *Rationale divin. offic.*, Bk I, n. 1 (ed. Venice, 1609): from the beginning of his work he distinguishes the *Ecclesia corporalis*, the walls, from the *Ecclesia spiritualis, fidelium collectio.*

42. See M. Grabmann, 'Die Erörterung der Frage, ob die Kirche besser durch einen guten Juristen oder durch einen Theologen regiert wurde, bei Gottfried v. Fontaines (nach 1306) u. Augustinus Triumphus von Ancona (1328)', in *Festschrift v. E. Eichmann*, Paderborn, 1940, pp. 1–19.

43. In his *Quodl. II*, qu. 8, quoted in connection with Vat. Lat., 1086, by J. Leclercq, 'L'idéal du théologien au Moyen Age. Textes inédits', in *Rev. S.R.*, 1947, pp. 121–48, see p. 127: *Dicendum quod multi decipiuntur per equivocationem ecclesiae, nam quidam bona ecclesiastica reputant ecclesiam, sed in veritate ecclesia pro qua Christus mortuus est sunt fideles quos prelatus major debet scire regere. . . .*

44. *Collyrium adv. haereses*, in R. Scholz, *Unbekannte kirchenpolitische Streitschriften*, vol. II, Rome, 1914, p. 506.

45. *De Statu et Planctu Ecclesiae*, I, art. 31: quoted by N. Iung, *Un Franciscain théologien du pouvoir pontifical au XIVe s., Alvaro Pelayo*, Paris, 1931, p. 150, n. 2.

CHAPTER THREE

The Christian Idea of History[1]

HISTORY—A POWERFUL WORD! ESPECIALLY IF by it we understand not simply the reconstitution of past events in their order, but a certain dimension of our view of the world. It is now one of the master-words of our generation.

Just one more slogan? I think not: it is something very serious, which for Christians represents a definite value of their faith. We have rediscovered, in fact, that faith is not simply intellectual adherence to a list of propositions, but something else, which includes also a hope.

Fundamentally, the Christian's situation is that of a man tied to a past fact and at the same time straining towards a hope. A religion lacking that dimension of hope would be disincarnate, detached from history, a religion, if you like, of the supreme being, the great architect, the eternal axiom (if it is not of the Catholic sort), but a religion without dynamism, without enterprise.

If the present generation has rediscovered this dimension of History, at the very heart of the Christian faith, it owes it partly, I think, to three facts which I wish briefly to recall to your minds.

First of all, the social movements: the very fact of having been concerned in great social movements or great movements of history—nearly always, alas, wars and strife! Through this we have discovered what has been well called the 'Community of Destiny': we might more accurately call it the community of struggle, community of hope.

Those know well what this means, who have belonged to a combatant unit, for example, or an escape team, or a social movement, a social struggle, a political party, perhaps! There can be no doubt that one of the attractions of Communism for the present generation is that being organised as a kind of church—laicised, secularised, of course—it has its hope; it has, dare I say, its eschatology, the whole state of things it hopes for, the sum of good things at which it aims. An earthly eschatology, I grant you, but all the same, dynamic. And it claims to be able to give an explanation of the facts of history. That is the first fact.

The second fact is, I think, the rediscovery of the Old Testament, rediscovery of the truth that we can only understand the gospel if it is not cut off from its roots in the Old Testament, and, by the same fact, rediscovery of the roots of the gospel in Israel, which is our source, as it were, from which we have received our first sap of life. And I think that here the unfathomable sufferings of Israel in the last fifteen years are a sort of mysterious condition for the rediscovery of the Old Testament by Christians themselves, the rediscovery by Christians of their roots in Israel, upon whom, says St Paul, we have been grafted. The fact is that Israel is from beginning to end a prophetic people: her special characteristic among all the other peoples and their history is to have been a people of prophets, a people always reaching out to hope, hoping in . . ., hoping that . . ., expecting something, a people of whom it may well be said that it has brought into the world the very category of the historical. It is certainly no mere accident that Karl Marx, the prophet of Communism and the historical explanation of the world, was of Jewish descent. Even there he carried on, secularised and laicised, the movement, the action of Israel, which will always be among us the people of the glorious promise, from whom Christianity has received the indelible mark of being, likewise, a hope.

As for the third fact, it is at the heart of questions which are extraordinarily acute and often painful for us: the need which Christians have found, to return to their own sources in order to drink from them afresh.

Now for Christians to return to their sources is the same thing as to be re-centred, it is always to return to Jesus Christ, the one centre of Christianity. It is to reconsider the meaning of the coming, the presence and the return of Christ, for those are the three great affirmations of the gospel about him: he has come, he is here, and he will return. Four times we read in the Apocalypse, *qui est, qui erat et qui venturus est*. Christ is he who has come, who is still here, and who will return.

With this point, are we not now at the very heart of the Christian notion of history? That heart is the centre, the root, the source, and it bears a very simple name, constantly blessed in our prayers: 'Jesus Christ'. It is before him that we must place ourselves as before our Centre: he who has come, who is here, who will return. He who, seated at the right hand of the Father, governs all things, their beginning, their existence and their future; he whom our magnificent Byzantine mosaics, in Italy and Greece, depict as the 'Pantocrator', the master of all things, that immense Christ who stands out against the unforgettable blue of the mosaics in the apses of Rome or Ravenna, the 'Pantocrator', he who governs all things and appears present at the origin, in the here and now, and at the end. That is really the essential affirmation of the Apocalypse, which four times uses the expression I have quoted: he who is, who was, and who is to come.

The Apocalypse also uses, in three places, another expression which really sums up all I have to say to you today: it calls Christ the Alpha and the Omega, that is, the first and last letters of the Greek alphabet, which is to say, again, the source and the end, the beginning and the consummation; we could as truly say, the seed and the harvest.

Christ is that, and if you understand that, my brethren, I believe you have understood the Christian meaning of history. It is that Christ is the Alpha and the Omega, the seed and the harvest: he is the seed, alone, for us: he is that grain which is planted in the earth, all alone, for the future. He is the seed, in the sense that everything comes from him, and that if the Church is a body, it is a body which is constructed, so to speak, from its head, which is the principle of everything, which brings life to all men.

He will be the end, with us, and we shall be the end with him: I tell you, the seed and the harvest! He is Alpha and Omega: He is Alpha, as our seed, all alone, for the ear, and he is Omega, the end, the consummation, as the entire harvest, sprung from the single seed, and all we are the harvest with him.

The whole of Christian history is set between those two

moments: Christ, alone, for us, in his state as Alpha and beginning,—and Christ with us, or we with him, in his state as Omega, end; and between the two is the whole history of the Church, filled with the presence of Christ, advancing from his state as seed to his state as harvest.

From this very simple view of things there flow consequences which we must carefully note, for they will tell us what is, from the Christian's point of view, the content of history, the content of the duration of time.

This duration is not empty for us. I do not mean empty merely of secular events—God knows they are plentiful enough!—but empty, I mean, of Christian events; from the Christian point of view it is even filled with them, and indeed, much is happening in it! It is a duration which is full, dynamic, fertile! Something Christian is going on in it, something Christian is being fashioned in it; I would even say that something of Christ is being fashioned in it.

It has been profoundly said that 'the man is the future of the man'. I would say too that there is a future of Christ, and that the Christian is the future of Christ. The Church, the mystical body, is the future of Christ, as the ear is the future of the seed. It is that growth of the single grain into the ear and the harvest which fills the history in which, as Christians, we are engaged. That history goes on, just like the great secular history, whether we know it or not.

You remember Stendhal's story of the battle of Waterloo: Fabrice, his hero, who was present at the battle without knowing it, and held his horse's bridle in a field of beetroot; then in the evening he learned that it was the battle of Waterloo!

Many men, obviously, are in the world like that. Thus there were many Parisians who woke up on the morning of the 26th August 1944, to learn that they were liberated. Something had indeed happened, but they had seen nothing, done nothing. In the same way, something is happening in the world, but those who do something in it are not always numerous.

Whether we know it or not, we are in that history. We are in a 25th August of Christianity, while a liberation is going on. The question is, shall we be actively part of it, or shall we be satisfied with waking up in the morning on the 26th, to hear—what? At that moment, when Jesus opens the books of history, will our names be in it? And if so, in which column? In the column of the active combatants? Or in that of the indifferent, or the tourists, or those who simply played cards while others freed them?

We are in that history, and we can, we must, do something in it actively.

The Christian must learn to co-operate in that building up of Christ, that passage from his state of seed, alone for us all, to his state of ear and harvest, we with him, and he associating us with his harvest-home in God's heaven.

So we must co-operate with Jesus: of course we don't know very clearly what we are doing from day to day: our case is, you may say, the opposite of Fabrice's. He saw the immediate foreground of his twenty-four hours in the beetroot field, but knew absolutely nothing of what was going on in general, or of the meaning of the battle, and obviously he didn't know what the result would be. The Christian's situation is the reverse of this: he knows the general meaning of the battle perfectly well, and he knows the result in advance, for his commander is victorious already!

But the Christian sees practically nothing of the meaning of the little things that happen in the twenty-four hours of his existence. He too is there, his eyes on his beetroots, holding his horse's bridle, and he sees nothing. To take another illustration: this time I compare our work of construction with a craftsman working on a Gobelins tapestry. You know that these tapestries are worked from behind, and the craftsman who weaves them sees a mixture or mass of threads of all colours, but cannot see their shape or designs. Those will only be understood when the tapestry is seen from in front. For us this will be from the other side of the veil, but on this side we must build as best we can, interweaving the threads known to God.

But we are making this history and we know the meaning of the whole. We don't know its detail: for the detail we live in faith, from day to day, as best we can, and that's all. But as to the end and the whole we are certain, and we know that we are thus called to build the Temple of God, to prepare the future of God's Kingdom, to build up the body of Christ, to work so that it may extend to more things and more men, and that its salvation may be richer. For God's Kingdom and his salvation do not float along above the earth, like clouds between earth and sky: they are truly within it, they are prepared in it.

Péguy says very neatly: 'the spiritual is always resting on the camp-bed of the temporal'. We can say that the Christian hope, which is the hope of the Kingdom of God, is always resting on the camp-bed of history: it is there, it rests there. The Christian hope rested on the camp-bed of Israel before Christ, and since Christ came it has been resting on the camp-bed of the Church. But it is truly there: we are doing something in it, it isn't a sort of meteor which will appear at the end, having never been present in the course of time and history. Truly, we are doing something in it. A development, no less. We are developing the Christ, from the single grain into the ear and the harvest.

Here we have to understand a sort of dialectic, that is, the simultaneous truth of two opposed terms, which are yet necessary to each other, conditioning each other. This dialectic is between the unique event, which happened once only: the Incarnation, the Word of God and the Apostles, on the one hand, and on the other, that which is being made present, and in a certain way is being renewed all the time in history.

Once again I shall draw on Péguy, this time on his mystery play, the Charity of Joan of Arc. Joan is wondering, and she says to herself: 'Oh, how happy were those who knew Christ, but what about us? We shall never see him. If only we could be like his contemporaries, see him, hear him speak, feel the touch of his hands! And Péguy's answer is his idea of beginning again, the idea that we can become real contemporaries of Christ, not merely mentally, by some sort of effort or tension of the mind (which after all would only be a pretence and an illusion), but in a concrete, real manner: by oneself living the realities of Christ, living out, day after day, in all the dimensions of time and its duration, that which has been provided only once, namely, the word of God (which lives in the tradition of the Church), the ministry of the apostles (which lives in that of the Christian hierarchy) and the Redemption by the cross (which lives by the sacraments and in the Mass). That is the Christian solution of that presence of the unique event—the Incarnation, the word of God, the Cross—which is yet lived and present in the whole extent of time and space, in such a way as to cause our single original grain, Christ our Alpha, to sprout and grow into its state of perfection and fullness, our Omega.

Equally this shows us the meaning of the Christian idea of salvation, which was wrought once for all on the Cross, but is applied and made actual throughout history, and will only be perfect at the summit, the end.

This salvation is not only individual, it is equally collective, I would even say, cosmic. See how St Paul speaks of it in his Epistle to the Romans: *Creatura ingemiscit*, *expectat*. The whole creation groans, waits!

This is not something individual, it is collective: it is not the purely spiritual, it is the corporal, the cosmic: it is not the purely static, it is dynamic and historical. 'The whole creation waits', says Paul, and waits for what? For its total redemption.

It still waits for something. Christianity, in its concept of salvation and of history, is able to combine two terms, two values, which many thinkers—and no mean or mediocre thinkers, either—cannot see how to bring to unity, to wit, the value of the person on the one hand and collective value on the other.

Read, for example, Albert Camus's *The Rebel.* You will see that the author considers the dignity of man to lie in being outside history, and he attacks Marxism precisely because it has brought man into history and so has reduced him to the level of mere material for history. For him, the very dignity of man requires that he should be outside history. For us, never!

Never! Christianity is able to combine both the highest idea, I think, of the value of the person and the idea of a collective work to be done together. The highest idea of the value of the person, for we affirm a kind of personal eschatology for each one of us, at death, in the particular judgement. We affirm that every life is so precious that the Church celebrates each person's individually, and that is what fills the calendar with the feasts of the saints, the whole *Sanctorale* of the Missal, that individual, personal celebration of each life, precious in itself.

Yet, along with this, we can affirm a movement of the whole, a collective salvation, because there is a transcendent destiny, because what persons have to do is to direct themselves towards the realisation of a unique, transcendent work, the Body of Christ, the Kingdom of God, the Temple to be built. And this work, because it is transcendent to persons, and is not only historical and earthly, can be for them both collective and personal, without in the least detracting from their dignity as persons, from what each has to do, or from the particular hymn of praise which only he can sing.

This work is accomplished in the course of history, in which Christ responds to the anguish, the triple anguish of men, in face of death, loneliness and sin. To his anguish in face of death he responds with immortality, or more exactly with the promise of the resurrection. To his anguish in face of loneliness he responds with the good news of the reality of Communion. To his anguish in face of sin he responds with the offer of the reality of holiness.

There we have three things which are accomplished on earth, by Jesus Christ. All this comes only from him. There is one sole principle, our Alpha, who obtains all that has to be developed in Christian history. There is neither immortality nor resurrection, nor communion, nor holiness, apart from Jesus Christ. He is their only source. He has opened that source once for all in the history of men, but from him it flows into that history, it fills the world.

That source, opened by him on the cross, like that spring of living water 'flowing from the side of the temple', which we hymn in the Easter season, that source truly waters the world, and time, and space: it can give immortality, communion and holiness to every man, to all men. But also it awaits its consummation. What it does here on earth is still a small thing in comparison with what we still wait for, for death still does its work, though by hope and faith we believe it is not final. Sin still exists in us and around us, everywhere, and makes men miserable. Enmity, division and loneliness still weigh on us all. We look forward to a victory, a complete liberation from these things. That victory, that liberation, we really have already, from Jesus Christ our source, but we look for them in their fullness, and we shall have them in their fullness only when he returns. That is why we look forward to his return with all our hearts, all our hope; we are utterly dependent on it. So long as here on earth there are tears and death, enmity and division, loneliness and sin, all the ills which surround us, we shall pray with all our hearts for the coming of Jesus Christ, his coming one day, for all the world, when he will bring us the fullness of those fruits whose seed he planted in his blessed Passion and Resurrection.

It is not for nothing that the Creed, in which our faith is summed up, that Creed we are about to recite together, begins with the words 'I believe', but ends with the words 'I expect'. I believe in God and in Jesus Christ his only Son, but I expect the world to come. Amen.

NOTES

1. Notes taken at a sermon preached in the church of St Séverin in Paris, 7th Dec. 1952 (Advent). Text from the *Bulletin de la Communauté Chrétienne de Saint-Séverin*, no. 21, pp. 11–17.

CHAPTER FOUR

Human Social Groups and the Laity of the Church[1]

SECULAR GROUPS EXIST ORGANICALLY. CAN this fact of the world's life be transposed to the plane of the Church, or is the Church composed only of atomised individuals?

The problem does not concern only the Catholic Church: it is the same with all denominations. Everywhere men are asking whether the commitments of working life have their repercussions in the actual nature of the Church, in the life of the community and in ecclesiology.

Starting from the more general and going on to the more particular, we shall examine:

1. The basic lessons of theology;
2. The lessons of history and tradition;
3. The conditions and limits of this sociological adaptation of the Church.

The basic lessons of theology

We must start with the mission of Jesus himself, when he said: 'I am come to seek and to save that which was lost.'

Reading through the Mass gospels for the Sundays after Pentecost, we notice that most of them are accounts of healing. Jesus heals men because nature is wounded; it needs a saviour. 'Creation waits for redemption': that means that creation has a relation with redemption, that God's response to men's needs is not to fly over their heads. God might have acted by a mere word, but he did not: 'the Word was made flesh'. He responded by an incarnation, by a coming into the world. This has immense consequences.

The mission of Jesus in regard to mankind is all-embracing. It is not only salvation from sin, it is the rescue of nature, which Jesus has taken on himself in its entirety—sin, of course, excepted.

The three functions of kingship, priesthood and prophecy are united in Jesus. His priesthood is kingly, in the sense that it is a priestly power, and his kingship is priestly, for he has not come to reign for reigning's sake, but in order to save. And his prophetic function, that is, his power of revelation, is both kingly and priestly, for it knows all things and is ordered to our salvation.

In Jesus these three functions are plenary. He has the power to change all creation in order to bring it to that perfection which God has willed for it from the beginning, according to a plan which has been spoiled by sin.

The mission of the Church is the same as that of Jesus in its object, but not in its conditions: it is to save man, the whole man, including all that is involved in the life of the world, in social life, in history. It is the same mission, but it is not accomplished in the same way. Christ has not, in fact, handed on all his priestly power to the Church. He himself, during his earthly life, did not exercise the whole of his kingship in its glory. Whenever it escaped him, so to speak, he immediately stopped, covering up, as it were, the light of his kingly power with a sort of extinguisher, which allowed only a dimmed ray to shine through. When men wanted to make him a king, he hid himself. In the garden of Gethsemani he said: 'It is I!' and the soldiers fell back. They felt the shock of his power, but at once he said: 'Put back your sword in its sheath: If I willed, the Father would send me twelve legions of angels, but the Scriptures must be fulfilled.' Jesus put the fullness of his kingly power as it were in parentheses, because he came rather to save than to reign, and it is in that line of action that the Church succeeds to him.

When we examine the conditions of Christ's different functions we can say that he is more king than priest, because he is king directly as incarnate Word, while he is priest because of sin. But the Church is more priest than queen, for in the Church the function of salvation by the cross and by sacrifice predominates over the function of influence and the transformation of things by power. For the Church follows Jesus, not in his condition of power, which he will reveal at his return, but in his coming in humility. On his pattern, she saves, more than she reigns, and that has immense consequences.

That is why there are more souls saved than there are members obeying her laws.

The energies proper to the Church, the energies of her priesthood, her teaching and her regency, which she draws from the energies of Christ, our king, priest and prophet, are essentially spiritual. The Church has no power over the temporal as such. By her ministry she has the obligation to guide men in their duties, even in those which are social or political, and in married life, but she has never had the authority which would allow her to appoint the kings and rulers of this world or to remove them from their seats. Though her power was used in this way during a certain period, that was not derived from her apostolic powers, but from the conditions of Christendom, unanimously accepted during several centuries. Pius IX laid this down very clearly just after the first Vatican Council: 'This right', he said, 'was exercised by the popes in extreme circumstances, but it has nothing to do with papal infallibility. Its source was not infallibility, but papal authority. This, according to the public law then in force, and from the consent of the Christian nations which recognised the pope as the supreme judge of Christendom, was extended to judging princes and states, even in temporal matters.'[2]

The Church reigns *directly*, by her jurisdiction, over the baptised, but over the world as such she has only an *influence*, with no strictly juridical power. Beyond her own subjects she has only an influence, pure and simple, but that is no slight thing: it is immense.

It has been observed for some centuries that the more the Church gives up the exercise of her juridical powers over the world (her clericalism, as we should now say), in order to exercise her prophetic influence and spiritual mission, the more really powerful she is. This seems to be written into the whole history of the world, and it helps to give us a clearer view of the functions of the laity.

In all that action by which the Church saves souls and acts on the faithful, it is chiefly the priesthood which is active, by communicating the fruits of the redemptive incarnation. The priesthood is like some great irrigation system, feeding the lake of the Church from all that flows from the pierced side of Jesus on the cross. It is the priesthood that nourishes the Church, that has the deposit of power, of truth, of the sacraments, of the charisma of truth and spiritual government. That priesthood is the apostolicity of the Church, it is the transmission by the Church of the treasures of the incarnation and the redemption acquired in Christ. If we may put it so, it derives from what is behind, but Jesus Christ is today, yesterday and tomorrow, as St Paul says: he is not in the past. When the Church draws on the fact of the Incarnation, that is chiefly the work of the priesthood. When, on the other hand, it is a question of that action by influence, where she acts, not by jurisdiction, but to bring into the world something in the direction of the kingdom of God, then the Church turns rather to the future, to the Parousia, the kingdom, and then it is rather the action of the laity.

So we ask, what exactly is a layman in the organisation of the Church?

A layman is not a secular man. The word comes from the Greek *laos*, which is used in the bible to denote the people of God. The other peoples are the *ethne*, *nationes*, *gentes*: the layman is a member of the people of God.[3] By what historical process has the word 'laic' come now to mean an anti-clerical, even an anti-Christian? That is the whole tragedy of the modern world, itself the result of the tragedy of Christendom.

The layman is, then, a member of the people of God. He is distinguished from the priest and the monk simply because these are *exclusively* dedicated to the kingdom of God. The working day for us priests is essentially Sunday, the day of the kingdom of God, at least in the parishes. It is the very day when the man who has been bowed down over his earthly work all the other six days, lays it aside and stands erect, just as the church in the village is a house standing up, a house which reveals the third dimension.

We priests are the men who work directly for the kingdom of God, and for that purpose are dispensed from earthly tasks: the bringing of men into the world, the advancement of mankind by science and the professions, that is, work and production.

The marks of the layman's engagement in the world, in the

secular, are marriage and profession. We are dispensed from these two things, but we have to help mankind to advance towards its transcendent end, the kingdom of God.

The layman is the man who works for the kingdom of God, but not at the expense of his earthly engagement. He has to serve God, not by setting himself above or apart from marriage and the professions, but through marriage and the professions, and in work. He does not take the short cut taken by the priest or the religious, who are dedicated solely to the kingdom of God. He follows a road which is longer and more difficult, but it is his own, his vocation.

This enables us to see the layman's place in the mission of the Church. For this purpose we must distinguish the 'sacral' order, in which the Church has power, from the order of influence, of which we spoke just now.

If we consider the sacral order, that is, the Church as an organism of grace, then, strictly speaking, the Church could exist in the bishops alone. That was the case with the apostolic body, but the apostles were not really alone: there were the disciples, the holy women and the Mother of Jesus, who is the first lay person. As an organism of salvation, however, sacramental, prophetic and kingly, the Church could exist solely in the priesthood and the episcopate.

Lay people exist, not in order to constitute the Church as a sacral organism, but to enable her to accomplish her mission fully; to recapitulate, to 'sum up in one' all the values of humanity in Jesus Christ. That is something the Church cannot do without the laity. So the laity are necessary, not that the Church may be a power of salvation, but that she may carry out the fullness of her mission.

Similarly, from the point of view of the apostolate, that is, the propagation and defence of the faith, the priesthood cannot be everywhere. At this moment, one third of mankind is practically without the Catholic priesthood; all of it, that is, between the Pacific and a line drawn two hundred miles east of Strassburg: thirty-one per cent. of the human race, and twenty-eight per cent. of the land surface of the earth. In those lands it is the laity who carry on the Church, as they did in Japan from about 1660 to 1864, when the first missionary set foot again in Japan. For more than two centuries the Church there existed entirely through the laity, who baptised, received consents to marriage, presided at prayer and handed down the catechism. The laity have often done the same in missionary countries. But though they can effectively start the Church, they cannot perfect her. The Church is perfected as the mystical Body only by the sacraments, and above all by the Eucharist, which only the priest can celebrate. So we can truly say that the Church exists in a certain way even without the priesthood, and we must not think that there can be no Church without the cassock and the priestly power. The Church exists through the laity, but she cannot be perfected without the action of the priesthood.

So much for the sacral order of the Church. Consider now her power of influence, without strictly juridical authority. We mean an influence affecting the laws, on the social plane, to make them more human, more open to the faith, and so more in the line of the kingdom of God. It means, on the one hand, creating conditions more favourable for the Gospel (guiding public opinion favourably, as Cardinal Saliège said), and on the other, spreading the faith in the while human field; domestic, cultural, professional, national, international. The only people who can do this effectively are those who are really engaged in these different spheres, who know them and are qualified to speak on them. There is therefore a whole section of her mission to the secular world which the Church can only carry out through the laity, not through the priesthood or the monastic orders, because these, by their state of life and their institution, are detached from secular tasks, outside the increasing of mankind, work and production, cultural creation. If some priests or religious have played a large part in cultural creation, it was a sort of extra; they did it *qua* laymen rather than *qua* priests or monks: here only laymen can extend the Church's influence.

In one of his finest documents, Pius XII said:

> The Church, while carrying out the command of her divine Founder, to 'preach the Gospel to every creature' [that is the sacral order of the Church], is not an empire in the modern sense of the word; she even follows a path opposite to that of imperialism. She advances, not in extent but in depth; she

> looks above all to man himself, she strives to mould man, to perfect the divine likeness in him: her work is done in the depths of each man's heart, but it has its repercussions on the whole duration of life, in all branches of the individual's activities. In men thus formed the Church prepares for human society a base on which it can rest securely. . . . Under this aspect the faithful, the laity, are in the front line of the Church's life: through them the Church is the vital principle of human society; they, in consequence, they above all, must be ever more conscious, not only that they belong to the Church, but that they are the Church.[4]

The text is very clear: the laity are the Church, and they alone are able to be the Church and to carry out her mission in all that zone of the Church's influence on culture, legislation, civilisation, seçular human creative work, outside her strictly sacral order. The laity cannot act on the structure of the world to carry out that mission of the Church which they alone can fulfil, unless they really enter into the destiny of the world, genuinely, according to their secular line. That is why the Church creates organisms which follow in general the natural sociological lines of the world, and groupings which enable her to have that influence and those responses in the secular order (where the Church also has her mission) which she can carry out only through her laity.

The Lessons of History and Tradition

Here we must consider three main stages: primitive Christianity; medieval Christendom and the old régime; Christendom since the French Revolution.

Primitive or apostolic Christianity made little attempt to develop the Christian's temporal relations. It was concerned above all with the primacy of his heavenly vocation, the primacy of eschatology, and did not consider the problem of his insertion in history. This is indisputable from the writings of St Paul. The first Christians thought that history would be short, that the Lord's coming would be very soon, and this world was so utterly opposed to them! There is abundant evidence that these Christians considered themselves to be the third race, *tertium genus*: there were the Jews and the pagans, and now the Christians. Jews and pagans were engaged in the world, Christians were outside the world. The Christians are *paroikoi*, strangers and foreigners. 'Our true city (*RSV*: our commonwealth) is in heaven', says St Paul. We read in Galatians: 'There is neither Jew nor Greek, there is neither slave nor free, there is neither male nor female, for you are all one in Christ Jesus.' It is the resurrection-state: they lived the resurrection.

We must always hold this message to be valid, in the sense that the Christian is always raised above the world by the call from above, he is always the man of the resurrection, and the kingdom of God: 'dealing with the world as though they had no dealings with it' and, in St Paul's paradoxical phrase, 'those who have wives, as if they had none'. It is part of the Christian condition.

But it was impossible for the Church, during the fifty years of the apostolic age, to experience everything that history had in store for her. The apostles could never have imagined what a Christian world would be; what the empire would be like after Constantine, the Carolingians, the Middle Ages. There have been other sociological experiences, which are providential facts of which the Church must take account.

In the Middle Ages, the active laity, the committed laymen, were represented almost solely by the princes: it was enough for the princes to make Christian laws, and the people obeyed. It was enough for the Church to act on the princes for society to be Christian. The laity of the Church was then extremely limited.

But there is an interesting lesson to be learned from an ideology which is no doubt limited in application, but its principle is worth noting: three orders were distinguished in the Church (an order being a stable state, having its rights and obligations and its own members): the *conjugati* or married, the *continentes* or monks, and the *rectores* or *praelati*, the bishops or prelates. This shows that the Church was organically constituted of certain conditions of life, in which the layman, characterised uniquely by the state of marriage, had his place. The idea is very interesting to bear in mind.

Among the *conjugati* sub-categories were sometimes recognised, such as *bellatores*, warriors; *laboratores*, cultivators, etc. Again the Church appears as constituted of laymen, *according to their condition*.

Under the old régime there was great activity on the part of confraternities. It was largely owing to these that the parishes were alive, and in them the faithful were grouped according to their occupations. Here, obviously, the concrete application needs to be revised: there is no point in restoring the confraternities of St Vincent de Paul or St Fiacre: it would be mere antiquarianism, unless these still survive somewhere or other. But we must retain the idea that the Church acted on men through organic groupings, linked to their earthly occupations, for it shows us that it is traditional to base our pastoral action on human structures connected with occupational conditions.

As a matter of fact, has this old régime come to an end everywhere? No: sometimes we have only to travel two hundred miles in order to go back two centuries in time. There are regions in our own country, and still more in others, where the old régime still survives, in the sense that we have to do with a 'good people', like that which once existed among us. I should like to explain myself a little on what I mean by a 'good people', for I think it is very important. What is distinctive about it is that we have to do with a community of men in which there are distinctions, but not by way of opposition: it is a strictly graded community in general, where ranks are much respected, but where men feel that they have something to do together, relying on the common tradition in which all trust.

I had this feeling in the Spanish Basque country. There you have a people full of vitality and joy: it is a people in which the ranks are respected. Once during an excursion we had to hire a big Spanish taxi, and a marquis, Under-Secretary of State in the Ministry of Fine Arts, was chattering the whole time with the driver, roaring with laughter because this good man talked 'Castilian' like a 'Spanish cow', by which he meant a Spanish Basque. This went on with complete familiarity, but with no loss of the sense of the ranks, and this let me put my finger on the meaning of a people's soul. This still exists in odd corners of certain regions.

People lived like this till the Revolution. They were less under the power of technology. In one sense they were poorer: it has been calculated that a workman in the eighteenth century earned only enough to buy a kilogram of bread a day per head. But in this extremely impoverished state they were not in the conditions which are now in course of debasing man. Modern man is so much in the power of industrial and political technology that he looks for ways of escape. A young doctor said lately that the motto of modern life was more and more becoming 'technology and touring'. More frivolously, but in the same sense, I should call it: 'jobs and bikinis'! Man wants to escape from technology, which is crushing him, but in fact he is not much more of a man in his leisure, and in all this there is a kind of suppression of the man himself, which is extremely serious.

But during the first half of the nineteenth century the word 'people' acquired a new meaning. That people before 1789, which I described rather idyllically, I shall call the 'good people'. After that we have a proletarianised people. It is interesting to note the origin of the words: 'sociology' was invented by Auguste Comte about 1840; 'proletarian' appears for the first time in 1817. It is a sign that the industrial revolution of the eighteenth century has begun to bear its fruit.

The essential fact of this period is industrial concentration, with uprooting; the uprooting of man from his traditions, including the religious. He has lost the sense of that strongly hierarchical society, in which there was yet a certain joy of life. That was real: it existed. In its place there is an awareness of class, a sense of class, a people defining itself as a fact of class. In a society which was hierarchical, but confident in its traditions, there was a people which felt it belonged to a whole. But now it is a people 'proletarianised', feeling itself as it were excommunicated, debased and deprived by a society of which it does not truly form a part, and which is no longer its own nation. Did not Toynbee define the proletarian condition by the fact of being in a society with the feeling that one is not organically an active member of it and has no rights in it?

Our Catholic social doctrine, our morality, our way of looking at our work among men, were all formed in the days of the 'good people', and the Church still preserves as an ideal that life of a 'good people', in which men have something to do together, and in and through all their ranks have still a certain joy in their common life.

To the 'good people' corresponded the virtuous 'good priest', of whom there were such fine examples in the seventeenth and eighteenth centuries. It seems to me that the 'Christian people' is not the people of the Middle Ages, which was far more ignorant, but that of the seventeenth and eighteenth centuries, fashioned by the bishops and priests of the post-Tridentine era, which lasted till about 1830, practically till the coming of the railways.

But what corresponds to the people of the nineteenth century is not the ideal set forth in the doctrine of the Church, but much rather the Communist manifesto of 1847, and especially the Marxist analysis. That concept of 'the people', a class opposed on the level of economic situation, is what created, developed and stimulated class-consciousness.

This new people is marked by a *certain* depersonalisation (I say 'a certain', for the workers who are most conscious of the class war are certainly not depersonalised), in the sense that it is dependent on all kinds of factors which dominate it, and which it cannot judge.

A few years ago an article appeared in *Masses Ouvrières* under the title, 'If the Curé d'Ars came back'. Would he, the author asked, convert his parish? No, he would not, for he would find men whose human reflexes were all formed outside the parish, by the trade unions, the co-operatives, politics, excursions, the attraction of the city, the radio: social problems which he never knew in his time.

In the new people man is formed by things beyond the reach of persons, things which he cannot judge clearly; the radio, the laws, the trade unions which are the princes of our modern feudalism, and control everything.

When the Church realised this, what was her reaction? At first it was to establish 'works', 'patronages', and so on. That was the great effort of the nineteenth century, and magnificent energy was displayed in it. It was an attempt to form a 'good people' outside the real conditions of history and the age, where there was no longer a 'good people', but a people in the sense of mass or class. They were really trying to lead it back into the bosom of the Church, where it could again become a 'good people', around 'good priests'. That was no doubt a great work, but it has had its day. We realised that we were gradually losing everyone, and that in any case we were not reaching the representative and really creative *élites* of the people.

What we now have to do is to recognise frankly the real truth, the new sociological structures, the new people, with its new conditions of life, the new feudalism, and to create spiritual movements of the Church inside them, movements of influence, not of power, provided with the necessary organisms, for a soul cannot live without a body. In old days, in the feudal and medieval times, the Church's laity consisted mainly of the lords: the rest of the people followed them. Now, among the staffs of the new feudalism, the factories, the radio and all the rest, which condition modern life, we have to raise up a new laity of the Church, which shall work to make all this conditioning permeable by the Gospel. On the one hand it will be Catholic Action; on the other, certain organisms which are partly in the Church and are like the supply services in the army.

The army, the queen of battles in the front line, is Catholic Action: the supply services are the technical organisms, more or less permanent, more or less *ad hoc* and temporary. An encounter in the course of a social conflict is like a temporary service; permanent organisms are those like the trade unions, the radio, UNESCO, with its present work for basic education. These are the constituent elements of the new feudalism and the new people.

It is incumbent on the Church to continue the tradition, not of the apostolic age, which did not know these problems, but of the Middle Ages and the old régime, and therefore to create organisms adapted to the sociological and especially professional conditions, organisations of lay people inspired by the priests. This is putting into practice the laity-priesthood team, which is like a kind of marriage, a couple. That comparison of the marriage goes far and is very accurate. In marriage the husband decides, but the wife influences the decisions, and so do the children. Similarly in the Church the priests decide and the laity, like the wife, suggests. A Catholic militant is strong if his wife is on the same 'wave-length' as he is, in communion with the same ideas. So the team is strong if the militants are on the same wave-length as the priest, in the communion of the same ideal.

I think I have shown, from the theology of the Church's mission and from history, that the organisms of the Church corresponding to natural sociological organisms are necessary, and have always been needed for the Church to fulfil her mission. It remains for me to define the conditions and limits of this sociological adaptation of the Church.

Conditions and Limits of the Church's sociological Adaptation

I lay stress on these concluding remarks, even if they are not so necessary for Catholic Action chaplains as for other priests, working in conditions less classically than those of the Church.

At all costs we must safeguard the transcendence of Christianity, the faith and the Church.

We must avoid the danger of letting our preoccupations and our conclusions be too coloured by sociology, for the essential thing is the proclamation of the faith; a too exclusively temporal commitment may harm the mission of evangelisation.

We must persevere in maintaining—or rather, promoting—the unity of Christians and preserving the conditions of social unity, by ensuring contacts without watering down commitments, by establishing in frankness and charity a dialogue which aims at understanding why others have other reasons or modes of solution.

We must also strongly desire human unity. The Church is always concerned for the fundamental unity of the society of men. Therefore we have no right to refuse the means at the Church's disposal; we must see things as a whole, together. If the struggle against injustice is a positive element, it is strictly only an element and a stage: it should never prevent us thinking also of the unity of men (which will modify the conditions in which the struggle is carried on). Christians, and priests all the more, who are engaged in the workers' struggle, should never press class-consciousness so far that they forget that wider perspective of the Church.

NOTES

1. Shorthand report of an address to the chaplains of *Action Catholique Ouvrière* (Versailles, 17th Sept. 1953). Published in *Masses Ouvrières*, no. 92, Dec. 1953, pp. 25–40.
2. Speech of 20th July 1871. Quoted by J. Lecler in *The Two Sovereignties*, London and Westminster (Md.), 1952.
3. This needs to be qualified in the light of the fine article by Fr I. de la Potterie, 'L'origine et le sens primitif du mot "laïc" ', in *NRT*, 80 (1958), pp. 840–53. While the noun is not found in the N.T., the adjective was known to secular Greek and the biblical Greek of the LXX, to denote things which were profane, not set apart for worship. Our usage, which was frequent from the third century, is derived from this and not from the word *laos* in its sacred use as 'people of God'. But what is said here is still perfectly true theologically. (Note added in 1961.)
4. Speech at the creation of cardinals, Feb. 1946.

CHAPTER FIVE

Outlines for a Theology of Catholic Action[1]

I. DIFFICULTIES

Since Catholic Action came officially into existence, few congresses have been held, few meetings have taken place, without the same question being raised, in one form or another: what forms part of Catholic Action and what does not? Yet the documents are there for all to see: those of Pius XI and Pius XII, of our cardinals and bishops, of sessions and studies plentiful enough to fill three or four shelves of a library. But in spite of all this, questions still remain, and certain works which professed to answer them have raised yet more.

Considering things rather as a theorist than as a practical man, I shall formulate my own inquiries in this way:

1. What is the exact relationship between Catholic Action, understood as a certain organisation of the Church, officially defined and confirmed, and the apostolate of the laity in its widest sense? It is clear, in fact, that Catholic Action neither creates that apostolate out of nothing, nor includes it entirely in its formations. Now there exists a certain disagreement, occasionally a source of discontent, between certain presentations of Catholic Action as purely and simply the apostolate of the laity, in direct subordination to the priestly authority, and the practice or experience of Catholic life, where things happen differently. Not only do Christians undertake all sorts of things to serve the cause of the Kingdom, but many have activities which they do not

hesitate to describe as apostolic, though they are not attached to any organisation of Catholic Action.

2. What is the 'participation in the apostolate of the hierarchy' by which Pius XI (not without divine inspiration, he used to say) defined Catholic Action? Does the definition preferred by Pius XII, 'collaboration in the apostolate of the hierarchy', represent a change in relation to the former definition? What is the rôle of the 'mandate'?

3. What is the relationship between Catholic Action and temporal action?[2] Within Catholic Action, what is the relationship between activities of evangelisation and those of civilisation?

4. The last question, in a more limited and concrete form, comes up again in this: does Catholic Action involve its members in responsibility for the general conditions of a given sector of life? The question arises chiefly in connection with Catholic Action movements for the young, because of the necessarily more global character of these organisms. They have to be a milieu which supports the young and takes them in charge—whereas adults are supported and taken in charge by more permanent and diversified structures—and also an educative milieu, in which they find formative elements corresponding to all their problems.

5. What are the boundaries of Catholic Action? What is its extent? What is its relation to the action of Catholics, that is, to all that Catholics do in order to serve, even remotely, the cause or the interests of the kingdom of God? Is every kind of collaboration by Catholics in the work of the Church 'Catholic Action'? If the answer is 'Yes', is not the notion of Catholic Action diluted by the whole range of very varied personal enterprises? If it is 'No', then once again, what are the criteria, the distinctions, the relations, between that special, specific activity of Catholic Action and the various activities of Christians? Must we, for example, adopt the distinction lately proposed by M. Jacques Maritain between 'acting professedly as a Catholic' (*agir en tant que catholique*) and 'acting like a Catholic' (*agir en catholique*)?

II. TWO ARTICLES[3]

Some readers will know the articles of Fr Karl Rahner and Fr Charles Baumgartner, and the reactions they provoked.[4]

1. Karl Rahner approached the question of Catholic Action and its relationship with the apostolate of the laity from the starting-point of a very vigorous study, aimed at defining the respective conditions of the laity and the clergy. The lay Christian, he said, is the man whose Christian being and Christian responsibilities espouse the conditions of his natural insertion in the world. He participates, according to his state as a layman, in the mission of the Church. Two types of apostolate, in fact, can be distinguished:

> The apostolate of the hierarchy is constituted by the mission which *takes the place* of the apostle and creates the ministry: the apostolate of the laity, if it possesses the features which distinguish it from the apostolate of the hierarchy, is that of the man in the place that he has originally received in the world (p. 20).
>
> The apostolate of the layman is therefore based directly on his essential nature as a Christian. What determines the extent and mode of that apostolate is not a particular mission received from above, but a mission received from below, that is, expressed by his situation in the world. The line of his Christian influence is the actual line of his relations in the world; it does not have to be constituted by a new mission or mandate (p. 22). If there is no official apostolic mandate, but there is still a genuine apostolate (that is, a legitimate influence on others with a view to their salvation), then we have the apostolate of the layman (p. 18, *n.*).

On the other hand, there is an ecclesiastical apostolate, properly so called. It is that which flows from the apostolic, hierarchic mission, positively instituted by our Lord. That mission withdraws those who receive it from the co-ordinates determined by their natural insertion in the world, and establishes them positively in a state of ministry, and presumes, in different degrees and manners, the exercise of powers relating to the mission received.

So long as laymen co-operate in the Church's task without receiving a part of the properly clerical functions, they remain fully in their lay state. On the contrary:

> . . . the real lay state ceases whenever there is a real, habitual participation in the proper powers of the hierarchy, so that the exercise of those powers characterises the life of those who hold them, that is, determines a state or condition (p. 13). . . . If we use the term in its strict sense, participating in the apostolate of the hierarchy can only mean receiving a part of the ministry of the hierarchy, and therefore also a part of the apostolate and of the mission contained in it: it is to cease to be a layman (p. 15).

Was this mode of defining the possession or loss of the lay state what Pius XII had in mind when he gave his discourse of 5th October 1957 at the opening of the Second World Congress of the Lay Apostolate? A layman, he said, did not become a member of the hierarchy unless he received some degree of the *powers* of Order (e.g., the diaconate) or of jurisdiction (e.g., a layman elected pope, being strictly bound to receive the sacrament of Order). But 'the acceptance by the layman of a particular mission, or of a mandate of the hierarchy, though it associates him more closely with the spiritual conquest of the world carried on by the Church under the direction of her pastors, is not sufficient to make him a member of the hierarchy'.

Rahner did not deny this. But he tried, as I did in Chapter I of my *Lay People in the Church*, to define the lay state not only negatively, by the absence of the powers of order and jurisdiction, but positively, by internal marks. He did so, on the whole, in the same way as I did, but in happier terms: the layman is the Christian whose Christian situation and responsibilities are determined from below, by his insertion in the life of the world, though he has to live that situation and those responsibilities as a Christian, in the strength of the resources of his baptism (and confirmation) and of the *vita in Christo* of a true believer, witnessing to his Lord.

These are two principles of definition, situated on different planes but not contradictory. One is taken from the internal structure of the Church, the other from her existence in the world: one starts from what formally constitutes the lay state. It seems clear that we can characterise this state positively only by considering the Church, not only in herself and her structures, but also in the mission she has in and for the world, in her relation with the life of the world. To do this does not mean moving from a canonical level, purely theological and formal, to a sociological level, depending on a material consideration. The positive definition of the lay state by insertion in the pattern and work of the world still characterises the layman as Christian and member of the Church, and therefore theologically. But, within a theology of the Church, it characterises him, not only in the setting of the internal hierarchic structure of the Church, but in that of the mission which the Church has in and for the world. We shall return to this later.

It would be interesting to hear the reactions of Rahner, and of other theorists of the laity and Catholic Action, to such a phenomenon as, for instance, the *Apostoliki Diakonia* or the Zoë movement in the Greek Orthodox Church.[5] In the Zoë fraternity we have a religious association of celibate laymen and priests (about one-third) who take temporary vows and share their goods in common. A sort of Secular Institute, in fact. The members of the fraternity direct and inspire movements and organisations similar to our Catholic Action. It is common for lay members of the fraternity to teach religion, even theology in University Faculties, and to preach in the churches, though of course not without canonical mission and approval by the hierarchy. Do they thereby cease to be laymen? Orthodox theology does not admit it. But I would entirely agree with M. G. le Bras, speaking of the members of the Secular Institutes, that they form a *quartum genus Christianorum*, alongside the clergy, the monks and the laity of fully lay state.[6]

2. Charles Baumgartner's aim was to show the diversity of kinds or forms of the lay apostolate. Unlike Rahner, who followed an independent line of thought on the idea of the lay state, Fr Baumgartner refers frequently to papal documents, especially to the discourse of Pius XII at the First World Congress of the Lay Apostolate.[7]

He distinguishes two forms of that apostolate: first, that which aims at actively procuring the salvation of souls: that is, the apostolate, properly speaking, in the strict sense of the term. That is Catholic Action. Second, the apostolate of Christian life and example. These two forms, Fr Baumgartner says, differ in their immediate origin, in their content and in their dependance on the hierarchy, and also in the obligation that the faithful have to practise them.

The apostolate, properly so called, represents a direct co-operation in the spiritual ministry of the hierarchy. It therefore places the man who practises it in direct dependence on the latter, a dependence which may admit of different degrees, as Pius XII expressly noted.[8] It demands certain gifts not necessarily possessed by all, so it is not universally obligatory. It does not turn laymen into curates without cassocks, but of its nature it is 'of clerical type or style, in varying degrees'.[9]

The apostolate of the Christian life has for its standard the duty of state: it flows from the very life of a baptised, confirmed Christian, communicating in the Body of the Lord, and therefore under obligation to be, by his life, a witness to Christ. It consists in directing towards God one's earthly life, which the Christian must make into a sign of the sovereign kingship of God. The hierarchy does not create that vocation, it can only remind men of its demands. Here it is a matter simply of living one's earthly life as a Christian, with the intention of letting God reign in it. Even when that temporal life or action is of Christian inspiration, it is not yet apostolate 'in the strict sense of the term'. 'It is not, properly speaking, a task of evangelisation . . . but a testimony of Christian life. It is a spiritual service; it not only builds the earthly city; it contributes, in its order, to the establishment of the kingdom of God, it promotes the active presence of Christianity in the natural structures of human life.'[10]

'If the layman's mission in regard to the world does not derive from a delegation or mandate of the hierarchy, if it is not properly speaking a collaboration in the apostolate of the hierarchy and the clergy, but a really autonomous apostolate inside the Church with its own responsibilities, it obviously does not follow that this apostolate is completely independent of the hierarchy.'[11]

It does depend on it, of course, but in a manner common to all, inasmuch as the Christian must always submit his action to the apostolic teaching.

This article, though very irenic and mainly descriptive, provoked some very sharp reactions. These concentrated mainly on the fact that, in order to distinguish clearly two forms of apostolate, they were labelled with two names and characterised by features which emphasised their differences. Moreover, to a distinction by origin of mission, Baumgartner added a distinction of content. Hence, while the words in which he himself described the Christian's action in his temporal life[12] gave it a *content* of truly apostolic value, he seemed, when speaking, on this subject, of an 'apostolate improperly speaking', to deprive it of the value of a real apostolate. The pope indeed employed the expression, but referring to *mission*. What *Masses Ouvrières* really found fault with in Baumgartner was his making an absolute division between the Christianly led life and a testimony of a really apostolic value: what the pastoral review of *Action Catholique Ouvrière* demanded was that the missionary or evangelistic testimony should be organically inserted in the Christian life, to which Baumgartner did not deny the value of a sign.

Perhaps, too, the reaction of *Masses Ouvrières* betrayed a rather characteristic Jocist tendency, the tendency to identify the Church with *Christian life* uncompromisingly led in the concrete conditions of work and the earthly task: in short, what certain theologians had recently felt they must criticise in the idea of the 'continued Incarnation'.[13]

Baumgartner himself noted[14] that the expression 'apostolate of the Christian life' was not found in the texts of Pius XII, although the idea was there. Since then he will have rejoiced to read, in the pontifical discourse of 5th October 1957, these words:

> Here we elaborate the concept of the apostolate of the laity in the strict sense, according to what we explained above about the apostolate of the hierarchy: it consists in the taking in charge by the laity of tasks which flow from the mission entrusted by Christ to his Church. We have seen that this apostolate always remains the apostolate of the laity and does not become the apostolate of the hierarchy, even when it is carried out under the hierarchy's mandate. It follows that it is preferable to describe the apostolate of prayer or personal example as apostolate in the broad or 'improper' sense of the word.

It is still not the expression 'apostolate of the Christian life' but, once again, it is the reality. But between the pope's text and

Baumgartner's there still remains a notable difference. The pope has previously stated that the 'apostolate in the strict sense' does not become an 'apostolate of the hierarchy' even when carried out with the mandate of the hierarchy: he has, in fact rejected the idea that that apostolate is 'of clerical style or type'. Baumgartner, who coined this expression, has retained something, on the other hand, of the idea of Rahner (whose study he had translated) according to which Catholic Action or the apostolate in the strict sense is, in itself, a clerical thing, being properly the ministry of the hierarchy. That is what has led him to appear, at least, to over-emphasise the distinction, if it is not actually an absolute division, between apostolate (improperly speaking) of life and apostolate in the strict sense.

With regard to our first question,[15] Baumgartner's article had the great interest of clearing Catholic Action's system (if we may put it so) of a possible claim to a monopoly of the apostolate. It has given fresh precision to an idea already recognised, but worth recalling, that there are other titles to the apostolate besides that of a monolithic and totalitarian Catholic Action—a salutary message of diversity and freedom.

III. SOME PRINCIPLES RECALLED

1. *Relations between the Church and the World*

The Church is not merely the spiritual animator of the world, or the internal sense of history, even of history in its Godward orientation. She does indeed enter history, and enters it to orientate it towards God, as far as that is possible in the 'flesh', but she is not confined to that, she is not identified with the fruit she has to bear. She exists herself, in herself, as a thing which comes neither from the world nor from history. She exists as an institution of salvation freely founded by God, as an order of holiness apart. *The Church exists in herself*, by an original, gratuitious and positive act of God, not to be reduced to the act of creation or to God's general governance of the world.[16]

Existing in herself, she yet does not exist *for* herself. She is not identified with her mission, but she has a mission for the world. She *is* not simply the animation of the world towards its divine end, but she has to provide this animation. The Church, like

Jesus Christ, is a gift made by God to the world, to draw the world back to him. That is why the relations between the Church and the world are very different from those, for example, between a jewel and the casket containing it, or between a prisoner and the walls of his cell. The Church and the world are two different entities, but they are united by a common end: with only this slight difference, that God is the *ultimate* end of the world, while he is the Church's *specific and proper* end. The Church is intrinsically specified by salvation, that is, supernatural communion with God and with all men together in God.[17] The world is intrinsically specified by a sum of temporal good things—civilisation, the content of history—but it is finally ordered to salvation, and the Church has the mission, in and for the world, of procuring that order towards God in which salvation consists.

All this produces a certain tension at the very heart of Christian thought. The existence of the Church in herself, existence of the Church in and for the world; order of holiness apart, mission of cosmic dimensions; these are the poles between which the tension exists. As always in such cases, the possibility or, if you like, the temptation, is to polarise one's thought on one pole only and thus, by suppressing the tension, to effect a simplification which is something like a betrayal. One could, in fact, consider the Church only in her existence in herself, as the order of holiness apart, the peculiar domain of purity, and care little or nothing about her mission in and for the world. Or one could be so interested in the world and the movement of history as to consider the Church only under the aspect in which she finds herself involved in it, or in the line of a maximum commitment, and to forget in practice, if not in theory, that before having a mission for the world she exists in herself, in her divinely instituted order of holiness.

No doubt these two attitudes do not exist as formulated theories: that would be heresy or very near it. But they exist as opposed psychological tendencies; at that level they are even the source of antagonistic parties who could be briefly described as integralists and progressives. It would be easy to give details and concrete examples of the two attitudes, whose quarrel burdens and renders sterile so many things in French Catholicism.

To return to our subject, let me define in a few words the content of that mission of the Church in and for the world. It consists in two points: (1) to convert men, to make them disciples;[18] therefore, evangelisation; (2) to guide the world towards God and to order it, as far as possible, according to God; therefore, action in the temporal sphere, or civilisation. The second is secondary to the first. Classical theology speaks, in fact, of the Church's second mission, when it is a question of that influence which she ought, and tries, to have in the human work of civilisation.[19] That influence is necessary, and is so for more than one reason, all grounded in the fact of the unity of the human person, and the unity of the total plan of God. From one aspect, in fact, the influence on civilisation is a necessary consequence of the Church's saving action in man: it is demanded by faith and love. A Christian cannot just accept any forms of social life and action: he wants the world in which he lives to be conformed as far as possible to the will of God, which is love, justice, brotherhood, communion, service. From another aspect, both experience and theological reason show that a certain human quality is invariably required for a man to become really Christian.[20] If one has no men, one cannot make any Christians. That is why, in the missions, the Church has constantly laboured to raise the condition of women and children, to teach men to work, to instruct them, educate them, care for them, carrying on all this simultaneously with the primary action of evangelisation; so that the work of civilisation pertains both to the magnificent fruits of the apostolate and to its 'preambles', to the signs and to the conditions of the approach of the Kingdom.

By converting men to faith and baptising them, according to the mission she has received from her Lord, the Church presents and actualises herself as the 'order apart' of salvation and holiness in the world. By acting in the sphere of civilisation, which means in the temporal order and in history, she fulfils her mission to be the soul of human society. She effects a beginning—here limited to the strictly human order, attaining the properly cosmic order only in some signs and adumbrations—of that *consecratio mundi* spoken of in the Martyrology of Christmas Day, and of which Pius XII said, in his discourse of 5th October 1957:[21] 'It is in essentials the work of the lay people themselves, of men who are clearly involved in economic and social life, taking part in government and legislative assemblies.'

2. *Definition of the Lay State*

The words of Pius XII we have just quoted, and which (as he himself remarked) echo the very illuminating words of his discourse to the new cardinals on 20th February 1946, show once more that there exists a consensus of fact on how we are to understand the lay state and define it positively. Going beyond the wholly negative canonical definition of the layman as one who is not a cleric, who has power neither of order nor of jurisdiction, agreement is reached in practice on a positive definition: the layman is the Christian whose contribution to the work of salvation and the advancement of the kingdom of God (and so to the double task of the Church) is made in and by his involvement in the structures of the world and in temporal work.

That was my definition in *Lay People in the Church.* The way in which Rahner formulates what is really the same idea is very interesting, and I would gladly accept it: the man who preserves in his Christian being, as such, the determinants of his natural insertion in the world.

It is because of that situation that the Christian laity is the point where the leaven of the Gospel is thrust full into the meal of the world and meets its historical reality. 'It is by the mediation of the layman's conscience that the divine law is written into the earthly city.'[22] In that sense, as Pius XII said in his allocution of 20th February 1946, the laity 'are in the front line of the Church's life; through them, the Church is the vital principle of human society; they, in consequence, they above all, must be ever more conscious that they not only belong to the Church but they *are* the Church, that is, the community of the faithful on earth.'[23] They *are* the Church insofar as she tries to be the soul of human society. They do not constitute her in her proper being as an institution of salvation: to think that would be to adopt a purely associationist view of the Church, as it is found in certain Protestant theorists, but also as it is absolutely contradicted by the biblical evidence on the institution, in the apostles, of an organ of salvation. If we view the Church as intrinsically existing by a positive divine institution, she is much more truly the mother of the faithful than made by them. But if we view her in *her mission*, especially in her second mission, that of being the soul of human society in order to guide it towards God and according to God, then we can say that the laity not only form part of the Church, but they *are* the Church.

3. *Mission and Apostolate*

In the term 'mission', it seems necessary to distinguish two different meanings. In a general way, a mission is a task entrusted to someone, in connection with certain means to be employed. But this definition, with its vague reference, can either be given its widest and most comprehensive sense, or restricted by a definition. There is, we may say, the mission as a simple responsibility or task, and the mission as a mandate.

Similarly we can define the apostolate in the wide sense, as the activity the aim or content of which is to 'lead men to Christ and his kingdom' (Pius XII),[24] or to exercise 'a legitimate influence on another with a view to his salvation'.[25] It needs little thought to realise that the apostolate follows from the mission either in its stricter or in its wider sense.

God has, in fact, a positive plan for the salvation of men and his reign among them. This plan is that of the history of salvation: before Christ it was called Israel and led up to Christ. He is its decisive and supreme moment. After him, everything comes from him and refers back to him. But he himself has determined positively the order of salvation which men must find in him; he has done it by the institution of the apostolate of the twelve, from whom are derived the various degrees of the hierarchical ministry, with the triple power of order, teaching and spiritual government. That is apostolate (mission) in the precise or strict sense. It is constituted by a positive and defined mandate, accompanied by the communication of appropriate resources, under the form of 'powers', properly so called.

But by engendering Christians the hierarchical apostolate forms men for whom the Christian life creates responsibilities and provides corresponding spiritual resources. For this reason, a mission in the wide sense exists for all the faithful, as so many papal texts have proclaimed.[26] Fundamentally, the apostolic organism of the Church, just like the Church herself, comprises those two registers: *Congregatio fidelium* is first *Ecclesia convocans et congregans*, and also *Ecclesia convocata et congregata*, to borrow an expression of de Lubac's.[27] The mission of the faithful in the wider sense is determined by the circumstances in which they find themselves placed, and the chief of these circumstances is obviously their situation in the world,[28] but also the occasions and, above all, the graces received and the inspiration of the Holy Ghost.

The same ideas and the same distinctions might be expressed in terms of the motherhood of the Church. We are accustomed to think of that motherhood being exercised almost entirely by the use of the particular, divinely instituted means of grace: the sacraments, the priesthood, official preaching. But Holy Scripture and the Fathers, and the facts of ecclesiastical life at all times, teach us that all the faithful also exercise that motherhood, in their own way, by faith, charity, prayer, and all the *vita in Christo* (*in Spiritu Sancto*), with all that this implies of value for the satisfaction, merit and co-operation in the redemption. The first to exercise that motherhood was our Lady, in the wholly exceptional conditions of her predestination as Mother of the Incarnate Saviour-Word, and of her grace. But it is *that* motherhood that she exercises on behalf of all mankind, she who has no hierarchical power, and is, may we say, the first lay person. The Fathers constantly point out how Mary realises the spiritual motherhood which they also attribute to all the faithful; *concepit fide, cooperata est caritate ut fideles in ecclesia nascerentur*.[29] There is a birth of souls through faith and charity, even without explicit testimony in words or activity expressing the faith. Texts are abundant. St Augustine provides the richest and most explicit. If, he says, we consider Christians as individuals in isolation, we ought to call them sons of the *ecclesia*, but if we consider them in the unity they form by *caritas*, we should ascribe to them the rôle and the value of mother, for it is in that unity, in that *caritas*, that souls are brought forth to God, sins are forgiven and the sacraments bear their fruit of grace.[30]

All this may seem theoretical. But it is extremely real and concrete, even if, unhappily, we take little notice of it in the elaborations of pastoral theology. It is proved in the daily experience of the Church's life, but sometimes God enables us to understand it more vividly. That motherhood by faith, love and prayer shines out, for example, in the wonderful and providential story of St Teresa of Lisieux.[31] For here was a young woman, who never left her Carmel, dying there at the age of twenty-four, but who became, not only in an officially recognised title, but in very truth, the universal patroness of the Missions. Installed at the heart of faith, love and prayer for the Church, she superlatively performed the function of spiritual motherhood, to which every Christian is in fact called. It would not be difficult to illustrate, by examples taken from the life of the Christian communities (where such really exist), the truth of this vocation to spiritual motherhood. But then we should have to envisage also, on the one hand, the value realised by such communities as signs of the Kingdom, and on the other, the part played by the Christian's witness, not only that which he shows by all his life (apostolate of personal example: Pius XII), but also that which he bears explicitly by the confession of his faith.[32] Better still, we should here refresh our biblical knowledge on the idea of witness.[33]

We should then see that the word in the bible meaning 'to bear witness' comes from a root which contains the concrete image of repeating, of impressing by repeating, and the idea of indicating one's will repeatedly and tenaciously. So that to bear witness means to lay down insistently, never daunted by contradiction, the affirmation of God's plan and its greater moments. So doing, the witness takes his stand on the past (and normative) acts and expressions of that plan, but he is also longing for its realisation, now and in the days ahead. By his testimony he advances the realisation of God's plan towards its final term, through all the circumstances in which he is placed by the passing of time. In these conditions the testimony is not only conduct, behaviour or speech; it is also every action which places the saving Plan of God before the world. From faith to action, passing through life and its value as sign; then by explicit speech, his *confessio fidei* is of one stuff throughout. The Christian life is all of one growth. It is, in the wider sense of the word, thoroughly apostolic.

It is clear that the apostolic mission in the strict sense is a priestly and hierarchical thing. If laymen are in some way taken on to it, it will be by participation in the mission proper to the bishops, and as assistants to the priesthood in its proper domain. Pius XII speaks of a 'taking in charge by the laity of tasks which flow from the mission entrusted by Christ to his Church'.[34] Mission as simple responsibility, on the other hand, and the apostolate in the broad sense, come to them from their ordinary quality as Christians, and in its commonest sense presume no further dependance on the hierarchy than the general dependence that all Christian life has in relation to the leaders of the Church in matters of faith, sacramental life and Christian conduct.

So it is one thing to take one's part, simply as a Christian, in the common task of the Church, another thing to receive a charge, as occasion arises, of part of the mission properly belonging to the hierarchy. Yet the two missions and the two apostolates are like concentric circles, they have the same aim and the same content. When we speak of the spontaneous apostolate of the baptised as 'apostolate in the wide and improper sense of the word' (Pius XII), we do not mean to deny to it the quality of an apostolate on the ground that it has any other content, any other intention than to 'lead men to Christ and his reign'; we simply indicate that it is an apostolate without mission in the strict sense, one, therefore, which is more diffused, imprecise, connected with God's plan in a more uncertain and precarious manner. We may certainly describe the hierarchical mission as an apostolate 'in the strict sense' (Pius XII), because it flows expressly and directly from the mission entrusted by Christ to the apostles. But we cannot distinguish apostolate in the strict sense from the spontaneous apostolate of the laity simply on the line of distinction between evangelisation and civilisation, or action on the temporal plane. These two things belong to the Church's mission, as its first object and its second or consequent object. But every man is called to fulfil that mission according to his condition. Priests are placed by their priesthood, as ministers, in the Church as an institution of salvation and an 'order apart' of holiness; they are therefore withdrawn from their insertion in the pattern of the world. The laity are consecrated by baptism to the kingdom of Christ, but are left free for their temporal commitments (provided that they are not contrary to God's law): for this reason, Christian influence in the temporal order to guide it towards God and according to God, is as it were, appropriated to them.

IV. SOME APPLICATIONS

The faithful perform, and have always performed, a great many activities with the aim of serving the cause of the Gospel and the kingdom of God. A mother, for instance, in agreement with her priest, teaches her children the catechism, or, it may be, in the course of ordinary day-to-day contacts, she says a word about some children who ought to be sent to church, or a sick person who is being prepared for a visit from the priest, or a marriage which needs regularising. The chances to do something for religion are endless. A man who is able to do so agrees to take on a collection for charity, or to defend the moral or material interests of the Christians in an organisation, a municipal council, or in his profession. Is this Catholic Action?

We should willingly call it the *action of Catholics* if this notion, endorsed in more than one official document,[35] did not seem to be confined in them to action in the temporal sphere—somewhat imprecisely, we think, for whereas St Pius X passed from 'the action of Catholics' to 'Catholic Action' and used the terms as equivalent, Cardinal Caggiano contrasted them, one being the action of the Catholic citizen in the temporal sphere, the other being every action done in the domain of the Church, as the hierarchy's instrumental cause. Was this not to transpose a distinction concerning the title-deeds of the action to one concerning the objects? This is not the same thing, and is liable to put too much separation between the lay people, weakened in the really religious field, and the clergy. However, if we really want to include in it an apostolic action in the wide sense, we could give the name 'action of Catholics' to all those enterprises undertaken by Christians in their personal or private capacity (*ex spiritu*), assuming that they are subject to the rules of orthodoxy and good order which govern the activity of all Christians. We should still be within this category even if the action were not that of an individual but the concerted action of a group: several women teaching the catechism, several men carrying out some action in their profession.

How then are we to place Catholic Action in relation to this action of Catholics? What exactly is it?

Catholic Action being an official organisation, constituted from above as a service of the Church, inasmuch as the Church is herself a positive divine institution, could be considered in the first place as taking over, at least in part, that action of Catholics, educating it, putting at its service wider means of training and action, and finally making that part of the action of Catholics into an official organ of the hierarchy, its *longa manus*, as some documents put it.[36] Catholic Action would then be an official organism of the Church (in so far as she is, in the world, an original and supernatural reality of positive divine law), by means of which all that Christians do in the world and among men to serve the cause of the kingdom of God would rise from the level of a mission in the wide and improper sense to that of a mission expressly received from Christ, which constituted the apostolate of the twelve and their successors. Such was the idea I proposed in an article in 1946 and in *Lay People*.[37] It appealed to papal documents and could appeal to the discourse of 5th October 1957: I still hold it to be valid. Here I part company with Karl Rahner, who says: 'Catholic Action as such cannot be the organism of the apostolate of lay people as such. Catholic Action and the action of Catholics do not coincide . . ., for what is called, in the concrete, Catholic Action, cannot penetrate where the apostolate of the laity is exercised: in the family, the profession and concrete activities.'[38]

The fact is that to Rahner the apostolate of the laity as such is simply the practice of the Christian life in the situation determined for each by his natural position in the world. For the exercise of that sanctification of life, only the laity, only individual Christian persons, are responsible. Catholic Action, however, is an organism *of the Church*, limited to the Church's competence: its function is (i) to form Christians spiritually for a total Christian life: (ii) to safeguard the rights of the Church in public life: (iii) to devise various aids for the clergy, in the *clergy's* special task.

We may wonder whether this interpretation does full justice, on the one hand, to the content of the apostolic mission received from Christ by the twelve and, on the other, to the content of the apostolic task of the Christian laity.

As to the first point, does it not exclude from the Church's apostolic mission the duty of ordering the world, as far as possible, to God and according to God? No, but it limits that duty to what pertains strictly to the apostolic mission: teaching Christians to act like Christians in all things. That is enough. Rahner really draws a logical conclusion from the distinction between

Church and world, which one is increasingly inclined to make, after the symbiosis and confusion produced by the régime of Christendom. The Church, as a supernatural order of holiness and a divine institution of salvation has no direct responsibility for the world as such: that belongs to men who, if they are Christians, will wield it in a Christian way. The Church is bound to teach them that: it is for them to wield it. That gives the action of the laity an autonomy (relative, of course, since it does not at all release them from apostolic authority) to the extent of the responsibilities which are theirs. There would then be room for detailing in this sense what we said above about the mission which the Church has in and to the world: to make a disciple of it, to order it towards God and according to God. It is true that the Church has this twofold charge, but the second part is really second and consequent: the Church achieves it by fulfilling the first: it is in the strongest sense that, in the words of Pius XI, she does not evangelise by civilising, she civilises by evangelising.

We should be less in agreement on the second point. It seems to me that Rahner too narrowly limits the apostolate of the layman to the sphere of his Christian life lived in the setting determined by his natural position in the world. 'Action and speech', he says, 'come into play only in so far as they form part of what the Christian must do in order to live as man.'[39] This is to say too little. It is to situate the layman too far outside the Church's sacral order. He too forms part of it. Faith and baptism consecrate him and impose on him the duty, besides the grace, of the *confessio fidei.*[40] I think Fr Rahner sets up an unwarranted barrier between the Christian responsibility of the laity and the work of the Church as such, flowing from the mandate she has received from Christ. There is more continuity between them. That is why, when certain activities of the laity are adopted by the hierarchy as fitted to help it in its own task, the laymen concerned are not thereby attached to a clerical or priestly type of apostolate.[41] For they are members, as Christians and baptised, of the body summoned to the kingdom of God, of that sacred organism which received, in the twelve, a mission in and for the world.

Here, too, it would be a good thing to make it clear in what conditions the faithful remain, as Christians, inserted in the frame of history and the world. It is not exactly as other men are. Faith and their membership in the body of Christ begin by withdrawing them from it. They raise them, in some fashion, above those earthly co-ordinates; they make them citizens of the kingdom, eschatological men, just as much as the priests or the monks, but in different conditions. In Christ, in whom they cause men to live, there is neither male nor female, employer nor employed, Frenchman nor German.[42] But because their particular service of the Kingdom consists in sanctifying these very elements of the world, the laity receive back these tasks of the earthly life anew, they receive them and have, as it were, to re-espouse them 'in the Lord'. They are called to live them as a portion of the work of God. Their insertion in the world is given back to them, but it is no longer exactly the same. The world has become for them the Father's domain, an adumbration of the kingdom of God.[43] These are neither abstractions nor sublime fancies: it is the very law of an earthly life lived in the love of God. But we can see how the fact that the laity's mission is set in the frame of the temporal order does not lessen their membership in the sacred order of the kingdom of God, which is adumbrated on earth in the Church, the body of Christ. These things must be borne in mind if we are to think rightly of the connection of the laity's special action with the mission which the Church received from Christ in the persons of the apostles.

In his important speech of 5th October 1957 Pius XII opened a new perspective. Not entirely new, for it is part of that line of thought in which the stages are marked, first, by the substitution of 'collaboration' for 'participation' in the definition of Catholic Action,[44] then by the great doctrinal discourses,[45] and even by the assimilation of the Spanish Marial Congregations to Catholic Action.[46] We know that Pius XII, even before he succeeded Pius XI, substituted for 'participation' (in his definition of Catholic Action, 'participation in the apostolate of the hierarchy') the word 'collaboration'. The new word expressed as forcibly as the old the fact that the apostolate, in the full sense of the mandate-mission, belongs to the hierarchy. In that apostolate, in the full sense of the word, the faithful only participate or collaborate, as the case may be. Catholic Action is not an *independent* work of the laity.

To speak of 'participation', however, might suggest the idea of a certain admission to the hierarchy itself, whereas in Pius XI's thought it only meant taking part in its task. To express that, however, the word 'collaboration' is undoubtedly better.

It has another advantage: it avoids suggesting the idea of a single, monolithic or even, we might say, monopolistic institution. It is more comprehensive. It makes it clearer that there are many ways of assuming a part of the task with which the hierarchy is invested. Many forms of those enterprises by which Catholics become active in the Church's task, whether of evangelisation or of civilisation, can thus be adopted by the hierarchy, as fulfilling a portion of its own mandate, and so become Catholic Action, an apostolate in the strict sense. It is in this sense that the papal discourse of 5th October 1957 lays down the definition of Catholic Action.

> Catholic Action has always the character of an official apostolate of the laity. Two points here must be noted: the mandate, especially that of teaching, is not given to Catholic Action as a whole, but to its organised members in particular, according to the will and choice of the hierarchy. Nor can Catholic Action claim a monopoly of the apostolate of the laity, for alongside it there exists the free lay apostolate. Individuals and groups can place themselves at the disposal of the hierarchy and be entrusted by it, for a definite or indefinite time, with certain tasks, for which they are given a mandate. It may then, certainly, be asked whether they also become members of Catholic Action. The important point is that the hierarchical Church, the bishops and priests, can choose lay collaborators when they find persons able and willing to help them. . . .

This doctrine is extremely clear, even if it leaves some questions open. The hierarchy is the inheritor of the mission entrusted by Christ to the apostles and furnished with powers in the strict sense. In this task the faithful collaborate on their own initiative in many ways, in the framework of their lay state. Certain of those activities, or others suggested by the bishops or priests, seem to the hierarchy to fulfil, at least partly, some one of the parts of their own mission. The hierarchy adopts them by a mandate, and this, it is emphasised (not without apparent, contradiction of what we were lately told), is not given to an organisation, to a sort of great formal framework, but to organised men. It is less a matter of organisations than of *tasks* undertaken by (organised) men. If this adoption is made and this mandate is given in a *stable* manner, there you have Catholic Action. If the group of organised laity and the activity it undertakes are adopted or mandated for an occasion or temporarily then it is a question whether it should be called Catholic Action, but that is of little importance. We must never forget the primacy of concrete *tasks* over *organisations*. The pope put an end, once for all, to the idea that Catholic Action is an organisation defined and privileged for all time, which could disqualify all groups not in its own Debrett, so to speak, even when these groups actually carried out the real objects of Catholic Action.[47] He suggests 'two practical reforms, one of terminology, the other of structure':

> First, the term 'Catholic Action' must again be given its general sense and applied only to the totality of lay apostolic movements, organised and recognised as such, nationally or internationally, by the bishops on the national level, by the Holy See for those which aim at being international. It will therefore be sufficient for each particular movement to be denoted by its name and characterised by its specific form, and not according to the general kind. The reform of structure will follow the fixing of the meaning of the terms. All groups would belong to Catholic Action and keep their own name and autonomy, but all together they would form, like Catholic Action, a federative unity. Every bishop would be free to admit or refuse a movement, to give it or not give it a mandate, but he would not be free to refuse it for not being Catholic Action by its very nature.

Thus, instead of a unitary organism, with multiple sections, Catholic Action would become a federation of activities and groups, adopted by the hierarchy as fulfilling part of its mission, freedom being reserved to each bishop to adopt a particular group or not. As early as 1951 Pius XII said that 'Catholic Action is a meeting point of those active Catholics who are always ready to collaborate with the apostolate of the Church'.[48]

But it is more than a meeting-point: it is also a co-ordination, a picked body of men, a tradition, a school of training: a service endowed with powerful central facilities: permanent chaplains, publications, congresses, inter-movement and international connections: a means of supervision and also direction: a means which is supplementary and more specific in relation to the task adopted, to ensure that the actions of the faithful are shaped by the Catholic mind.

After what we have now recalled or explained, several questions formulated at the beginning of this article seem to have found an answer: certainly questions 1, 2, 3 and 5. It remains to outline an answer to question 4. This included two questions, which we must deal with in turn:

(*a*) Does Catholic Action involve its members in taking charge of the general conditions of a given milieu of life?

After what has been said, the question simply means: does the mission entrusted to the apostles by Christ involve such a taking in charge?

We might answer by not merely distinguishing but separating the task of evangelisation and sanctification (considered as the exclusive concern of the hierarchy) from the task of civilisation, the peculiar concern of Caesar and the citizens as such. But this could be ambiguous and lend itself to an ambiguous interpretation. The popes, Pius XII in particular, have often protested against the idea of a purely spiritual sphere, cut off from all influence on society. Man is, without any possible separation, both Christian and citizen: the Christian in him must both inform and animate the citizen.[49] But the papal documents are as prudent as they are clear. When they speak of the 'Church', meaning mainly the hierarchy or the priesthood acting in their sacral order, they say that the Church must form the whole man. When they speak of effective action in public life, they usually speak of Catholics.[50] This fully agrees with what has been said above. It is the duty of Catholic Action to be the link between these two levels of execution of the same mission.

However, the primacy of evangelisation over the temporal activities inspired by it necessarily entails a fact which is one of the constants of history. In the life of the Church the demand of the spiritual for transcendence and purity perpetually raises the question of the manner in which the spiritual enters into the temporal. To many facts of missionary history[51] or the contemporary history of the country[52] could be added the memory of what happens in mission lands or the recent crises in France. Prolonged study of the history of the relations between the Church and State, between the spiritual and the temporal, has sufficiently convinced me that there has never existed, and no doubt never will exist, before the coming of the kingdom, any formula fully adequate to, and therefore definitive and normative of, their difficult relations. If the Gospel formulates a thesis—'Go, make disciples of all the nations'; make every man, the whole man, a Christian—history, on the other hand, shows us a series of hypotheses, adumbrations, adaptations and approximations: a succession of inquiries and more or less satisfying formulas of an agreement both necessary and difficult. Here on earth, tension between the two can never be suppressed. Now, these relations between spiritual and temporal, which were formerly sought almost entirely in political and juridical terms, are now being expressed increasingly in much wider terms of civilisation, because there increasingly exists a purely human civilisation which demands to be purely earthly.

(*b*) Catholic Action for the young exists in particular conditions. Is this not because it represents, for its members, (1) a milieu which is educative, and therefore more total and exclusive, (2) a milieu which ought to support them when they have not yet found their total insertion in the world, a full insertion which comes with the family, the job and complete civic and political responsibilities? The fact that for them it is a matter, not so much of active commitments as of educating consciences with a view to future commitments, means that the Christian educative movement itself will tackle problems which are temporal in themselves. The Catholic Action youth movement ought, however, to stop short at the point where taking a stand would practically involve political action. The criterion is, I admit, difficult to maintain, especially in moments of crisis, when pure moral or spiritual testimony has the effective value of action.

We must be equally awake to the fact that in our day youth is seen, far more than formerly, as a world of its own, with its own set of facts. This is something we have only to open our eyes to see, and the whole development of philosophical and sociological studies tends in this direction. In former days the child or the adolescent was scarcely considered as anything but a future adult, a still very imperfect adult—a state from which there was a tendency to escape as soon as possible. That is one of the reasons why children and young people matured sooner than now. Nowadays they are considered as a world of their own. Further, the fierceness of competition characteristic of the modern world, and the fact that youth needs both to adapt itself to that competition and to be defended against its devouring and destroying character, gives increasingly a sort of independent existence to the problems of youth as such. No pastoral plan for the young, and therefore no Catholic Action for the young, can avoid assuming these data and envisaging these problems. This tends to give them a character more global, more total, more indistinct than that of adult Catholic Action. In times of quiet, this does not present too difficult a problem, but in troubled times the problems are insoluble. Then, it seems, all one can do is to state as purely and clearly as possible the principles of distinction and the hierarchy of values, and for the rest, to be patient and tolerant, not to insist in season and out of season on final demands; to explain our problems and reasons to one another; to emphasise resources, the demands and the reality of full communion in the Church (the bible, the liturgy, charity).

At this level, in fact, the problem is not peculiar to youth movements. It is that difficult problem of communion between Catholics as soon as they are really treated as responsible people, which is the very condition of their effective action. Insofar as Catholic Action does not confine itself within the sacral domain of the life of the Church as divine institution of salvation, but seeks an influence in the world and to that end assumes at least a part of the action of Catholics, it is committed to a path of tension for which there can be no advance solution, once for all, except by suppressing one of the terms of the tension. This might happen in two ways. We might claim to align everyone on positions uniformly and officially defined as obligatory: that would mean either skating over problems or giving the hierarchical Church a political aspect.[53] Or, as Karl Rahner wishes, we might separate the apostolate in the strict sense from the action of Catholics. If Catholic Action takes over, at least partially, the action of Catholics, it must at the same time conduct it on the lines of a work of the Church and admit a margin of freedom in action. Only on this condition can the action really be that of responsible persons, the only persons who can carry it out.

NOTES

1. Article written in Dec. 1957 at the request of the chaplains of the Jeunesse Agricole Chrétienne, and published in *Les Cahiers du Clergé Rural*, no. 200, Aug.–Sept. 1958, pp. 387–405.
2. I use 'temporal action' in the widest sense, to comprise not only political and civic commitments (municipal or trade union affairs) but all the activities by which men seek to organise their collective earthly life.
3. I here restore section B, which was omitted from *Les Cahiers*, all the subscribers being familiar with the debate. This may not be the case with some readers of this book. Also, Karl Rahner has reproduced his article in his *Theological Investigations* (note added in 1961).
4. Karl Rahner, 'L'apostolat des laïcs', in *NRT*, no. 78, Jan. 1956, pp. 3–32; C. Baumgartner, 'Formes diverses de l'apostolat des laïcs' in *Christus*, no. 13 (Jan. 1957), pp. 9–33.

Reactions in German reviews (on which see A. Z. Serrand, in *Vie Int.*, May 1955, pp. 107–13); add also H. Schauf, 'Ueber die dogmatisch-kirchenrechtliche Grundlage des Laienapostolates in der Kirche', in *Aachen 1958 Dioz.-konferenz*, pp. 8–31 (see *Herder-Korr.*, 13 (1959), pp. 223f); A. Sustar, 'Der Laie in der Kirche', in *Fragen der Theologie heute*, Einsiedeln, 1957, pp. 519–48. In Spanish: Alonso Lobo, 'Concepto teologico-juridico del apostolado seglar', in *Rev. Espan. Derecho Can.*, 13 (1958), pp. 5–42. In English: J. Fitzsimons, 'Pius XII and the Apostolate of the Laity', in *The Clergy Review*, 43 (1958), pp. 530–8. But for France I specially mention Mgr Tiberghien, 'Une controverse sur l'A.C.', in *Masses ouvr.*, no. 127 (Feb. 1957), pp. 41–52 and the collective article in the same review, no. 128 (March 1957), pp. 1–30; G. Dejaifve, 'Laïcat et mission de l'Église', in *NRT*, 80 (1959), pp. 22–38; G. Philips, *L'état actuel de la pensée théologique au sujet de l'apostolat des Laïcs* (*Folia Lovaniensia*, 12 = extr. from *Ephem. Theol. Lovan.*, 1960, pp. 877–903), Louvain, 1960, pp. 880f. (I have borrowed from it some of the items in the bibliography given in this note).
5. See *Unitas*, French edition, Jan.–Feb. 1953, pp. 8f; G. Dejaifve, 'Le "revival" de l'Eglise orthodoxe de Grèce' in *NRT*, April 1955, pp. 400–7; P. Hammond, *The waters of Marah. The present state of the Greek Church*, London, 1956, pp. 37, 115f (on *Zoë*), 128, 138f, 159 (on *Ap. Diak.*).
6. *Prolégomènes* (*Hist. du Droit et des Institutions de l'Église en Occident*, I), Paris, 1955, p. 36, n. 1.
7. 14th Oct. 1951.
8. Speech of 14th Oct. 1951 to the first World Congress of the Lay Apostolate.
9. P. 18.
10. P. 25.
11. Pp. 25–6.
12. See *supra*, from his p. 25.
13. A. Z. Serrand, 'Réflexions sur l'Action catholique ouvrière', in *Vie Int.*, Oct. 1945, pp. 40–61; L. Bouyer, 'Où en est la théologie du Corps mystique?', in *Rev. S.R.*, vol. 22, 1948, pp. 313–33.
14. P. 19.

15. *Supra*, A.
16. This runs directly counter to certain Protestant pronouncements to the effect that the Church is nothing else but the sinful world, as pardoned and confessing the sovereignty of God: a position which reveals Protestant misunderstanding of the Church as an institution (see the third part of *Vraie et fausse réforme dans l'Église*).
17. Augustine, *Societas fruendi Deo et invicem in Deo.*
18. Mt 28:19.
19. See *Lay People*, pp. 335f.
20. See below, chap. 6.
21. *AAS*, 49 (1957), p. 927.
22. *Directoire pastorale en matière sociale*, no. 32.
23. *Doc. cath.*, 17th March 1946, col. 176; *Lay People*, pp. 366–7.
24. Speech of 14th Oct. 1951; exhortation to members of Roman Youth C.A., 8th Dec. 1947; allocution to episcopate of Italy, 25th Jan. 1950.
25. K. Rahner, p. 18, note.
26. See the collected texts, either in E. Vauthier, *S.S. Pie XII et l'apostolat des laïques*, Langres, 1953, pp. 13f, 22f, or in *L'apostolat des laïques dans l'enseignement de S.S. Pie XII*, Rome, 1956, pp. 20f.
27. *Méditation sur l'Église* (*Théologie*, 27), Paris, 1953, pp. 78f.
28. Rahner's idea fits in here; see *Lay People*, p. 406f.
29. Abundant texts in A. Müller, *Ecclesia-Maria. . .*, Freiburg (Switz.), 1951; Hugo Rahner, *Marie et l'Église . . .*, Paris, 1955. See especially Augustine, *De Virginitate*, cc. 5 and 6. On this spiritual motherhood, and the part of the faithful in it, according to the Fathers and the early Church, see now K. Delahaye, *Erneuerung der Seelsorgsformen aus der Sicht der fr hen Patristik*, Freiburg, 1958.
30. See especially *Guelferbyt.* 16, n. 2 (ed. Morin, p. 62: 'Ligatis et vos, solvitis et vos'); *Epist.* 98, 5; *In Ioann. Ev.*, tr. 80, n. 3; etc.
31. A point remarkably clarified by F. Heer, 'Die Heilige des Atomzeitalters', in *Sprechen wir von der Wirklichkeit*, Nuremberg, 1955, pp. 177f, on the basis of the fine studies by Abbé A. Combes.
32. J. Hamer writes, in *RSPT*, 1957, p. 555: 'When the subject is the apostolate, before determining where and in what conditions it can be exercised, before examining the circumstances, we must consider what resources of the Church it brings into action. Now the layman has at his disposal the sacraments of baptism and confirmation, resources common to all Christians. The proper act of the Christian who by confirmation has reached adult status in the spiritual life is *homologia*, the confession of faith. That is the foundation of the apostolate of the laity.'
33. The most complete biblical study is Protestant and German: R. Asting, *Die Verkündigung des Wortes im Urchristentum . . .*, Stuttgart, 1939; see also R. Koch, 'Témoignage, d'après les Actes' in *Masses ouvr.*, nos. 129 and 131 (April and June 1957).
34. Address of 5th Oct. 1957.
35. See especially Pius X, encyclical *Il fermo proposito* of 11th June 1905 (*Actes*, Bonne Presse, vol. II, pp. 90–104) and the doctrinal address of Cardinal Caggiano to the first Congress of the Apostolate of the Laity, 'Natura della Chiesa e del suo Apostolato', in *Actes du Premier Congrès Mondial pour l'Apostolat des laïques*, Rome, 1952, vol. I, pp. 196–229; pp. 210f. See also *Lay People*, pp. 344–5.
36. The phrase is sometimes found in papal documents, particularly in the speech of Pius XII to the first World Congress of the Lay Apostolate (*AAS*, 1951, p. 789; *Doc. cath.*, 1951, col. 1052), but it is also explained in a sense which

excludes the idea of the hand guided by the clergy. See also G. Philips, *Le rôle du laïcat dans l'Église*, Tournai-Paris, 1954, pp. 47 and 157–8.

37. 'Sacerdoce et Laïcat' in *Vie Int.*, Dec. 1946, pp. 4–39, and *Masses ouvr.*, Dec. 1946, pp. 19–56; *Lay People*, pp. 354–5.

38. P. 29.

39. P. 24.

40. See n. 32 above.

41. I would admit, however, that permanent officials of Catholic Action, paid by the Organisation, or professional catechists paid by the Mission, while still canonically laymen, and in many cases married, are sociologically no longer in the fully lay state, being allotted to a function of real ministry, although without hierarchical powers in the proper sense. See above, n. 6, *quartum genus Christianorum*.

42. See Gal 3:27–8; Col 3:11.

43. I venture to refer those who seek a full treatment of this subject to *Lay People*, Part II, chap. VI, and 'Vie dans le monde et vie "dans le Seigneur" ', in *Vie Sp.*, April 1957, pp. 401–8.

44. See *Lay People*, pp. 348f.

45. 20th Feb. 1946 and 12th Oct. 1952 to the Italian Catholic Action; 14th Oct. 1951 and 5th Oct. 1957 to the World Congresses of the Lay Apostolate, etc.

46. Letter to the General of the Society of Jesus, 15th April 1950 (*AAS*, 1950, pp. 437f; *Doc. cath.*, 1950, col. 577f).

47. See Speech of 5th Oct. 1957: 'It is reported that a regrettable and fairly widespread discontent is now prevalent, originating largely from the use of the term "Catholic Action". This term, in fact, is being reserved for certain determined types of organized lay apostolate, for which it creates a sort of monopoly: all the organizations, it is said, which are not included in the framework of Catholic Action as thus conceived, are represented as of less authenticity, of secondary importance; they seem less supported by the hierarchy and remain as it were on the fringes of the essential apostolic work of the laity . . .' (*AAS*, 49 (1957), p. 929).

48. Speech of 3rd April 1951 to the Italian Catholic Action: *AAS*, 1951, p. 378. The idea of Catholic Action as a federation of movements was not unknown to Pius XI.

49. See *Lay People*, pp. 366f; Vauthier, *op. cit.*, pp. 5f and 45f.

50. See the texts quoted by Vauthier, *op. cit.*, pp. 46–8.

51. Well interpreted by Jean Daniélou, e.g. *The Lord of History* (London and New York, 1959).

52. See *Lay People*, pp. 369–70.

53. History shows that the Church accepts the risk when the whole of a population or of a given group is morally agreed. We in France have paid dearly for other such history lessons!

CHAPTER SIX

Temporal Efficacy and the Gospel Message[1]

IS TEMPORAL EFFICACY ESSENTIAL TO THE gospel message? Let us first be quite clear about the meaning of the question I have been asked to answer. It is a question of principle, as is evident from its formulation. It is not 'can the gospel message foster effective temporal action?' or 'has it done so?' but 'is it essential for it to do so?'. We must be careful, too, to note the expression 'temporal efficacy'. The programme of our conversations well defined it: it concerns 'the ability (of Christianity) to modify the conditions of temporal human life so as to give man material well-being', or again, 'to inspire civilisations, to transform this world and make life more comfortable'. 'Material well-being' is therefore to be taken in the broad sense and means, rather, 'civilisation'. Such also is the wide and pregnant sense very rightly given to the word 'temporal', which must not be reduced to 'political': 'the temporal' is not exactly the 'temporal power', for it includes the whole earthly work of man, and in this sense is identified with the human march of history.[2]

To the question as thus defined my answer will be both Yes and No, or rather, in the order I shall follow, No and Yes.

I

In the first place, no, for the three following reasons:

1. The essential content of the gospel is a message of salvation addressed to men plunged in a sinful world. It does not tell them

how to organise the world: it shows them how treacherous it is, and how it is the object of the wrath of God, but also of his pardon in Jesus Christ. To this pardon, won for us on the Cross, and to this salvation, for whose total achievement we are still waiting,[3] we are made fast by faith and hope, somewhat as a ship, tossed by storms is fastened to *terra firma* by an anchor, fifty fathoms down.[4] This is the essence of being a Christian: to escape from a perverse world,[5] to use it as though not using it.[6]

The gospel message has also a more positive aspect and speaks of a new life, but it is eternal life. It begins, indeed, in this world, and St John never tires of telling us that by faith and hope we already have eternal life. But it is still a heavenly life, the life of *another* world than ours. Its actions are not designed to further the work of this world; it makes us live, while still mortal, in the heavens.[7] The essence of the gospel message is concerned with the fight against the devil and our own lusts, with faith, with the love of God and our neighbour. We may say with Pascal that it has its own order, which is not that of outward conquests, not yet of the discoveries of the mind, but that of charity and holiness: 'Jesus Christ, without goods and without any untoward show of learning, belongs to his own order of holiness.'[8]

Here we must guard against the temptation to apply to life in time, and to the earthly achievements of Christians, texts which in the Gospel apply to the Kingdom of God, which is the kingdom of grace and charity. With the passages on the grain of mustard seed or the leaven in the meal we could easily produce optimistic pronouncements of social or even cosmic implications, but they would be unwarranted. We had better recognise that the gospel is firmly pivoted on personal salvation and the person's position in the other world. If we had to express its message in a single verse we could surely do it in this: 'What does it profit a man if he gains the whole world and loses his soul?'[9] It is possible, we know, to draw up a list of social and cultural achievements inspired by the gospel; it is impossible to find in the gospel systematic programmes in the field of culture or social achievements. Its essential point of view is quite different.

2. We can even say that this point of view, transcending the world, makes the gospel indifferent to culture. Not opposed to it; nothing is less Manichean, less hostile to the earthly as such, than

the gospel. We may even feel that behind the parables, in the way in which Jesus approaches men and speaks of their life, there can be detected a sort of sympathy with the life of men, perhaps even with the benefits produced by their work.[10] But Jesus' true attitude, which includes and explains that sort of sympathy itself, was indifference to the events, creations and efforts of human history. This indifference is such that anyone who had read only the gospel, and did not know from other sources of the political crises which formed the setting of our Lord's life,[11] would gain the impression that the Gospel had been preached in a world idyllically calm, outside time.

The writings of the apostles, like the gospels, clearly reflect a struggle for Christian existence and the freedom of the apostolic preaching, but also a profound indifference concerning culture, political or social facts as such, riches or poverty, etc., in so far as they do not challenge the fundamental attitude required by the Gospel itself.[12] The Christians before Constantine respected the outward order of the empire as they did the outward order of creation;[13] towards society their attitude was as to things,[14] but with a bias towards sympathy, a great wish for peace and a desire to have the esteem of man.[15] Certainly, Christians often continued to occupy the same place in the state which they held when they first came to believe: the apostles had given them that rule;[16] with some exaggeration the apologists, like Tertullian, represent them as filling the city.[17] All the same, they are not really concerned about the world, and a man like Celsus reproaches them for it. They do not systematically create schools. The only question they ask about secular activities, the only question Tertullian raises, is: can a Christian practice them?[18]

Jesus had said: 'I do not pray that thou shouldst take them out of the world, but that thou shouldst keep them from the evil one' (Jn 17:15). He had given them in advance the rule for Christian conduct: neither systematic flight from the world—except from its sinfulness—nor positively active interest in its work. To use it as though not using it:[19] the form of this world is passing away![20]

The first Christian generations certainly thought that the end was near.[21] I think it is beyond question that their historical experience was too short for them to have learned all the possibilities of the diffusion of grace in the world of men. Too short in time: too short also in the content and variety of opportunities offered. The Church at first knew only one situation, marked by the opposition of a world which already had its own body and its soul. We recognise that we are bound to honour pronouncements which are still normative for us, but we may hold that the texts of the Gospels and the epistles have not told us positively all the possibilities of the faith with regard to the world. In the course of time Christianity has had other historical experiences, in new conditions which have imposed new duties and demanded new answers: conditions, duties and answers which are indeed suggested by the words of Pius XII in his Christmas message in 1942: 'The Church, which has now arrived at her mission as universal Mother of the believing people . . .'. The Church has received a kind of new responsibility for the world, obliging Christians to shoulder its burden even in the temporal order. We shall recall this remark later.

3. The world has not waited for the gospel message in order to live its history and do its world's work. About 1296–7, during the quarrel between Boniface VIII and Philip the Fair, the partisans or spokesmen of the king put out a little work which began with these words: *Antequam essent clerici, Rex Franciae habebat custodiam regni sui et poterat statuta facere quibus ab inimicorum insidiis et nocumentis sibi praecaveret.* 'Before there were any clerics, the King of France had the guardianship of his kingdom, and could make laws with which to protect it from the plots and injuries of his enemies.' There could be no more striking expression of the notion that the temporal work of the world is the responsibility, not of the Christian as such, but of the natural man, who is presupposed by and anterior to the Christian. In spite of the temptation, to which more than one partisan of the lay princes succumbed, to conclude that neither the Christian nor the Church has anything to do with the political scene, it must be firmly held that the Christian ought to be active in temporal matters as a Christian, and that the Church has the right, and therefore the duty, to give him guidance. But we can admit that it does not fall to the Christian as such to carry on the world's work.

This line of reasoning of course requires corrections, which I shall suggest later. Moreover, it does not form the basis of a compelling argument, for it might be essential for the Gospel message to have temporal efficacy without the temporal, and in particular the political, world looking to Christianity for its elementary existence. Nonetheless, this line inclines the mind, once again, to the idea of two autonomous orders, each defined in its own limits, without reference to the other. In these conditions, is one not impelled to think that it is not *essential* for the Gospel message to have temporal efficacy?

The question is important. In particular, it concerns the right of the Christian to say No to the world, to withdraw from it, not by the selfish and sterile path of suicide, of course, but by the total and exclusive *consecration* of self to the service of God. Here is an indefeasible right of the Christian, which, as we shall show later, expresses his royal condition. Before this was realised in the life of the hermit or the monk, it was expressly vindicated by the martyrs, especially by many of them who refused to accept the profession of arms.[23] If, as some authors have shown with great depth,[24] the monastic life is simply the Christian life, absolutely pure and consistent, we must clearly admit (again, subject to the qualifications I shall make later) that it is not *essential* for it to have temporal efficacy. For what the monk does is precisely to leave the world behind: he does not do its work, and he anticipates, as far as that is possible on earth, the life of the heavenly kingdom. In seeking exclusively the Kingdom of God and his justice, the monk cannot avoid, incidentally, the earthly increase promised by our Lord. It is a fact that monasticism has everywhere been a marvellous inspirer of culture, an educator of the nations.

II

1. *The Evidence of the Facts*

And yet, have we not very strong reasons to assert that temporal efficacy is essential to Christianity—reasons drawn from the *facts*, first, and therefore indisputable as they are? No doubt we cannot proceed directly from a statement of fact to a statement of essence. But when the facts are constant, they proclaim an essential disposition, and at least the first facts of those I am about to select appear to me to be really constant.

(*a*) In a brief but penetrating study of Paul's Epistle to Philemon, the Protestant scholar Theo Preiss has shown how the 'mystique' of life in Christ preached by Paul, though situated on a plane far transcending the problems and categories of earthly society, was necessarily effective in them.[25] Paul sends Onesimus back to his master, but neither here nor in his other epistles does he urge the slave to shake off his fetters, nor does he attack the institution of slavery. But the 'mystique' of the presence of Christ in every brother, and the 'mystique' of communion, as he preaches them, are such that new relations between the faithful necessarily follow from them. Faith and charity, which make them all one in Christ,[26] are not simply sublime sentiments *alongside* the social order, *alongside* natural realities which they cannot change. There is a realism in Christian life which sooner or later must find expression in earthly life at its most concrete.

Then we have the words of Pius XII:

> In carrying out the mandate of her divine Founder to spread throughout the world and win every creature for the Gospel,[27] the Church is not an empire, especially in the imperialist sense that word ordinarily has nowadays. Her progress and expansion is in the opposite direction to that of modern imperialism. Before all else she progresses in depth, only thereafter in extent. In the first place she seeks man himself, using all her endeavours to form and fashion him, to perfect the divine likeness in him. She does her work in each one's heart, but it affects the whole of life and every individual activity. In men thus formed, the Church prepares a secure foundation for human society.[28]

Because faith and charity are principles by which the whole personality is educated, they cannot help having an effective result, even in the field of our historical enterprises and our temporal conduct in the world.

(*b*) History bears witness that this has certainly been the case. To draw up a full account of the temporal efficacy of the Gospel message would obviously exceed the bounds of the present essay.[29] It would mean writing the story of Christianity and that of a greater part of civilisation itself. Here are a few examples, rather stated or suggested than developed.

The transformation of the state of the poor, the suffering, all the outcasts of society: the creation of hospitals, leper-houses, etc. Christianity, which proclaims heaven and calls this world a 'valley of tears', has never ceased, wherever it has set foot, to care for the bodies of suffering men and to better their lot.

Chesterton once said that for the pagan hierarchy of father, mother and child, Christianity had substituted the reverse order! Obviously we must not make too much of a statement made more than half in jest, but it is true that Christianity has established the dignity of woman and the child on new and remarkably effective foundations. The dignity, too, of the servant, of the manual worker, in short, of man as such. It has been a powerful factor in the assertion and development of personality.[30]

And what has it not done for education? It has indeed been the inspirer of art, culture, thought. Etienne Gilson's work on Christian Philosophy is well-known: it is not the thesis of a theorist, though it has theoretical value and has had theoretical developments: it is the thesis of an historian, who simply interprets facts.

When it has had the chance, Christianity has brought about some remarkably inspired political achievements. Whatever is produced in history, of course, risks contracting the impurities of history; many things in Christian countries do not spring from Christianity but, for example, from absolutism, from a revived paganism, from the mercantile spirit, etc. On the other hand, from what I know of the history of political ideas and institutions, and from what may be read, for example, in the six volumes by the Carlyle brothers,[31] I believe that there is such a thing as a political genius of Christianity. When it has been free to create political forms corresponding to its genius, Christianity has brought forth kingdoms of moral inspiration,—*rex a recte agendo vocatur*, said Isidore, to be followed by all the medieval West—combined with some expression of the consent of the community. A régime, then, of both order and liberty, in which the hierarchical spirit and the community spirit are allied; one of its highest points was the corporative ideal of the thirteenth century.

That Christian order tried, with some measure of success, to bridle the violence of war itself. The 'Truce of God' was not only a fine idea: for a certain time it imposed peace for some four or five days in the week. In this connection, therefore, we can speak of temporal efficacy.

Christianity has also been an awakener of freedom. Its contribution in this respect has been immense,[32] so much so that it is one of the historical sources of the modern sentiment of freedom, which often degenerates into libertinism or rebellion. Berdyaev has noted that rebellion appears, historically, in a world formed by Christianity.[33] Similar things could be said about the sentiments of equality and fraternity, spiritual offspring of the Gospel, even when they are unfaithful to it in one respect or another.

All these remarks apply to the ancient lands of Christendom, but they are equally true if we consider the temporal efficacy of the gospel in missionary countries. There it is conspicuous, and at the same time lamentably inadequate to the need, as we have been able to observe recently, for example in China. The spirit is willing, our Lord said, but the flesh is weak. The Gospel is, as he said, a powerful leaven of efficacy, and even of revolution. But Christians too often treat it like a talent hidden away by the slothful servant, which he gave back to his master intact, but unprofitable. Why is it that Christian tasks of real reform, too often deserted and betrayed by the faithful, have to be resumed by others and carried on, for better for worse, under the sign of false reforms?

It is clear, then, that Christianity appears, as a matter of history, to have a temporal efficacy which is both very real and also limited. It was the Gospel that eliminated slavery; one day it will eliminate war and the proletarian condition. But it has only done this, and it will only do it, slowly and indirectly. For the demands and appeals of the gospel to be realised in societies and in history, the strictly historical and mainly economic factors must first bring about conditions in which the structures can be effectively changed. The example of slavery is famous: it was the invention of collar-harness and the use of horse-shoes which, by transforming the efficacy of animal traction,[34] did as much on the plane of technical or economic conditioning to abolish slavery as the preaching of the fatherhood of God and the brotherhood of man on the plane of deeper spiritual motivations. The finest, truest idea can succeed only through the mediation of history and the appropriate techniques. The gospel too—who would dare think otherwise?—desires that wars should be no more and that men should devote the resources of their work, not to preparing the destruction of its fruits, but to multiplying, increasing and widening their opportunities of earthly happiness. Nevertheless, the gospel will not attain the desired result till the laborious evolution of a good many very complicated human factors has given it, so to say, the possibility of being at last fully effective.

That is not the only limit to its efficacy. As we have seen, it changes temporal things because it changes man himself, and only by changing man himself. At the necessary technological level, Christianity is very weak. What is more, it has nothing to say, at least nothing positive; here it is, in the strict sense non-existent. As the Message of the kingdom of God, it touches the temporal only through man, who is its agent. That is its strength and its weakness: its greatness and its limitation. It has temporal efficacy only through a spiritual or, may we say again anthropological efficacy. That is, its temporal efficacy is conditioned by human freedom and has nothing automatic about it. That is why the ineffectiveness of which it is often accused is the fault of Christians, not of Christianity.

(*c*) The facts show, however, that at least a certain temporal efficacy is necessary for a wide diffusion of the gospel itself. I said earlier that the gospel demands a certain temporal efficacy, because faith and charity are totalitarian. Now I would note the fact that certain conditions of things make the faith socially very difficult, if not impossible. In the great years of the founding of Catholic Action, when the clergy became aware of the real state of the apostolic field of work and of the concrete conditions of the faith in the modern world, we discovered how very far men are conditioned in their behaviour, even (and especially) in their spiritual behaviour, by their surroundings, that is, the social groups, the structures and institutions, the laws, the material position, social pressures. We found that we not only had to preach the faith (though that is strictly sufficient and is always, in any case, essential), but also, if men were to be socially capable of receiving it, we had to protect or create really human social structures and outward conditions of life. Just as faith, in the modern age, has had to undertake to establish the *praeambula fidei*, so the apostolate has often to undertake the task of a sort of *praeambula apostolatus*, which involve action in the realm of culture, of social questions, in short, what I have called the temporal.

In particular, this is the primary function of Catholic Action, whose scope Cardinal Saliège once defined in these words: 'To modify social pressure, to guide it, to make it favourable to a full development of Christian life, to use it to create a background, an atmosphere, in which man may develop his human qualities . . . in which the Christian can breathe comfortably.'[35]

For the moment let us stick to the plane of observations and facts: we shall soon go on to interpret them in terms of the Church's mission; see below, 2(*b*).

Medieval Christianity was dominated, at least till the thirteenth century,[36] by the monastic idea of flight from the world. It is always valid in the Church, and it is indeed remarkable that in many countries (Spain and the United States, for example) we are witnessing at this moment a real spring of religious, and especially contemplative, vocations. But our age also seems to show that God's providential guidance is drawing the Church as a whole to a form of holiness less opposed to the earthly life, towards a less narrowly monastic spirituality, one more adapted to men and women who desire wholeheartedly to practise the Gospel perfectly and live the Beatitudes, but feel called to do so in the world, without being dispensed from actively doing the world's works,—only without sin.

We all know the facts in this connection (we are still on the plane of facts). That they represent, not a falling away, not a regrettable pact with the spirit of the age, but the fruit of a guidance of God, is clearly enough signified in the directives of the pastoral magisterium. But it is also seen in the fact that God has given us, for the last century, saints of a new type, who have reached a high degree of sanctity, revealed in startling canonisations, by performing ordinary actions, identical with those we are called on to do, and often in a world which is precisely our own. We think of saints like Anthony Claret, John Bosco, Teresa of the Child Jesus, Pius X, and with them all the holy men and women not yet canonised, like Pietro Frassati, Frederic Ozanam, Garcia Moreno, General de Sonis, Marius Gonin, Elisabeth Leseur, Jaeger, Brother Mutien, Antoine Martel, Maximilian Kolbe and so on. They did not flee to the desert, they did not kill their bodies with extreme asceticism, they did what we do every day. Antony Claret and Kolbe published newspapers: John Bosco taught children to play; Ozanam and Antoine Martel gave lectures; Brother Mutien taught in school; Jaeger was a bank manager. In short, they did one or other of those temporal works in which we are engaged.

Indeed, when we hear popes calling us to co-operate boldly in the movement of the age and in progress, we cannot help thinking that a providential guidance is leading Christians as a body to develop, through the Gospel, an effective temporal action, and to find in that work itself the framework of a new holiness and the actual means of their sanctification.

2. *The theological principles*

Those are the facts. Now we must try briefly to understand them by considering the theological principles which are capable of explaining them.

(*a*) There is first the notion held by Catholic tradition of the relations between nature and grace: the two realms, the two realities, are not foreign to each other, although they are different and sometimes, in the concrete practice of activities, opposed.[37] Nature, in the ontological sense of the word, is the very thing which is saved and will be glorified. We expect, St Paul says, the redemption (= the total salvation) of *our bodies*, yes, of our mortal bodies, which are still carnal.[38] That redemption is already acquired in Christ, but the grace of God, with our active co-operation, is now producing its spiritual effects, and sometimes even external effects, so that Christ, who lives for God, reveals himself by the Christian life, in us.[39] Catholic theology has expressed this view of things in the idea of 'healing grace', *gratia sanans*. The meaning of this idea is certainly, in the first place, that human nature is profoundly insufficient, its condition is imperfect and diseased, but also that grace is ordained to the healing and restoration of that nature. So one cannot say that an earthly efficacy, 'temporal' in the sense which describes the work of culture pursued by man on earth, is outside the range of grace, and therefore of the Gospel message. That is first and foremost a message of eternal salvation, but it includes also an aspect which is turned towards human nature, and even the cosmic.

The same conclusion is reached if we consider the God of salvation. One of the most essential statements of Scripture is that this God is identical with the God of creation. Throughout her history the Church has condemned in turn Marcionism, Gnostic or Catharist dualism, and the Protestant disjunction between a wholly corrupt nature and an all-transcending grace, passing over but not penetrating it. God's gift of grace was not a 'passing over' but an incarnation: God became *man*, and the most theological statements of that fact in the New Testament insist precisely on the profound bond it implies between creation and redemption.[40] Christ saves the world, he resumes the plan of creation and brings it to his goal. So no one can say that an action in the temporal order is outside the scope of the Gospel: that would be to reduce the Gospel to a mere response to the sense of sin, dramatically perceived in the conscience and to empty it of a cosmic but very real aspect. It is not for nothing that so many of the Gospel stories, often told in the liturgy of the Sundays after Pentecost (which represent the life of the Church), are stories of healing, in which Jesus appears as the restorer of a sick human nature.

(*b*) The Fathers also saw a figure of the Church in the inn where Jesus, the Good Samaritan, provided care for the man he had found wounded and half dead on the road from Jerusalem to Jericho.[41] If, as the Gospel and tradition tell us, the Church continues the mission of Christ, it is natural for that mission to include, in the first place, the news of the gift of an eternal salvation, but also a work for the restoration and healing of nature. We have seen that the apostolate, at least on the social scale, is engaged in an activity to humanise the social structures. It must also be said that the Church's action, her mission, comprises an action (coming from Christ and leading to Christ) on man, on man's bodily work, on the structures of social life; in short, on civilisation. This is precisely what St Pius X said in one of his letters, in which he was already speaking of Catholic Action, or at least of the action of Catholics.

> It excludes absolutely nothing that belongs in any way directly or indirectly, to the divine mission of the Church: *To restore all things in Christ*. To restore in Christ not only what is directly incumbent on the Church in virtue of her divine mission to lead souls to God, but also whatever flows spon-

taneously from that divine mission: Christian civilisation, in the totality of every one of the elements which compose it.[42]

Let us note again how the Church touches the temporal *through man*, because it is in man that she does the work of God. She touches the temporal, not because she has a political programme, or is competent in architecture or music, but because the temporal is the product, the framework and the means of fulfilment of any man worthy of the name.

All this is extremely important, especially for a theology of the proper function of the Christian laity. If the Church had nothing but a mission of pure spiritual salvation, she could be composed of none but priests and religious. If she has a mission with reference to the world as such, it is essential, not to her particular structure as institution of salvation, but certainly to her mission and her life, that she should be composed of lay people. Here we must beware of two pitfalls: on the one hand we might so relate the Church to the world that in seeking her cosmic aspect and her human catholicity we lose sight of the fact that she is not the world but something else, that she comes from above and constitutes a heavenly and supernatural order of salvation. On the other hand we might see in her only a refuge of holiness, the ark of the pure floating above a world doomed to perdition, and forget that she has a duty to be Catholic and a mission with reference to the world. Her task, to quote St Paul again, is 'to bring all things to a head' in Jesus Christ, who is the New Adam; to make 'all things grow into him, who is the head'.[43]

This presupposes that Christians are engaged in the world and the world's work. Priests and monks are dispensed from it, being directly ministers of the Kingdom, but lay Christians ordinarily receive, in the form of 'vocation' and so of task and responsibility, an engagement in the work of the world, to carry out God's plan for his creation. I believe I have been able to find indications, in this situation, for what is commonly called a 'spirituality of the laity'.[44] For the laity, who thus carry out a part (which is their own) of the mission of the Church, a temporal commitment is part of their Christian life. This does not imply that there are two Christianities, one for monks and priests, the other for people in the world. But the vocations are different, and it would not be difficult to find texts in the Gospel to illustrate the point.[45] Jesus did not call everyone to the exclusive service of the Kingdom: he left the centurion to his command, Jairus to his home and Joseph of Arimathea to his rank as a counsellor. Only, those who thus use the world, who *must* use it in order to follow their vocation, are no less called to live as children of the Kingdom, and must use it 'as though not using it'.

I have spoken of every man's vocation in the most general terms, but we have only to imagine any one such vocation to see that it necessarily implies some temporal commitment. We do not live alone, but in the society of other men: our duties of justice and of charity as well, are expressed concretely and every day in acts in the temporal sphere. Furthermore, there are some things, forms of art, leisure activities, laws, social structures, with which the Christian conscience cannot make terms. For every man living in the world and socially, the gospel message always implies, in some degree, the obligation of temporal efficacy. But it is not so much on this moral aspect, which can scarcely be questioned, that I now wish to dwell, as on what we may call the ontology of things.

(*c*) What I have said about healing grace, about the relation of salvation to human nature and even the cosmos, and then about the mission of the Church and the common vocation of the laity, is all directly based on the universal Kingship of Christ.[46] Universal and cosmic: such is the affirmation of Scripture, for which theology has no difficulty in giving reasons. From the fact that God has resolved to lead the world to its destiny, not simply from the heights of heaven, if I may put it so, but through a humanity, the humanity of Jesus, which he has united personally to himself, that humanity has been raised far above every creature and possesses a royal sovereignty over the world, visible and invisible. I wish I had space to quote here the principal texts.[47]

The universal kingship of Christ is characterised by the fact that, in order to reduce all things to unity by re-establishing their hierarchy, it extends both over things below and over things above, things in heaven and things on earth. The Kingdom, which will be the adequate and perfect effect of the exercise by Christ of his priestly kingship (reconciling and saving), is characterised precisely by the perfect subjection of the bodily to the spiritual, of knowledge to light, of the corruptible to the incorruptible, because of the perfect subjection of all things to the Spirit of God. In this subjection, created beings, and especially man, find their integrity and perfection. It is the perfect accomplishment of the programme outlined rather than effected, and foretold rather than outlined, in the reality of healing grace.

Plainly, the Kingdom is eschatological: the sovereign exercise of his Kingship by Christ is eschatological; and that is enough to nullify all claim to achieve a Christian civilisation, a Christian state, a Christian order, or even a Church, which shall be the Kingdom of God. Here on earth, the 'Thy kingdom come, . . . on earth as it is in heaven' can never be perfect and must often be confined to the order of personal spiritual life.

There are, however, real anticipations and, as Paul says of the Spirit,[48] 'earnests' or guarantees of the kingdom of God. Christian action can accomplish, here or there, parables, as it were, of that perfect order, precariously, partially, mixed with impurities, and the more so, the farther we depart from God and persons and towards things. But these anticipations are also *real*, and that is sufficient to furnish a positive conclusion to our problem: a temporal efficacy is native to Christianity, because Jesus Christ is King, the King *of the world* and *our* King. How then can we not strive to extend his reign to the utmost before his triumphal return?

(*d*) Finally, we may briefly mark the truth to be found in what may be called the cosmic point of view, to which Teilhard de Chardin gave what is no doubt its most extreme expression. We shall in any case be in no danger of going astray if we look at things from above, starting from that first level, the highest and firmest there is, God's plan, the purpose of the holy will of God.

That purpose is to save all that he has called into existence—except those free wills which persist in rebellion against him, for he respects the freedom of the creatures whom he has made such, so that he will not, he cannot save them unless they consent and co-operate. St Paul says it is to bring everything under Jesus Christ, as under a sovereign head of reconciled and filial life. It is for that end that Christ is supreme priestly King.

Once again, the full completion of that plan is eschatological, reserved for that world to come, which at the end of our *Credo* we say we 'expect'. But even in this world a certain accomplishment of it is so to say roughed out, in such a way that the sketch is not lost, and what is valid in it is resumed, transfigured, in the final accomplishment, which will be the work of the Master's hand. This fact, that God's plan involves, for us, a sketch, implies two consequences, which can be briefly stated, but are of the greatest importance.

(1) We must strive to do our best to realise some anticipation of the Kingdom, that is, a reign of the Holy Spirit over our souls and, by our faithful action, over what we can model according to a Christian ideal: (2) We must therefore try also to offer to this reign as much of creation as possible. The Christian programme of consecration to God presupposes a world to consecrate. Whether we are concerned with art, science or politics, we cannot fulfil the programme unless we practise them according to the proper laws of each, which are ultimately willed by God. Once again, a temporal commitment and efficacy, that is, in the activities of one's earthly human work, are part of the Christian vocation, and are therefore required by the Gospel message.

CONCLUSION

To sum up the results of our reflection: the Gospel is from heaven and for heaven, but the work of the world is not foreign to it, for it is not foreign to heaven. Jesus, who effects the link between this world and the other, invites us too to make it real in the extent to which he calls us to co-operate, by the offering of our efforts and our adumbrations, in a salvation which he wills to be cosmic. In this life, however, this salvation begins only in souls: the heart of man is the point where, by its spiritual reign, the Kingdom of God is inaugurated. The Gospel and the Church work essentially to change hearts. Yet, in so far as mere things concern men and are human, they are drawn into our submission to the reign and come to represent humble adumbrations of the Kingdom. Thus a temporal efficacy really forms part of the Gospel message: it is a consequence of our obedience.

This conclusion is not without relevance in giving us a sort of practical criterion for our action and guiding our social, political and cultural choices. It is by seeking everywhere for what is most human, most genuinely human, that we shall place ourselves most fully in the area of the Gospel's temporal efficacy, and at the same time we shall have the best chance of being accepted and of finding a kind of complicity even with those who do not positively share our faith. Christianity has nothing to fear from such a truth as that formulated by a French novelist of the Left in these words: 'Victory, in the last resort, will go to the most human.'[49]

One last remark before I conclude. No purely systematic consideration can exhaust the whole Christian reality. One can propose a view of Christianity as the agent of temporal efficacy: or one can show it as a pure 'mystique' of salvation and the heavenly life. Whenever, in particular, one speaks of the relations between Christianity and the world, the theory leaves unsatisfied some still genuine aspects, which another theoretical exposition would present in a better light. As I know by experience, this is especially the fate of explanations of the relations between the spiritual and temporal powers. It is somewhat similar with explanations of the relations between the Gospel and temporal efficacy. I know perfectly well that we have not said everything: I have said too little, for example, about the demands of charity. But that is one of the difficult problems which ordinary Christians solve every day, by living.

But allowing for all that, since I must formulate theoretical propositions, I shall say, in reply to our question, that for any particular person it may not be essential for the Gospel message to involve temporal efficacy, but that if we consider the Christian programme in its entirety, and so the Gospel as it has to be realised by the whole Church, then it is certainly essential for it to have, as a whole, a certain temporal efficacy.

NOTES

1. Paper read to the international Catholic 'Conversations' of San Sebastian, in Sept. 1952. The dialectical form of the paper was purposely chosen in order to start a 'conversation'. Published in *La Revue Nouvelle*, Brussels, 17 (Jan. 1953), pp. 32–49.
2. See J. Caryl and V. Portier, *Les exigences sociales de l'apostolat*, Lyons, 1951, pp. 98–100.
3. That is to say: salvation (Rom 8:24; 13:11; 1 Pet 1:3–5), the glorious redemption, including the resurrection of our bodies (Eph 1:14; 5:20; Phil 3:20–1), the freedom of the children of God (Rom 8:21), glory (Rom 5:2), the life of our bodies (Rom 8:9–11, 23).
4. See Heb 6:19.
5. 2 Pet 1:4; 1 Jn 2:15–17.
6. 1 Cor 7:31.
7. See Phil 3:20; Col 1:12–14, etc.
8. Pascal, *Pensées*, ed. Brunschwig, fr. 793.
9. Mt 16:26; Mk 8:36; Lk 9:25.
10. After rightly noting that 'Christ was not a social reformer, he was a reformer of man', H. C. Link (*The Return to Religion*, 37th ed., New York, 1943) discovers a real sympathy for property and the production of wealth in the parables of the king and his servants (Mt 18:23–4), the labourers in the vineyard (20:1–16), the talents (24:14–30), the faithful steward (Lk 12:42–8), the dishonest steward (16:1–13), the master and the servant (17:7–10), the nobleman and the 'pounds' (19:12–27). This is perhaps going too far, but Link is right in noting also that Jesus visited the rich as often as the poor.
11. See *Hist. de l'Église*, ed. Fliche and Martin, vol. I, pp. 30, 43–4; J. Bonsirven, *Le judaisme palestinien au temps de Jésus-Christ*, Paris, 1935, vol. I, p. 14; J. Lebreton, 'Jésus et son peuple sous la domination romaine', in *Construire*, 4th series, 1941, pp. 79f.
12. See O. Cullmann, 'Le christianisme primitif et la civilisation', in *Verbum caro*, 5, 1951, pp. 57–68.
13. For political order, Rom 13:1–7; 1 Tim 2:1–3; Tit 3:1; 1 Pet 4:7. For the order of creation, 1 Tim 4:1–5; see Jn 3:3, 10; 1 Jn 3:9; 1 Tim 4:4; etc.
14. There is not only the indifference of Christian liberty concerning external practices (Rom 14:6f, 19; 1 Cor 6:12; 7:17–24; 8:4f; 10:23; Col 2:16–23), but indifference to wealth (1 Tim 6:17–18; Jas 1:9–12; 2:1–7; 5:1f), a certain mistrust of worldly high position (1 Cor 1:26) and the advice not to try to change one's state but to stay in that in which one has been called; see n. 16.
15. The apostles constantly urge doing good *before men*, earning their esteem, being at peace with all men: Rom 12:17–18; 15:2; 2 Cor 4:2; 6:3f; Phil 4:5; Col 4:5–6; 1 Thess 4:12; 1 Tim 3:7; Tit 3:2; 1 Pet 2:12, 15; 3:15–16; Mt 5:16.
16. 1 Cor 7:17–24; 1 Tim 6:1–2; Tit 2:9–10; 1 Pet 2:18f.
17. *Epist. ad Diognetum*, 5; Tertullian, *Apol.*, 37, 7–12; see 26.
18. See A. Bigelmair, *Die Beteiligung der Christen am öffentlichen Leben in vorconstantinischer Zeit*, Munich, 1902, pp. 293f. On the question of the schools,

see H. Marrou, *Hist. de l'Éducation dans l'Antiquité*, Paris, 1948, pp. 421f (English translation, *History of Education in Antiquity*, London, 1956).

19. See 1 Cor. 7:29f; (cf. 2 Cor 4-7f); 2 Cor 6-4–10 (12:5–10); etc.

20. 2 Cor 4:16 to 5:5; 2 Pet 3:11.

21. See Rom 13:11f; 1 Cor 1:8; 7:29; Phil 4:5; 1 Pet 4:7.

22. See J. Rivière, *Le problème de l'Église et de l'État au temps de Philippe le Bel*, Louvain and Paris, 1926, p. 99.

23. See, for example, the passion of Maximilian in 295 at Theveste in Numidia (*Ausgew. Märtyrerakten*, ed. Knopf, 3rd ed. by Krüger, Tubingen, 1929, pp. 86–7), and that of Marcellus, in 298, at Tangiers (*ibid.*, pp. 87–8).

24. G. Morin, J. Leclercq, L. Bouyer.

25. T. Preiss, 'Vie en Christ et éthique sociale dans l'épitre à Philémon' in *Aux sources de la tradition chrétienne*, Mél. Goguel, Neuchatel and Paris, 1950, pp. 171–9.

26. Gal 3:28.

27. See Mk 16:15.

28. Speech of 20th Feb. 1946 to the new cardinals; *AAS*, 1946, p. 143; *Doc. cath.*, 17th March 1946, col. 172. Translation from *Lay People*, p. 366.

29. In French, on the general subject, see E. Chénon, *Le rôle social de l'Église*, Paris, 1911. Each point would need a special bibliography: I quote only a few studies.

30. A rather curious sign of this fact can be found in the development of the Romance languages from Latin: see H. F. Muller, *L'epoque mérovingienne*, an attempt at synthesis between philology and history, New York, 1945; *A Chronology of Vulgar Latin*, Beihefte z. Zeitsch f. romanische Philologie, 88, 1925, Halle.

31. R. W. and A. J. Carlyle, *A History of Medieval Political Theory in the West*, Edinburgh and London and New York, 6 vols., new impression, 1940.

32. See the reports by myself and others in *L'Église et la liberté, Semaine des intellectuels catholiques*, (4th–10th May 1952), Paris, 1952.

33. *L'Esprit de Dostoïevski*, Paris, 1929, pp. 80–1.

34. Cdt Lefebvre des Noettes, *L'attelage, le cheval de selle à travers les ages. Contribution à l'histoire de l'esclavage*, Paris, 2 vols., 1951. M. Bloch clarifies the subject in 'Les "inventions" médiévales', in *Annales d'hist. économique et sociale*, 1935, pp. 634–43: see pp. 640f.

35. 'Action catholique incarnée', in *Semaine relig. de Toulouse*, 18th Feb. 1945. There are countless similar statements.

36. On this point, and the whole of this paragraph 4, I refer the reader to *Lay People*, Part II, Chap. VI. I think I have there given historical and documentary evidence for everything I have said here. I have added, in Appendix III (p. 444) 'Some utterances of the Church's Magisterium calling on Christians to be active in the work of mankind'.

37. Hence the famous chapter in the *Imitation of Christ* (Bk IV, ch. 53), on the effects of nature and grace.

38. Rom 8:11, 13; Phil 3:21; etc.

39. See, among others, Rom 6:10–11; 12:1; 1 Cor 6:15, 20; 2 Cor 4:10; Phil 1:20; O. Cullmann, 'La délivrance anticipée du corps humain d'après le N.T.' in *Hommage et reconnaissance à K. Barth*, Neuchatel and Paris, 1946, pp. 31–40.

40. See particularly Jn 1:1f; Heb 1:1f; W. S. Boycott, 'Creation and Christology', in *Theology*, 52 (1949), pp. 443–8; L. S. Thornton, *Revelation and the Modern World . . .*, Westminster Md., 1950.

41. For example, St Augustine, *Quaest. in Ev.*, 2, 19 (*PL*, 35, 1340); *Tract. in Joann. Ev.* 41, 13 (35, 1700).

42. Encycl. *Il fermo proposito,* 11th June 1905 (*Actes,* Bonne Presse, vol. II, pp. 91 and 93).
43. Eph 4:15 (Westminster Version); 1:10.
44. 'Au monde et pas du monde . . .', in *Supplément de la Vie Spirituelle,* 15th Feb. 1952, pp. 5–47 (= part of last chapter of *Lay People*).
45. For example, Mt 19:11–12; comp. 1 Cor 7; etc.
46. On what follows, see 'Royaume, Église et Monde', in *Récherches et Débats,* July 1951, pp. 2–42 (= part of Part I, Chap. III of *Lay People*).
47. Ephes 1:9–10, 20–3; Col 1:15–20; 1 Cor 15:27–8.
48. 2 Cor 1:22; 5:5; Eph 1:14.
49. J. Guéhenno, *Caliban parle.*

CHAPTER SEVEN

Problems of competence between Society and the Christian Faith[1]

I. HOW AND ON WHAT GROUNDS DOES CHRISTIANITY IMPOSE RESPONSIBILITIES IN THE TEMPORAL SPHERE?

The first point to note, which seems to me quite decisive, is that Christianity does not change the cosmic, that is, the physical structures of the world. In modern philosophical language one would call them the 'ontic' structures, as distinct from what concerns the subject, the person. It is extremely important to start with this commonplace but decisive fact.

A tap is a tap, regardless. A toothache is a toothache; you can't have a Christian toothache. The rules of football are the rules of football; there is no such thing as Christian football. There is a certain structure of things which Christianity does not change. What does Christianity do from the point of view of things? Only from time to time, in order to proclaim the promise of the Kingdom of God, where things will be transformed and brought into a state of truth, does God work a miracle, in which the power of the kingship or Christ over even the physical world is revealed. What happened in the Gospel—as when Jesus walked on the water, made lame men walk—happens from time to time, at Lourdes or elsewhere. Or again, the Church in her liturgy takes a certain number of the elements of the world: water for baptism, oil, human actions, to make them sacred and so to make a sort of sign or project of what the Kingdom of God will be. But it does not, strictly speaking, transform them, except in one case, that of the eucharist, which all the same is decisive. Its elements are natural, simple and noble: bread and wine—natural, for they come from the earth, but at the same time they are natural elements which have been *worked on* (the earth produces grapes, not wine; corn, not bread), natural, worked elements, incorporating both man's work and the produce of the earth. These elements are made sacred in their substance, in token that the world will be changed into a state of subjection to the Spirit of God, in a state of the kingdom of God. But these are the only elements, the only cases in which Christianity touches the cosmic structure of the world. Normally it does not. It touches the heart of man, transforms man's heart and gives him a new end. In place of a merely terrestrial end (to obtain comfort by practical means) it gives him a supernatural end, the kingdom of God, an order of things in which God asserts himself, God reigns, and in which man, for that reason, finds his equilibrium, his happiness, his full development as a creature, the friend and child of God.

That transformation of the ends of life at once imposes on the Christian a certain number of obligations to intervene in the temporal sphere. I shall name three grounds of intervention, three rather different levels, each of which approaches a step nearer to what is your responsibility, that is, public life.

1. The fact that the Christian has different ends, a different 'chief end', the kingdom of God, transforms the *significance* of what he does, and therefore also the *intention* he gives to his temporal work itself. But that is still a private matter, a matter of personal conscience. For instance, one tends the sick in an epidemic, or after a riot; there are atheist doctors there, along with Christian doctors, agnostic or 'lay' nurses (in the French sense) along with staunch Christians. The Christian doctors or nurses treat those sick with charity, for the love of Jesus Christ, of God. They put an intention into it, the significance which they give to their actions, but that makes no difference to their action being medical, necessarily and primarily medical. I like that saying of Etienne Gilson's: 'They say the west front of Notre Dame in Paris is a work of faith. So it is, but first of all it is a work of

geometry.' The sick are treated with charity, but not just with charity. They are treated with a lancet, with a knowledge of medicine, which must be as highly qualified, as accurate, as it possibly can be. We see then, that this order of intention is extremely important, because that is how the Christian, while performing the same acts as anyone else, gives them an additional value which, from the spiritual point of view, is amazing. For example, I said that you can't have a Christian toothache. No, but the Christian can give his toothache a spiritual meaning which becomes part of the redemption of the world, and that is why I refuse to follow in the steps of a certain number of thinkers, including even Christians, who of late years, influenced by the dialogue with Marxism, have been criticising what is called the morality of intention in the name, and for the sole benefit, of a morality or ethic of efficacy. Of course we want to be effective, but we must not criticise the morality of intention indiscriminately. In most cases it is at that level that the Christian adds something to the non-Christian. In the spiritual sphere, of course, in faith and charity, in the Holy Spirit, he validitates even what is cosmically or physically similar in his actions to the actions of any other man.

2. The Christian 'ends' give the Christian other rules of action, on the level of *use*. To take an example from our religion at this moment (Lent), the use of food. It is quite natural for us to make very good use of it, since it is a gift of God and gives man pleasure and increases his faculty of communion with his fellow men. But the Christian can deprive himself, for example by fasting, or by accepting a privation which may be very small, but which stamps the effort with a religious intention. The use is transformed. I take an extremely feeble example, but whether it is the domain of marriage or wealth, or any kind of 'having' (for wealth is only one kind of having: I have not only money, if I have any, but I *have* health, I *have* strength, I *have* intelligence, I *have* credit, I *have* knowledge of this or that, I *have* a car), it is obvious that in all domains, all 'having' is the object of a use in which Christian faith and charity make new rules. That is still in the private sphere, even if it is done collectively. A family, for example, living in a certain style: that is collective, but on the juridical plane that is still in the private sphere.

Now we come to the collective order, which, if it is expressed on the level of law and public regulation, may reach the properly public level, in the juridical sense of the word, by which public powers and rights are distinguished from private powers and rights.

On the collective level, too, the Christian is obliged, as a Christian, to intervene in the temporal level, on several grounds.

In the first place, he cannot just accept anything, and that obliges him to make a certain number of choices. There are situations which are absolutely unacceptable to a Christian, situations involving the oppression of man, the dishonour of woman, the destruction of the family; all sorts of situations. It cannot be denied that here the Church, churchmen, Christians, throughout history have been far too slow to protest.

It is very striking to see how, in ancient times, they had not the collective and historical sense we have now. We see saints, holy men and women, true Christians with very delicate consciences, purifying themselves, and refusing, for example, to profit from the produce of a property they thought unjustly acquired, but changing none of the objective structures of the thing. They had a very acute sense of justice, but on the personal level. They had never thought that this ought to be carried to the level of possibly unacceptable situations, against which they ought to protest. My previous examples are rather negative. Faith and Charity evidently imply something positive. There is an extremely clear and interesting example in the New Testament, the situation in which Paul found himself, related in his letter to Philemon. Philemon had a slave called Onesimus (Philemon was a Christian), and the slave left his master: ran away. This often happened, and there were severe penalties for it. But having fled, the slave did not know what to do and took shelter with Paul. What was Paul to do? Would he say: slavery is unjust, I am keeping Onesimus: that is settled? No: Paul sends Onesimus back to his master. But he sends him back with a letter, that letter which we have, which is a marvel, where St Paul says, in effect: 'Look, I am sending Onesimus back, but if you have understood what Christianity is, and if you realise the debt you owe me, because you owe me faith and grace, then you will arrange for Onesimus not to be your servant any longer, but you will give him back to be the Gospel's servant with me.' We see from this letter that Christianity does not change the structures, which would mean other changes in the economy and society. Slavery could not be destroyed at one stroke. (I shall return to that point.) But Christianity has introduced spiritual and human modifications, like Christian brotherhood, which were bound to modify things, and this necessarily implied changes at the level of relations between men, and finally, more and more, on the level of legislation and social structures. But we may think that, here again, Christianity has been and is too timid.

Last night at Mulhausen I was quoting Bernanos's words: 'God does not choose the same men to preserve his word as he does to carry it out.'[2] Paul Evdokimov has written to the same effect: 'It is the Church which has the message of liberation, but others do the liberating.'[3]

3. A third ground: there are situations and human structures which are more, or less, favourable to the faith, to the Christian life. Obviously, it must be recognised that the faith and the Christian life transcend social structures. I have no use for any theory which says: let us first change society, then we can preach the gospel. No, we can and must preach the gospel always. I know cases, we all know them, quite amazing sometimes, of men who have been born and brought up in the most unlikely social conditions. I know of one very near to my own family. Brought up in a family where the children hadn't even a shirt, they used to run about naked in the next street. As for their morality, they did the best they could. Well, one of them—he is about thirty-five—is now a man of the most extremely delicate feelings and faithful heart. I have rarely known such refinement of sentiments, fine, noble, pure, faithful. Flowers grow even on the dung-hill, but in spite of all that—and this is an essential element, of which we are better aware in this generation, taking things statistically, all round—it is certain that there are situations which can crush man and alienate him, and that one of the first things to be done, in order to help in the direction of faith, is to re-establish situations and social pressures which will reconstitute the noble, human tissues of man.

Cardinal Saliège said once that one purpose of Catholic Action was 'to make social pressures favourable'. I find that a very interesting definition, though it cannot be exclusive. Catholic Action is first and foremost a fact of apostleship, but in the second place (essential, but second) there is the aim to make social pressures favourable, so long as there are social pressures which are unfavourable.

Ever since modern unbelief has existed on a collective scale, a phenomenon which began in germ in the eighteenth century and acquired political structures and expressions in the French Revolution, we have realised the fact that, while evangelising and proclaiming the faith, we must at the same time remake bases for the faith. In the nineteenth century the problem was how to remake the rational bases of the faith, and they spoke of the *praeambula fidei*, the preambles of faith: it was to re-establish the solidity of reason, the rational certainty concerning the existence of God and the immortality of the soul. That is still relevant. The Vatican Council of 1870 dealt with it. Today, I believe we are chiefly sensitive to the social bases of the faith, to the sociological conditioning of faith or unbelief, and I think the next Council will have to deal chiefly with that aspect. Now it is not so much the *praeambula fidei* as what I should call the *praeambula apostolatus*; to establish healthy human foundations for social possibilities of the apostolate.

These are the grounds on which the intervention of the Christian as such, in the temporal sphere, is decisive, and they bring us, especially the second and third, practically to the level of public life and legislation.

Historically, there is here a lesson which we must learn, one which theologically is explained extremely well in the perspective of what I have begun to say: that Christianity is effective for changing anything in society in the precise degree to which it touches men. The nearer one goes to things, the less Christianity has to say. In the extreme cases, on things which are purely and simply things, it has nothing to say. It does not change the cosmic structures of the world. We have nothing to say on the rules of football, or on how to build a bridge or to calculate the weight and resistance of materials. The more the subject-matter is 'things', the less we have to say. The more it approaches man, and the more we have to say, the more effective also is Christianity.

Though it has been very slow, partial and insufficient, there has been, historically, a certain transformation of the world by Christianity. It has been studied. There are all kinds of works on the subject, on the influence of Christian princes on legislation, on how the appalling penal code of antiquity was modified, on how the status of women and children, and even that of servants was gradually improved. That was all very slow. There was a certain transformation in art. There is a Christian art, or rather a Christian climate of art. There are certain Christian conditions of art, but they do not concern the rules of beauty as such. We have not done any better than the Greeks of that miraculous fifth century before Christ. We have not excelled Praxiteles or the Parthenon, but we have created other forms which deal with man, not so much in his strictly physical beauty as in the radiance of the face, the special expression of man. We have created other forms of harmony which help to dispose man for inner recollection. That, essentially, is religious art: it is an art which helps man to dispose himself for recollection.

There is also a Christian philosophy, as Etienne Gilson has shown.

There is something Christian in all that, only when it touches man, and in exact proportion as it touches man, as it concerns man. That is extremely interesting for us, for it shows us what our field of action is going to be, both of responsibility and of efficacy.

I believe that Christian efficacy is far from exhausted when it concerns man. Now, man is always man. What finally concerns us is what touches man in his simplest feelings, in those realities of his, home, love, the family, justice, his profession, his creative power. Here we have something to say. I am convinced that the interesting and fruitful part of what is called the social doctrine of the Church (a rather ambiguous term) is really Christian anthropology, the Christian doctrine of man, unfortunately too little studied, too little worked out, even by the theologians.

This is also extremely interesting because it shows us why and how we can collaborate with others, which is the case with all of you and of us, in one way or another. We have to collaborate with non-Christians. It is a problem, a tough problem, but it is possible, because it is always a question of man, and because the power of grace aims only at giving nature back to itself. Really, all that is demanded of a Christian policy is that it should be genuinely human (of a policy called Christian, for there is no *one* Christian policy, there are all sorts of attempts to act Christianly in politics or economics). On that level we and others can understand one another, because we have reached a genuinely human level. True, we start from a light of faith, from a teaching of the Gospel and the Church. For example, what we believe about healthy family life, what we hold against divorce as a common, easy possibility, we hold, for our part, from the Christian teaching of our Lord. But granted that grace simply restores nature to its true state of health, we ought to be able to meet an unbeliever on that ground, and we can do so because in point of fact psychology, medicine, sociology and criminology all lead to the same conclusion, that man's health lies in the stable, monogamous family, and that what the child needs is essentially security, a home of assured kindness. We know very well that homes which are without it—when the child tells you, as so often happens: 'Father isn't my dad, it's someone else now'—we know that homes like that are doomed, I don't say to crime, but to social maladjustment. So we know, sociologically, psychologically, medically, that it is true, and here we join hands with Christian doctrine, starting from a purely natural study, which in reality is found to agree with the conclusions of dogma, since grace only gives back nature to itself.

Fundamentally, what we wield in the temporal sphere is essentially the healing function of grace. It is not so much its function of salvation in the strict sense as its function of healing nature, enveloping nature in order to heal it and set it up again on its sound bases.

You may, perhaps, ask me, in what does this function consist? I do not undertake to make a complete list, but in reality it is a matter of a whole Christian anthropology, of a man's whole concept of human truth, of justice, of respect for the person, of the ideal of service, of brotherhood, of mutual help, and also of that value peculiar, I think, to Christian social doctrine, the value of personal responsibility. The Church always sets a limit to 'planning', which may become too total, because she likes to stake much on personal responsibility. If the Church criticises integral socialism, it is essentially, I think, for that reason, so that the exercise of personal responsibility may be safeguarded, it being granted that from the Christian point of view it is always a question of the destiny of a person.

There are, then, all these immense values. I should just like to draw your attention to some points.

There are some things—and personally this touches me deeply, for I love man—which destroy man, and there are some things which build man up.

(*a*) What is it that helps to build man up, independently, I mean, of his inner life, his soul and therefore the grace of God, his instinct, his conscience and the homely education of his parents?

Christianly speaking, I think, and pastorally speaking, one must give the very first place to the dwelling. I know an admirable priest in the outskirts of Paris, a man of the Gospel, with a considerable experience of thousands of people, who has told me more than once: 'I take dozens of marriages every year. Well, if they have no place of their own to start in, it's a broken home before the year is out. To me, that's clear and certain.'

Pius XII had a phrase which I think extremely significant and expressive. He called the home, including the most immediate property in the things one used, 'the person's living space'. I think we ought to meditate on that expression and its profound truth. That the human person should have living-space: that is the first condition for building up the man.

Here, obviously, comes in a question with which you are all familiar, which is very complex, the question of the great concentrations of population. I pass on to you a suggestion which came to my knowledge a little while ago. It originates from Berrurier, who is Secretary of the Association of the Mayors of France, and is himself mayor of a French commune. We make great industrial concentrations, he says, we concentrate men to work in a factory or group of factories. Instead of concentrating men, could we not leave them in a certain state of dispersion, more favourable to the human character of the dwelling, in contact with the soil and with natural life? Every morning we transport men, who in these mass transports acquire the rather crushing and crushed mentality of men reduced to the mass, and losing a great deal of time—you know that many workers leave home when it is still dark and don't get home till after nightfall—well, instead of all that, could we not leave the men dispersed in their dwellings and transport the material to them? A sort of conveyor-belt, not on the scale of the factory but on the scale of a region. I pass on the suggestion to you. What is it worth? It has to be examined from the technical angle. There is a profits aspect, but also a human aspect, which is paramount, and has its own force, which includes the point of view of total profit, that is, in the taste for work, in social peace, in men's happiness, in the building up of man himself.

The point is that one cannot pretend only to make products in plastics, or what have you. You know what Pius XI said in his encyclical: 'in our factories, where matter is ennobled, man is degraded.' All the same, it is a tough problem!

I think that among the things which build man up a very high place must be given to the things which confront man with other thoughts, for the opposite of building up the person is precisely unification, making uniform. It is then that men cease to have dialogue about anything at all, but are faced only with their own ideologies, their own view of the world, which in the end is always poor. That is true for us too, both clergy and laity, in the field of our philosophical reflections. Dialogue is clearly a condition of the real person; there must be a condition permitting dialogue and contact with other persons. Many of you know, for instance, the *Institut de Travail* at Strasbourg, a product of the law faculty. It is something very authentic, where a very fine work goes on, bringing Trade Unionists, full-time and responsible officials, into touch with a university type of thought, a type of thought which is disinterested, not sectarian by definition, which looks at things with a certain detachment, a scientific objectivity. Here is something noteworthy, which can be produced at different levels: clubs, lectures, cultural activities, representing so many elements of dialogue and contact.

Also those non-conforming elements which bring out the need for dialogue, which oblige you to dialogue, must not be eliminated, but on the contrary, in a certain way, must be cherished. We can no longer avoid it. I know myself that one of the disastrous things about certain situations among the clergy is just that it no longer has contact with non-conforming elements: contact and information are too exclusively of a certain type, a certain level, and their hearts no longer suffer the shock of an idea which is different, bitter.

(*b*) What is it that destroys man?

There are certain frameworks and structures which depersonalise man, rob him of the element of personal reflection, or even of dreaming, the element of the beyond, of transcendence: there is a certain saturation of the surroundings by over-organised activities, including those in the order of leisure. Here I would refer you to a passage which for me is immense, decisive. I used to read it to my students once a year. It is the legend of the Grand Inquisitor in *The Brothers Karamazov*, and it is a passage which calls for reflection at all levels, including the Christian and even the ecclesiastical.

Again, everything which depersonalises, which destroys, I don't say morality, so much as the moral sense. For I think that deeper than morality in the narrow sense (how boys and girls behave, for example), in a more radical, more fundamental way, at the deepest levels of the man, lies the moral sense.

One day I had a long conversation with the manager of a big magazine over some private matter, and we wandered from the subject. I said to him: 'I don't like your paper. I know there is always a "religious" page, and your stories have happy endings. In all the romantic press there are happy endings. They are not immoral stories, they are not all divorces, things turn out well. The fault I find with you is that you destroy men's faculty for reflection, you dissolve their capacity for fair judgement.'

There is an enormous problem, the problem of the cinema. The French Assembly of Cardinals and Archbishops published a statement on the subject. Personally I should not react only on the point of morality. A kiss on the mouth lasting five minutes—I don't think many people are affected by that! We are somewhat immunised to the virus. I don't approve everything, you understand, but I can see something more serious on the level of the moral sense: one ends by putting one's conscience to sleep, enervating one's faculty of reacting and judging sanely, and this destroys a certain number of essential human attitudes in the man. In my opinion, the most destructive thing about the cinema is not so much, as I said, the sexual immorality, which is great; it is the fact that by its very structure the cinema is violent, it is the school of perpetual violence. Because the cinema has to work out a drama or an idyll in a matter of minutes, in a few images, they have to be made violent, they are emphasised. This has to be expressed in a face, or by a violent gesture. The cinema is a terrible school of violence. Modern psychologists, as you know, have made a great study of aggressiveness, which the old psychologists called irascibility. The cinema is the perpetual school of disordered aggressiveness, in which the ideal of human action seems to be nothing but violent action, brutal action which is dramatised in a few minutes and is marvellously rendered by the camera.

Another factor, I should say, is *noise*, which destroys men's nervous systems. So many children never have really quiet nights and so have lost the power of attention. Last summer I met the women of an organisation for popular leisure activities, holiday colonies, sports, etc., who told me that their experience went back a good thirty years, but year after year they could see the children losing their faculty of attention. They had a holiday house in the Vosges. They told me that at the beginning of a holiday period the little girls are incapable of looking at even one picture in a museum; absolutely incapable. After three weeks one can get them to stop in front of a picture for a minute or two. I think that here you have a destruction of nervous control for which noise is partly to blame.

Obviously, in all this, very great efforts will be necessary to effect any Christian influence in this temporal sphere, of which I have given you some extreme examples. There are no formulas for it. There is no such thing as a 'Christian policy', any more than a Christian art or a Christian literature. There is a Christianity which transcends these attempts at expression in the temporal, for the temporal is not only the political, it is the whole of man's effort to arrange his earthly life. There is a Christianity which transcends the temporal, and stimulates or suggests a certain number of efforts, which have to be adapted as best they can.

I have myself made a fairly profound study of what are called the relations of the Church and state. Formerly the temporal was conceived principally in political terms. Today it is still political, but also, decisively, sociological, juridical, economic, cultural, sporting, etc. You know that in the nineteenth century was launched the slogan of the distinction between the 'thesis' and the 'hypothesis'. Well, I say that there is only one thesis and no other: 'Go, make disciples of all the nations', and that is all inclusive. All the rest is hypothesis, including what are called Catholic states, whether Franco's or any others, which some would call the thesis, because it seems that there is to be found an ideal state of legislation. Let us admit that in it there is some approach to such a state. It goes against the grain to admit it, but let us admit that there is a nearer approach to an ideal of legislation. But it is only a hypothesis of history: everything concrete is included in the hypothesis. And what does the Church do? She is accused of accepting any sort of government. Hindenburg is in power; we salute him. Hitler; salute him too! Adenauer is there; give him a blessing! But in and through all this, the Church aims at one thing only, to carry out to the full her mission, 'Go, make disciples of all nations.' Make all men Christians. So the Church makes use of all she can—but not of evil, I hope. Pius XII said he would treat with the devil himself if it were a question of peace. He treated with Mussolini: I think it was a clear enough indication. The Church uses everything to the full, as far as she can. If a door is open, she goes in. All that is hypothesis. There are only approximations, which always have to be revised, which are always extremely imperfect, always sinful, always needing forgiveness. One does one's best. It cannot be otherwise.

II. WHENCE AND HOW DOES THE CHRISTIAN IN PUBLIC LIFE DERIVE HIS STANDARDS OF ACTION?

Undoubtedly, we must here distinguish between what is given or received, and what has to be done. I could almost say, if it would not misrepresent my thought, the 'ready-made' and the 'still to do', in the sense that the Christian in public life is first of all a Christian. But as a Christian he has next a public responsibility, in which he tries to be a Christian still, and always. As a Christian he is subject to the gospel, as we are all, and also to the interpretations placed on the gospel by the Church, the bishops (the teaching Church). That is what I call the given. It is chiefly the encyclicals, the papal discourses and the elaboration of the Church's doctrine.

But here there are several planes to be distinguished in the given. I can see three different planes, which are often mixed. One passes naturally from one to another. In the concrete one does not make such sharp divisions.

There is the plane of doctrine, in the strict sense: obviously it must be received as it is. Then there is the plane of spiritual government or pastoral directions. Many elements in the papal discourses and the encyclicals, especially in the reign of Pius XII, are of the pastoral order, the pastoral *magisterium*. The pastoral *magisterium* clearly derives from doctrine, but there comes into it an element of appreciation of the facts, of opportuneness, which can change with the evolution of the facts or the opportuneness. So here it will be not so much direct or integral faith, but rather an obedience, and obedience is never of the barrack square, totalitarian type, but always has a certain element of dialogue, without thereby lessening the rights of authority. Obedience always involves co-operation. If I pay my taxes because in the end they will be raised by ten per cent., because there are penalties, I am not obeying, I am merely complying. I obey truly if I collaborate, if I enter with the authority into its intentions. On the pastoral level there is already a certain element of dialogue between the circumference, or the base, of the Church, and the summits or centres of that same Church.

And there is a third level which is not to be despised, though it is lower in the scale of values than the other two. It is not doctrine, nor is it pastoral direction or government; it is what we may call ecclesiastical policy, which exists, which can scarcely help existing, since the Church is in the world, and the Holy See is an authority of international type. One ought to pay great attention to it, for if the Holy See or the bishops demand things of us in the field of ecclesiastical policy, they don't do it in order to take part in politics, nor for any temporal interest as such, they do it in the interests of the cause of God's kingdom. But all the same, it is less directly tied up with the truth of the faith than preaching or the pastoral care of souls. In this field there are political judgements on which we may differ. It is perfectly legitimate for a Catholic to diverge in some points from the policy of the Holy See.

The best known example is the attitude of the German *Zentrum*, the Centre Party, when Leo XIII, in order to liquidate the after-effects of the *Kulturkampf*, had asked the Catholic parties and the Catholic or Christian parliamentary deputies to accept Bismark's views on a point very important to him, the Septennate. This consisted, you remember, in voting the military credits for seven years together, which would make possible an extremely active militarist policy. The Holy See, wishing to make its peace with the German government, called on the *Zentrum* to vote for the Septennate, but the party refused and renewed its refusal some months later, in another connection but similar to the former. I am going to read you the text of the declaration of Frankenstein, who was Secretary of the *Zentrum* at that time. He was writing to Mgr Galimberti, author of the Holy See's directives under the authority of Cardinal Jacobini, Secretary of State. This is what he wrote: 'It is absolutely impossible for the Centre to obey directives given for non-ecclesiastical laws. In my opinion it would be a misfortune for the Centre and a source of very serious troubles for the Holy See if the Centre were to ask the Holy Father for instructions about laws which have nothing to do with the rights of our Holy Church.'

This is extremely clear and a major example. There are other lesser examples, which you certainly know. All the same, it is very important. In other words, the element of dialogue here implies a greater degree of liberty than when it is a matter of pastoral questions, where liberty has still a certain place, and far greater than when it is a matter of the strictly doctrinal field, where liberty has no place at all.

The Christian in public life will then be dedicated to his conscience, which has to be the mediator of the application of the Church's doctrines. In the last resort, I think, public life consists in finding structures of justice, that is structures for the organisation of human relations, in which the indicatives or imperatives of charity may be expressed better, or less badly.

And here, clearly, we enter an extremely delicate field, the field of the moral nature of every action which is human in its aim, for no action is strictly technical. A machine is not human, but the use of the machine is already human and therefore moral. A factory is not human, but a factory time-table, or a scheme for security or health, necessarily concern the human element. As soon as you enter the human field you enter the moral field, and therefore a field in which the Church has something to say, because it concerns man's ends, his chances of being a Christian and winning the kingdom. All the same, one cannot judge of the collective as such in exactly the same way as the individual action. The collective, inasmuch as it is human, is moral, certainly, but by itself it includes factors which are outside any strictly personal moral obligation.

Think, now: we have in the Gospel our Lord's command to turn the other cheek, that is, not to take the law into our own hands. But in Romans 13 we have it that the prince, that is, the public authority, bears not the sword in vain, he bears it for punishment and the terror of evildoers. We cannot transpose exactly to the public plane what is true on the personal: to turn the left cheek, not to do justice. The prince has to do justice. In the same way Paul asks Christians not to take their suits, their quarrels, before the pagan courts, but to settle them in a friendly way. Notwithstanding, the public authority must set up courts, and that is its primary function; the function of justice is primary.

So they are not the same thing. We cannot judge them in the same way, because the conditions of existence are not exactly the same. A society has to last, therefore it must preserve its own existence, it must defend itself. It is, in a way, in a perpetual state of legitimate defence, and that state has different rules from those of ordinary life. We could apply this, for example, to certain problems which have been discussed in the past few years in connection with Algeria. There is a certain collective state of society which must go on, and this allows, or even forces on it, a number of decisions which one could not take on the level of personal life. Here, I know, I raise a difficult problem, which cannot be solved in a few words: it would need a detailed and complete treatment, in which, for one thing, balance would be assured by a very strong assertion of the Christian's duty to try to inspire *even political life* with the Christian principles of love and forgiveness. What I say of political life I should equally say of economic life. Besides, political society is economic to an extremely profound degree, and in a more complex way than a commercial undertaking of one kind or another.

I therefore maintain that the problem is fundamentally a moral one, but its moral nature is active in conditions which are not exactly those of personal morality. This seems to me extremely important.

But having said that, and still with the idea of giving you some reflections in all Christian simplicity, I would insist on one point which I think very important: the holiness of the work of justice. By the work of justice I mean not only judging, condemning or acquitting, but justice in its entire scope, creating structures of justice, the just regulation of human relations.

When one is a Christian, one loves Jesus Christ, one loves the gospel, one wants to act like a Christian, and I think one often envies the little Sister of Charity, going to look after the sick, or her children, because really her task is hard, but it is simple. And then, whenever we have done an act of charity or forgiven someone, or made a sacrifice, every time we have given, it warms the heart.

When we do an act of justice it doesn't warm the heart. The manager of a business says: 'I sack a workman, and I have to sack him; it is just. That doesn't warm the heart. Personally, as a Christian, I would much rather take him by the arm and say: "How's the family?" But I have to sack him.' That is only one example, but all the time you have to be doing things like that, acting on that level.

I think one has to have a double faith, in a way, when one has to do one's duty without feeling that warmth at the heart which comes from charity and the generous action. We must *believe in the holiness of justice* and in the real sanctification we can acquire from it. There is the example of St Louis. It is one of few, and there are not enough of them. All the same, here was a man who had children, who ruled a kingdom and did justice. We see him in the old pictures, under his oak tree, crown on head. But in reality he was dealing with party walls, stories of inheritance, family feuds. And when he arrived in sight of the Egyptian coast on his crusading expedition, he was the first to leap into the water and fall upon the Moslems, as the worthy Joinville relates. Was this sanctifying? We see him again, crowned with a halo, but in the meanwhile, in the Crusade, he was there to kill men, to make war, and war has never been a game for choirboys. That wonderful example of St Louis, who was sanctified in justice, with the admirable rulings he gave! One day they set St Louis a problem, which he used to set himself, because he was very fond of the Franciscans and the Dominicans and all the mendicant movement of the age. As a Christian, he would gladly have been a poor man with the poor, and from time to time he would go and sup with the friars, from a bowl, and play the poor man. But at the same time he was King of France, he gave receptions, he could not be less than a baron. And Joinville says that he gave this rule: 'So act that the young men will not think that you are doing too little, and wise men will not think you are doing too much.' With the Franciscans, saying his Office, living like a monk, he could have warmth in his heart, but in a sumptuous reception he had none. He sanctified himself solely at the level of justice.

I shall conclude by rapidly noting some of the spiritual conditions of this Christian work.

First of all, the frequent practice of reflection: detaching ourselves often from the immediate business we are engaged in, to have a moment of reflection, and so we must procure the means of reflection. What are they? You will say, silence, recollection every now and then. Then, there is what is now recommended to Christian husbands and wives, the well-known 'art of the sofa', the settee, which means sitting down from time to time, sitting down so as to get out of the exhausting round of action, meetings, receptions. Simply to see each other, husband and wife, to talk, which usually they can't because life is so hectic. So I should advise the 'art of the sofa' too, learning how to sit still. But also, having some material for reflection, such as a review which makes you think.

Then there is something which seems to me absolutely decisive: real contact from time to time with the 'base', the rock-bottom of society, plain and unadorned, the people of the people. Contact with someone who will tell you frankly his reaction as one of the people, with no regard for manners or conventions.

Another thing I think absolutely indispensable, if you are to be effective, is meeting in small groups. Experience has shown that this has been one of the great blessings of the Church in the last fifteen or twenty years: reflection in little like-minded groups. It is only in such little groups that one can, in the first place, inform oneself thoroughly about a question, know it completely, because contributions are made which enrich you surprisingly. And also it is in such little groups that you can go all out to the limit of your own conscience and its demands, and can in the end find some of the practical ways, often so difficult to devise, which will enable you to realise an ideal, the ideal, in fact, of conscience.

I will say this too; having a conscience indwelt by a very pure, very exacting ideal. Being a conscience to oneself. In the bible story of Susanna,[4] there is an aspect which should not be forgotten, the aspect of Daniel. Here is this young man who is not a conformist. For all the rest, clearly, the elders had pronounced sentence, the crowd had agreed and were going off cheerfully to stone the poor girl. But there was one who said: 'I do not agree with what you do', and he stood up solely on the ground of a movement of conscience, which is ascribed to the Holy Ghost.

I think it is absolutely necessary to preserve in our souls and consciences a corner of non-conformism, of resistance to the slogans, the trends, the judgements of our group, our set,—even of ourselves in so far as we are creatures of habit—so as to question things again, because so often it is the one who has been guided by conscience who turns out to be right, and in any case it is conscience which is right. It has to be criticised, informed and advised, certainly, but in the end it *is* conscience, and if after criticism and information one sees *thus* in conscience, conscience must be followed.

In the world of today, in our twentieth-century scene, Christians above all others have an extremely urgent duty to be truthful. The world is full of lies. Our newspapers lie, they tell us only part of the facts. We are badly informed, and that partly excuses us, in so far as we could not be better informed. But people juggle with the facts. We are victims of constructions, more or less sincere, of the truth. There is a duty always to criticise the slogans, criticise words, come back always to the facts; to try to be informed about the other side of the barricade as well, where things are not seen as we see them in our groups, which in the last resort are always interested groups.

I believe that the Christian is called thus to be an upright, free conscience, a free man. A free man is one who is bound only by the truth. We need consciences which are free, upright, critical, non-conforming if necessary, filled with the love of truth. I believe that in the end, for that purpose, the purely Christian and spiritual activity of prayer, adoration, is something essential. It is its own value. Of course you can't measure the value of adoration by its usefulness in comforting your conscience. It is its own value. Guardini has written some admirable pages on adoration as an anthropological value; adoration, apparently useless, but in reality one of the most immediate factors in the construction of a free man, an upright man.

Here some examples might be quoted. But there is one example which I think should make us reflect, the example of Gandhi, not a Christian, though a sympathiser, but he is an extraordinary example. I refer to the action of conscience, his famous Satyagraha. You know this is formed of two Sanskrit words meaning 'power of truth'; action purely by the power of truth. I was reading in a number of *Informations Catholiques Internationales* an article about La Pira in Moscow, in the Soviet Union last summer. Something rather incredible: the man who begins by saying to his Soviet friends: 'Today, Saturday, is the 15th of August, the Assumption. I am going to Mass. Our meetings will be later.' Next day the officials approach him: 'Well, today?' 'No, today is Sunday. I am going to Mass again. . . .' Finally, La Pira declaring, '*I* came here to pray!' You will say: if I am an economic delegate to a conference, that is not what it is about. But it can be about that, in the inner forum of the soul, at the level where the new man is being formed in us and will finally shine through. Because there is nothing to be done; when one is in the presence of a man like that, it is felt. When one is in the presence of an upright man, possessed of the truth, that is felt, and a certain number of things fall into place. There are men to whom one cannot lie.

NOTES

1. Report of a paper read at Mont Saint-Odile, on 26th March 1960, to a gathering of Catholic men occupying executive posts in the political, social and economic life of Alsace.
2. *Lettres aux Anglais*, p. 245.
3. *La femme et le salut du monde*, Paris, 1958, p. 18.
4. It was the Epistle for the Mass of the day, on which the archbishop had preached in the morning.

CHAPTER EIGHT

The Theological Conditions of Pluralism[1]

I AM SURE THAT IT WILL NOT BE A WASTE OF time to begin by explaining and briefly justifying the two terms of my title. My subject is pluralism. By that I mean not only the bare fact that there are a number of ideas or positions on the destiny of man, held by men living together in the same community, but rather the way in which they accept such a situation, and the actual scheme of collaboration which they adopt as a result. We see at once how the question is posed immediately and concretely in the problem of co-operation and the conditions on which such co-operation is possible.

But we have spoken, more definitely, of theological conditions. That is because for the Christian, and especially for the Catholic, conduct is neither the simple resultant of empirical observations, nor yet a mere deduction from reason: it depends on normative indications taken from scripture, and from doctrinal and canonical tradition, interpreted by the teaching authority: indications bearing on man's destiny, the demands of faith, our position in the Church and that of non-Catholics, etc. The object of this paper is to bring to light, from the point of view of Catholic theology, the conditions or principles of co-operation between men of different beliefs or even, apart from all positive religious faith, between men who do not all profess the same doctrine on the 'last things' and ends of man.

Anyone who is at all in touch with the situation and needs of the present moment will readily agree with Jacques Maritain that the elucidation of this question is one of the most urgent tasks facing the theologian.

The first thing the theologian seems to meet when he approaches it is an impressive *videtur quod non*. This is in the name of indisputable principles which, if forgotten or ignored, could lead to the false liberalism so often condemned by the Holy See, and again recently in a letter to the bishops of Brazil.[2] As we all agree, there is only one last end, which is the same for collective bodies and States as for individuals. That end is in fact supernatural, and so we only know it by Revelation, propounded and interpreted by the *magisterium* of the Catholic, Apostolic and Roman Church. By definition, the last end subordinates to itself everything else, step by step, as so many means; in relation to it there is no such thing as a morally indifferent act, and therefore no such thing as a neutral zone, except in the purely technical order. Hence it follows that the rules of action form a closely connected whole; that they exist in their purity and integrity only in the body subject to the Church's *magisterium*, and that in consequence it is impossible for non-Catholics to hold the whole of the true norms of action or for Catholics to agree with them in action as a whole.

We shall reach the same conclusion if we start from the idea of the Church's mission, which determines her competence. That mission is clearly to obtain for men the supreme blessing of supernatural communion with God, but also to guide and train the whole man in that direction, by rejecting the false and ruinous separation between the order of private sentiments and that of outward action, including the sphere of economic, social, civic or political life. Pius X expressed this very clearly when he defined what even then he called Catholic Action, by way of commentary on his motto: 'To restore in Christ not only what is directly incumbent on the Church in virtue of her divine mission to lead souls to God, but also what flows spontaneously from that divine mission: Christian civilisation in the totality of each and all of the elements which compose it.'[3]

This Catholic ideal, with its all-embracing and monolithic character, is not, I should add, a chimera: it existed in the West from the conversion of the barbarian princes, especially under the Carolingians, at least until the destruction of religious unity by the Protestant Reformation, and even long after that. Society as such was then Christian or Catholic: it expressly intended to be ordered to man's supernatural end, and therefore to be regulated by the principles of the faith. The principle according to which error, which is an evil, indeed the gravest of evils, has no rights, could then be put into practice not only on the ecclesiastical and dogmatic planes, but on the social and political also. One knew, not only on the ecclesiastical and dogmatic plane, but also on the sociological, *who* were in error and who in the truth, and therefore *who* had rights and who had none.

The teachings of Aquinas must be seen in this perspective. Their statements are well known. Non-Catholics have not the true knowledge of the end, therefore they cannot have true political prudence, which is wisdom. They can, however, have a prudence which is valid in some particular field, so one can call upon them occasionally, for some special undertaking. But usually one must avoid associating with them or entrusting them with executive functions. In any case, mercy requires that heretics should not be destroyed, so that they may have time to be converted.[4]

But to paint a historically complete and therefore fully accurate picture of the medieval situation we should have to reserve a place for certain pluralist experiments imposed by the facts, in the Sicily of Roger II, for example, or the Syria of Baldwin I, regions where Christianity had to coexist with Islam.[5]

The Reformation struck a mortal blow at the medieval *Respublica christiana*. From then on the states, which in the same period were developing towards modern forms of royal or state absolutism, had to take account of the fact that their subjects were divided in faith. Following at the same time a Machiavellian policy—of which the Roman Curia itself was not wholly innocent—they hastened to form a political or national interest independent of denominational or even religious points of view, and to make alliances with powers which were non-Catholic, non-Christian or even anti-Christian. As soon as one state had started on this path, the others had to follow. With Richelieu, with the Treaty of Westphalia, the purely political and secular interest of the state, and a pluralism in fact if not in intention, became the certainly definitive marks of the constitution of society.[6] The problems which were then raised potentially became absolutely acute and unavoidable when the French Revolution, extended by Napoleon's campaigns, had succeeded in overthrowing the ancient structures of hieratic Christendom and had given the secularity of national life a political and juridical form.

For nearly a century the Church reacted by refusing, by condemning—she had already condemned the Treaty of Westphalia—by struggling to hold on to what remained faithful to her in the logic of ancient Christendom, and also by condemning the various attempts to introduce among Catholics the revolutionary ideas of the separation of the orders and the secular nature of the state and social life. The Church accepted the new state of affairs only as a state of fact; in a relative and historical sense, said Lacordaire; as 'hypothesis', not as 'thesis', said *Civiltà* a little later.[7] Forced to accept the situation of hypothesis outside herself, the Church tried as far as possible to retain the Catholics in a régime of thesis by constituting, within a mixed and secularised society, a Catholic body, provided with Catholic social institutions, and so in a position to order her life, as in the past, according to the regulation of the supernatural end, interpreted by the hierarchy. This was without prejudice to the restoration of hieratic dominance over the State itself and the whole of social life, whenever this might seem possible. In the nineteenth century this attempt produced, as part of a grandiose and indeed prodigious effort, those substitutes for ancient Christendom, the Catholic schools of all degrees—this was the most urgent as now it is the most serious demand of modern Catholicism—the Catholic parties, the hospitals, the Catholic *patronages*, and later the Catholic trade unions. The most successful example of such organisations is, no doubt, that which has given us the live Catholicism of the Netherlands.[8]

The case of the trade unions is certainly one of the most instructive, and the texts concerning it, though less spectacular than the Syllabus, are remarkably explicit.[9] They start from the principle that both by virtue of educative grouping and on the ground of common action necessarily obedient to a certain doctrine, the trade unions imply an idea of the end and the means and must therefore be Christian, for Christians. It is impossible for them, having different views on the end and the means, to make common cause with men of another doctrinal obedience, and equally impossible to educate Catholics by anything but Catholic doctrine. Hence the conclusion, still held in France,[10] that wherever possible, denominational trade unions should be formed: that inter-union cartels or united action should be allowed only in particular cases and for limited objectives, every precaution being taken to avoid the dangers which might arise from such co-operation.

These are the principles, this is the *factum Ecclesiae*, which constitutes for a pluralist programme what I have called a *videtur quod non*.

As with Aquinas, however, the series of objections is followed by a *Sed contra*, which we must now consider, to see if it is such as to counterbalance the preceding arguments. It does not involve principles, as they do, and that is all to the good, for we are not obliged to deny the force of those we have already been able to recognise, but rather to see if there is another way of respecting them. It is based on facts, but facts to which the theologian will ascribe a real value all the more legitimately, in that several of them are part of the Church's own practice, and so they too constitute a *factum Ecclesiae*.

First group of facts

In the new conditions of the modern world, a new type of relationship has emerged between the Church and the world of temporal society; a new way, that is, for the Church to exercise her mission with regard to the world or society. To explain all that would require a special study;[11] here I must confine myself to some brief indications. The Church's essential mission is to lead all men, and the world too, to their last end, which is in fact supernatural. It involves trying to bring about the subordination of man and society to that supernatural end. Yes, but how? Not necessarily by the way of direct subjection to the Church's juridical power, the way which characterised medieval Christendom. That way is one of the hypotheses presented by history, but it is not necessarily required by the thesis, the one and only thesis expressed in the dogmatic statement concerning the Church's mission to the world, and the obligation which lies on all men to direct all their human activity to the aim of communion with

God. That mission and obligation can be carried out by way of the prophetic word and the teaching Magisterium, indicating to men and the world the demands of the truth—the sword of the Church is the word of God.[12] Then, when this apostolic word has been received and obeyed by the faithful, it is carried out by their action and influence, and again by the prophetic word of the Church, reaching the consciences even of those who do not believe. Here the initiated will have recognised what is called, by a rather misleading name, the directive power. Now it certainly seems as if this were a line of action which the Church is actually taking in this modern age. Here are the facts:

1. History shows that this is the line the Church has followed since the seventeenth century. To prove this in detail would need too many facts and quotations. I must refer you to the historians.[13] But I add a consideration which they do not offer. Pius XI and Pius XII presented Catholic Action as *the* real solution of the evil which they called 'the plague of laicism' and as the secret of the regeneration of society in the Christian direction: this shows that the formula approved by the popes as appropriate to the historical situation in which the Church of today is obliged to fulfil the thesis of her integral mission is that of a Church acting on the consciences of her members, and through them having, not a *power*, but a very real *action* on the temporal plane. Simultaneously, moreover, there has been a development of presentations of Catholicism as an atmosphere, a general view of the world, organic fullness of values rather than a system and a *magisterium*. But more, there has been developed an exercise of the Church's magisterium which is one of appeal and witness rather than of authority, of influence rather than commandment. Many papal speeches and messages, episcopal utterances, theological writings, and many developments in the encyclicals on work, the family, the state, education, etc., are really addressed, far beyond the circle of the faithful, to a world which, we know, does not submit to the Church's authority, yet seeks—often unconsciously—and sometimes explicitly welcomes the content of her message, agreeing in its convictions with many elements of Catholic teaching. In her apostolic tactics the Church has largely replaced the 'works' by 'movements'. The change I am trying to define will be clearly seen if we consider historically what has

happened to the application of the body-soul idea to the relationship of the Church and temporal society. It used to be understood in the sense that the soul commands the body in an organic unity: now we hear much more of a soul which inspires, which is a spiritual leaven and a stimulus, something which Pius XII, speaking expressly of the rôle of the Christian laity, called 'the life-principle of human society'.[14]

2. In their search for a theory of the relations of Church and society, the theologians are moving more and more in the direction so well defined by the Dominican friar, John of Paris, at the time of the quarrel between Philip the Fair and Boniface VIII.[15] At the same time, historical study of the documents enables us to see more clearly how the position formerly held and described as the 'indirect power' depended strictly on a certain state of affairs, still hierocratic, and how historically and theologically speaking it is practically a mere limitation of the direct power, itself bound up with particular historical circumstances which vanished long ago.[16] It cannot be denied that certain papal texts, especially those of Leo XIII and Pius X, seem to favour a theory of the indirect power, that is, in Charles Journet's words, 'a jurisdiction of the Church over the City'. But it has been shown, from a study of the utterances of the last five popes,[17] that none of the three theories (direct, indirect or directive power) can claim the support of the papal teaching. Further, the doctrine of the Church in this domain is presented in very different conditions from those of the strictly dogmatic domain, conditions which include possibilities of considerable development and adaptation. Signs, some of which we have just indicated, are not lacking to suggest a development or application in a sense approximating to what is called the directive power.

The facts show clearly enough that in a world so divided and given over to its secularity as is the modern world, the Church finds her interest, if I may put it so, and fulfils her mission better, when she is purely Church, more purely limited and devoted to her spiritual task of apostolate and her strictly sacred activities. Her action then takes place in two stages, or rather in two concentric circles. The apostolic body exercises its powers (in the twofold order of preaching the faith and celebrating the sacraments, which are its field of competence) over the faithful, and thus shapes the Christian or Catholic community, the earthly body of Jesus Christ. It fashions the complete Christian man. That Christian man, sown and scattered among the wider community of the world, plays in it the part of leaven and provides it with the influence of the gospel and what may be called the 'Christofinalisation' of human civilisation. He does this by releasing energies and convictions received from the Church, but made interior and personal in men's consciences, and there, in such conditions, he can enter into co-operation with other convictions and other human spiritual energies. This enables Catholics to be potential collaborators in the temporal work of the human city and, without clericalism, to make a very real Christian influence felt in it.[18] We shall find this point to be of capital importance at other stages of our enquiry.

Second group of facts

The break between the secular, modern world and the Church was abrupt. It was made in an atmosphere, on the one side, of aggressive revolt and, on the other, of resistance, peevish ill-humour and a narrowing of the defences: the atmosphere which prevails when an adolescent throws off the yoke of a too prolonged tutelage. With the rebound of history, from which theological thought itself has profited, many now think that beneath the excesses and sometimes aberrations of the revolt, there was at bottom, at least in part, a normal historical process. In a régime of sacral Christendom, with an essentially monastic spirituality, certain things had finally been oppressed and as it were alienated to the immediate, exclusive service of God, and these things were now restored to the world and its secularity. In a monastic order of life—which uses the world as not using it, for the fashion of it passes away—it is natural to consecrate everything to the angelic life of praise and union with God. Why look for the scientific explanation and the technical mastery of perishable things when we profess to be interested only in the one thing necessary? Thus, except for the search for wisdom and for such beauty as is fitted for praise itself, an interest in things or in secondary causes is wiped out, so to speak, by the interest devoted to God. The claims and rights of what might be called the priesthoods of the secondary causes are dominated and as it were abolished by the higher priesthoods of the first cause. Is it surprising that they rebelled and took their revenge?

After a necessary resistance to the secular world, vowed to secondary causes, Catholics became more clearly aware of the intrinsic value of things and of the inherent demands of the temporal. From being, in a way, unconscious pupils of monasticism, they became *laymen*, men called to work out their salvation by serving God, not only in himself, but also by doing the work of the world: men, in short, for whom, without prejudice to the first cause, secondary causes exist. Nothing better marks this rediscovery of the intrinsic though relative value of things than the human and sociological realism which now marks our efforts in the pastoral field. Catholics have acquired a loyalty to man and to things, the often real lack of which was the most fundamental charge brought against them by the 'laics'—that word then meaning (in France) not simply the lay state but the party of laicism, that is, the ideology of revolt which I have described. To this change among Catholics must be attributed the new fact, so characteristic of the present day, that Catholics no longer shut themselves up in a closed sociological world, which was in danger of becoming a ghetto, but mix with others in pursuit of man's work and the activities of the world, and are found today in the most varied camps and different kinds of activities: always respecting, of course, the indefeasible demands of a faith which is for them a conviction as much as a discipline or an obedience. Interchanges of positions, overlappings of sociological groups, have occurred and are occurring every day. Far beyond the supposedly 'right-thinking' positions, Christians are interesting themselves in all legitimate domains, along with others, in the various elements of men's work on men's earth. I need only remind you of the now familiar distinction between Christianity and the Christian world, Catholicism and the Catholic sociological world.

Once more we note how this development made them available and fitted for collaboration, without their having to deny any of the demands of their faith. Once 'things' were no longer in danger of being sacrificed to the sacred, or drawn into the sociological frameworks of Catholicism, once the faithful recognised the essential secularity of things, those same faithful could be received as worthy companions in the pursuit of the human task. They could not be refused on the ground of being believers (their faith being an interior personal conviction), except in the name of some totalitarianism; either ideological (and finally political), like that of scientism and militant secularism; or political (but fundamentally ideological), like the totalitarian dictatorships which it has been given our age to know.

But the secularists—those of the radical and 'republican' movements in France—have also had their experiences and some discoveries. After the violence of the first revolt, so sadly destructive of many things which will never be restored, they have become increasingly aware that along with Catholicism they had undermined some of the most precious foundations of morality, or order, or respect, of the greatness and even the freedom of man. This was all the more so because, in countries like those of the West, the very idea of man, moral judgements, and even more radically the profound conviction that human life is moral by nature; all this obviously springs from Christianity, and in the Latin countries is fundamentally Catholic. Thus there began to be convergences, possibilities of co-operation, to which the circumstances, as we shall see, were to give relevance and reality.

Third group of facts

Our age has produced the new phenomenon of challenges and trials which affected, at a deep level of their existence, both Catholicism on the one hand and, on the other, communities which were Christian or even non-Christian but still religious; they even affected purely secularist groups which but yesterday were still bitter against the Church or indifferent to her troubles, but sincerely concerned for the dignity of the human person. The new and decisive facts in this connection have been the rise of the totalitarian régimes and their survival, with many other affirmations and negations too, in atheistic communism. There have since been the persecutions of the Christians, the struggle against the very idea of religion and then, even more radically, the formidable challenge to the grounds of respect for the human person, for his use of reason and his freedom. Catholics have striven and suffered at the same time as Christians of other communities and often together with them. All who care about a way of life which respects the primacy of the human person have been able to salute Pius XI as the intrepid defender of their ideal against the Fascist, Nazi and Marxist totalitarianisms. Speaking of a certain evolution then taking place among our French intellectuals, 'Christianus' wrote in *La Vie Intellectuelle*: 'The political citadel has many floors. Is it indispensable to agree on the plan of each one in order to undertake building together? Not always. If there is disagreement on the plan of the foundations, collaboration seems impossible. But if there is agreement on the substructures, there seems no reason why disagreement on the superstructures should prevent a start being made at building together, since all parties need shelter. . . . For a long time, as the substructures were not in practice threatened by anyone, it was in the superstructures that they fought one another. Now, when the very bases of society and civilisation are gravely menaced on the extreme left and the extreme right by the totalitarian régimes, the preoccupations of the radicals extend to a lower floor.'[19]

Events thus favoured the emergence of a positive field of action, which was held in common. Under the pressure of a common danger, men became aware of a certain common heritage, even of a certain unanimity in their concrete ideals. After all, it is a general law that we only fully realise what we hold and value when it is faced with obstacles, challenge and opposition.

Now here we come to a point which all must recognise to be important for our subject. It was not only distinguished Catholics, acting as Catholics but speaking only for themselves, it was the Church through the voice of her princes and the pope, in the most solemn documents, which expressly recognised that solidarity of spiritual treasures and appealed to all men of good will who were really devoted to them. Remember the manifesto signed jointly by Maritain, Claudel, Mauriac, Du Bos, and by Desjardin, Gide, Brunschvig and Schlumberger. Maritain, moreover, did not fail to justify this step in his *Lettre sur l'Indépendance*.[20] Recall, among so many others like it, the attitude and declarations of Cardinal Verdier, the providential man for such a time. Remember above all the great documents of Pius XI, earnestly carried on by Pius XII. Here let me quote only a few:

In his encyclical *Nova impendet* of 2nd October 1931, Pius XI, in order to avert the social consequences of the economic crisis, appealed to all men with true hearts. But a little later he saw more clearly the situation created by the great spiritual battle of materialism and militant atheism against an idea of man and social order as indefeasibly in need of God. He then addressed 'the whole world, to exhort all men to unite and to oppose with all their strength the evils which burden mankind and those worse evils which threaten it.' 'We appeal in the Lord,' he said, 'to individuals as well as nations, that they may all unite. In such a union of minds and strength, those should naturally be foremost who glory in the name of Christian . . .: but let all those, too, who still acknowledge a God and address their worship to him, bring their sincere and cordial assistance. . . .'[21] A few years later the encyclical *Divini Redemptoris* of 19th March 1937 against atheist communism renewed this appeal.[22]

And now for some teachings of Pius XII:

'In order that this (the social question in the light of the inspiration of the gospel) may be carried out under favourable auspices, forces should not be weakened by dispersal, but increased to the utmost by union. To this healthy unity of ideas, to this agreement which generates great actions, we also invite, moved by charity, all those whom Mother Church weeps to see separated from her.'[23] In his speech of 24th December 1939, in which he indicated in five points the conditions of a happy peace, he declared that 'regulations and the letter of the paragraphs will never serve this (*sc.*, peace) unless all those who rule the nations and the nations themselves are penetrated by that sentiment of intimate and living responsibility which weighs and measures human constitutions by the rules of the divine law and that hunger and thirst for justice which is proclaimed a blessing in the Sermon on the Mount, of that universal love which is the compendium and summit of the Christian ideal, and thereby throws a bridge even towards those who have not the happiness of sharing our faith.'[24] On 21st December 1941 the pope's five points were expressly subscribed as the foundation of a Christian work of reconstruction, in a joint letter signed by Cardinal Hinsley, along with the Anglican Archbishops of Canterbury and York and the Moderator of the General Council of the Free Churches.[25] Incidentally, it was this document which formed the basis of the movement called the 'Sword of the Spirit'.[26] Thus work in common became a reality, the facts showed that it was even possible to express the charter of such a common work in other than vague terms of 'spiritual values' and of appeal to men of good will. It was no doubt more specially to this agreement, originating in England, that the pope alluded in his message of 24th December 1941, when he said: 'May our blessing descend also on those who, though they do not belong to the visible body of the Catholic Church, are near to us by faith in God and Jesus Christ, and agree with us on the organisation and the fundamental aims of peace.'[27]

But Pius XII's most urgent appeal was certainly that which he published on the fifth anniversary of the outbreak of the world war:

> To all our sons and daughters of this vast world, to all those who, without belonging to the Church, feel themselves united with us in this hour of perhaps irrevocable decisions, we address an urgent exhortation. . . . Let them consider how, over and above all divergent collaboration with other ideological tendencies and other social forces, which may be suggested in certain cases by purely contingent motives, faithfulness to the patrimony of Christian civilisation, its intrepid defence against atheist or anti-Christian currents, is the keystone which cannot be sacrificed to any fleeting advantage or any combination subject to change. This appeal . . . aims above all at honest and effective collaboration in all domains in which a healthier juridical order appears to be particularly required by the Christian idea itself. And this is very specially the case for that set of formidable problems concerning the constitution of an economic and social order corresponding more closely to the eternal divine law and to human dignity.[28]

Still more recently, in the allocution pronounced on 2nd June 1948, on the occasion of his name-day, Pius XII, addressing Catholics of the whole world, declared again: 'They should not hesitate to combine their efforts with those of men who may not be among their ranks but are none the less in agreement with the social teaching of the Catholic Church. . . .'[29] Since the present report was written and published, other papal texts have appeared, which must be added to those I had then collected: I reproduce some of them at the end of this paper. There are still other passages of the same tenor from Pius XI, Pius X and even of Leo XIII before them.[30] Others will be found in the directives given collectively to the Churches of different countries by the local episcopates.[31] Such documents certainly mean something and imply something. From now on—we shall see better with the passing of time—I expect them to presume and recognise a certain common area, wider than Catholicism and even Christianity, in the idea of man and his destiny, and therefore a field of possible co-operation, in spite of the pluralism of philosophical or dogmatic convictions, a field wider and deeper than that of occasional and limited objectives or purely technical levels. In all this it is a matter of more than a merely outward collaboration in the neutral setting of civil life. It means a community of action on a strictly moral or even religious plane, that of the bases of human civilisation, of the foundations of the very order in which man must range himself, personally and collectively, with regard to his destiny, which in fact is supernatural.

Fourth group of facts

For some generations, but especially since the two world wars, men have been feeling their way, not without difficulties and setbacks, towards the creation of institutions for organising their life in common, not only empirically and by way of compromise, but rationally and on the basis of certain moral principles; in short, on the level of that human civilisation which the Church, as we have seen, included in her spiritual mission. I need only mention the efforts to work out a morality and a code of labour and of social life, the League of Nations, Unesco, the United Nations Organisation, the Council of Europe and so many national or international organisations. The search for a moral basis is so explicit that the UN was willing to promulgate[32] a declaration of the Rights of Man which expressly professes to represent the demands of the dignity of the human person and the ideal common to all peoples.

We know that some Catholics found this declaration inadequate on the ground that it did not state that the rights expressing the dignity of the human person had their foundation in God. Reservations of similar inspiration have been made about Unesco's undertakings.[33] The Church knows, too well not to say it, that she alone can supply to the overgrown body of mankind, from sources higher than herself, that reinforcement of soul, of which Bergson spoke.[34] Pius XI, when he issued his invitation to co-operation, quoted above, [35] warned Catholics to guard their independence in relation to political groups and sometimes to be content to follow a path parallel to theirs.

None the less, the parallel paths do not exclude a certain companionship. If Catholics could often wish for a closer conformity to the truth, a less grudging admission of the true divine foundations of the dignity of man and the social order, they can already perceive appreciable convergences, a greater or less coincidence of the formulated declarations with the principles they hold themselves. It has been pointed out, for example, that the preamble to the thirteenth section of the Treaty of Versailles proclaimed, on social reforms and the organisation of labour, a certain number of principles which seemed to have been almost all borrowed, word for word, from the encyclical *Rerum Novarum* and other papal documents.[36] We could say the same about many other documents, even political ones, and note a striking agreement between, for example, the principles of the Atlantic Pact and the Five Peace Points, already mentioned, of Pius XI. Not so long ago, Pius X pointed out[37] that the principles of the Carnegie Foundation for international peace harmonised with the ideas and traditions dear to the papacy. Cardinal Roncalli, later John XXIII, while expressing the wish that Unesco's Christian inspiration could be more positive and explicit, insisted, in accents of lively conviction, that there was a common denominator, bound up with the structure of man, in certain basic moral and religious principles, between Unesco and Christianity.[38] It is clear—and the facts fully confirm this deduction—that such a common denominator provides a real basis for co-operation in a domain which is not, I repeat, of purely technical action or empiricism, or even of occasional opportunities of meeting (I have purposely refrained from quoting examples of this kind, though they are sometimes interesting),[39] but of considered human edification and, in short, of civilisation.

From the Catholic point of view the situation might perhaps be profitably defined by means of a distinction which seems to me to be applicable in several problems where, at present, there is conflict among us, between what we might call a monolithic, closed attitude and one which is open, though free from a wrong sort of liberalism. It is not always remembered that the word 'Church' covers several components which are not all on the same plane. There is the Church as dogmatic organism and apostolic *magisterium*. As such, she can only assert purely and integrally the deposit of truth which she holds in trust, and denounce the lack of truth in whatever does not purely and simply conform to that deposit. She can only be intransigent. Moreover, holding her *depositum veritatis* from above, and containing it all in herself, she has, as such, nothing to receive from outside her. But there is also the Church as a religious organism loving in history, which she transcends in its origin and essence, but in which she has her concrete life. In this respect the Church exists in and by her members and is subject to the same conditions as they are. They learn and receive from others and from history, she learns and receives in them. They live in a mixed world and are themselves a mixture of Christian and non-Christian. Only, they try to make the Christian prevail over the non-Christian, in themselves and in the world. It is only as *magisterium* that the Church exists in a state of pure *thesis*: in her members, in the historical life she leads in them in the world, she is always in a state of *hypothesis*, and the consequences of that state go far beyond the question of a subjection of the political power to the authority of the priesthood.

As is generally the case with Aquinas, my *sed contra* has given me, not only an abundant supply of facts and considerations, but the gist of my reply. What I have now to do is to clarify the principles of that reply and to define its conditions, its limits and its consequences. Let us call it my *Respondeo dicendum*, followed, as is sometimes the case, by a short *Et per haec patet responsio ad objecta*.

The problem, you remember, is to justify, by defining their conditions, not only a merely factual co-operation, but a pluralism and a collaboration with men professing other beliefs than our own, in pursuit of the task of humanity, understood in all its universality and depth.

Maritain has answered my question in a broad sense, on the lines of his *True Humanism*.[40] First of all he scouts the idea of a theoretical common denominator, a minimum of identical ideas or statements. It is not there, he thinks, that the foundation of the companionship in question is to be found, but rather in the fact of Christian charity and human friendship. The love which brings men together has certain implications: that love and its implications express a basic unity of human nature and its innate inclinations. There is an objective reality independent of the representation or subjective construction that we may make of it. These implications of love are chiefly: (*a*) the existence of God and the fact that man is ordered to him, which gives the law of love an absolute value; (*b*) the holiness of truth; (*c*) the dignity of the human person, with that on which it is based, namely, the spiritual nature of the soul and its eternal destiny. These implications of love are not understood by all in the same way. But we have agreed from the outset that human good companionship is not founded on a common theoretical or speculative minimum. On the other hand:

> in another sense, there is far more than a common minimum between those who, though belonging to different religious families, allow the spirit of love to possess them, since the implications of brotherly love create—in the principles of practical reason and action, with regard to earthly civilisation—a community of likeness and *analogy* which, on the one hand, corresponds to the fundamental unity of our rational nature, and on the other hand is not concerned only with a minimum number of points of doctrine, but is rooted in the whole series of man's practical notions and principles of action. There is therefore a community of analogy between principles, movements and practical proceedings, which is implied by the common recognition of the law of love, and corresponds to the primary inclinations of human nature.[41]

A solid ontology and a sane intellectualism prevent M. Maritain from offering us at this point a step in the manner of Kant, concluding by the postulates of practical reason what is not demonstrated by speculative reason. Doubtless he does not deny that the analogy of practical notions reflects an analogy of theoretical notions, mediating between the unity of nature with its primary inclinations and the said principles of action. But it is not exactly in this line that I want to continue the interesting reflections I have just summarised. It is rather in the line, more familiar to me, of ecclesiology and ecumenism. Maritain, speaking as a philosopher and addressing a majority of non-Catholics, started from below: he has analysed descriptively what happens in persons who obey the call of a companionship or a community of constructive action. As a theologian (and therefore speaking *von dem christlichen her, von dem katholischen her*) one can try to supplement his ideas from the angle of an interpretation and of the principles of that association, considered in its objective elements and from the point of view of the truth of Catholic doctrine, which we accept as final.

Maritain himself admitted that for his part that community of analogy presupposed 'a previous analogy, purely and simply true, and that it is implicitly to Christ, known by some, unknown by others, that all genuine love finally tends, under more or less perfect, pure forms, working in the world for the reconciliation of men and for the common good of their life here on earth.'[42] Cardinal Roncalli, whose thought I have already noted, expressing this community of heritage, as I do, in terms of elementary principles of a moral and religious character, said that those principles, 'more or less indeterminate among certain peoples, perhaps confused for others, transfigured (or disfigured) or counterfeited by the superimposition of ulterior ratiocinations, are yet clear and resplendent to the mind of a Catholic, who reads in them the immediate solution of the great problems of life and history.'[43] It is definitely from the idea thus expressed by these authors that I want to start, by resuming what has been said elsewhere on the question of ecumenism.

The Church is one, but with a unity of fullness. She is an organic totality, the only pure and integral one there is, of numerous elements. If the metaphor were not so material and materialising, we could say that the Catholic totality is like a bundle of realities, increasingly specific from the periphery to the centre, increasingly her own and intimately linked to the personality of the Church. This is unique and indivisible: there is only one soul of the Church, which binds together the organic bundle of *all* the elements and makes it that integral body which is, precisely, the Church. There is a bond, a reciprocity, between that soul of the Church, which ultimately is the indwelling of the Holy Spirit in her, and the integrity of the elements which make up the body. Wherever all the elements do not exist in their purity, there is not purely and simply the Church, there is not purely and simply the real gift of the New Covenant. On the other hand, it is possible that *some elements* of the body of the Church or of Catholicism exist outside it. They are then to some extent wounded, disfigured; they cry out to be reintegrated, in communion with all the others, into the body to which they belong. None the less, they are elements of Catholicism, though in an abnormal condition. If our subject were now strictly ecclesiological or ecumenical, we could trace these various elements from the centre to the circumference. The most central are inalienable: they would draw all the others with them, like a cylinder when its axis is moved. If the centre and criterion of unity were 'there' instead of 'here', it would take the whole body with it, and the Church would quite simply be 'there' and not 'here'. But beyond the centre, to which the supreme graces are attached, there are the sacraments and the episcopate, which suffice, where they exist, to constitute a community in the quality of a local church.[44] Beyond that again, there is the minimum of baptism and faith in the Apostles' Creed, which suffices to form a Christian communion. Beyond that we should leave the domain of the positively religious and Christian and, in fact, of what we call, in general, the *sacra*. I shall define later in what conditions Catholicism continues, beyond the domain of the sacred or supernatural things, in that of nature herself. Before going further, I simply remark here that there can be no communion with non-Catholics in those *sacra* which constitute and specify the Church herself and her inner personality, that is, in the practice of her worship, which is based on profession of the articles of the Faith. Whatever accidental events may be found in history, Catholic tradition has always forbidden *communicatio in sacris* on principle; the acts which are distinctive and specific of the Church can only be performed in the Church, with those who are her members, and according to her discipline.[45]

But as I have briefly noted elsewhere, Catholicism extends beyond the strict domain of the *sacra*, of the positively supernatural, and embraces nature itself, giving it its health and integrity, either by providing it with order in God, its creator, or by showing its true nature and communicating to it the powers which flow from Jesus Christ, through the sacraments and the other channels of grace. That is why God, who is man's creator, has also willed to be his lawgiver, and so the Church possesses and hands on, as part of her tradition received from God, not only the articles of the faith and the sacraments of grace, but the truths of the natural law.[46] The Church's tradition (*id quod tradit Ecclesia*) includes also the principles of nature, in so far as nature is restored to its reality and health, that is, conformed to the intention of its creator. Grace is inclusive of nature, as the revelation of the incarnate Word is inclusive of the truth-in-God of creation, whose eternal artisan is the Word, he who enlightens every man coming into the world.[47] The liturgy and the Fathers, too, begin their paschal instruction, their teaching on the truth of redemption, with a chapter on the creation and with a *Hexameron*: as does the bible itself, in fact.[48]

Catholic doctrine holds that all creation, and especially the spiritual creation, to which man belongs, forms a single order, in which the lower elements derive the integrity of what they are in their own nature only from their relation and subordination to the higher elements, and ultimately to God. It is a position common to the fathers and to theology that nature derives its integrity, and the powers enabling it to be ordinarily faithful to its own law, only from grace. Accordingly the principles of the moral life, of the dignity of the person and of the social order, appear to the Catholic as a consequence, as an application and a dependence of faith and the life of union with God in Jesus Christ, *in quo omnia constant*. But this consequence of dependence of Christianity in the order of nature, though wholly effected by the work of the Church, are none the less intrinsically and substantially natural. Therefore, in the one hand, they can be produced, at least sometimes or partially, by the purely natural action of man and, on the other hand, when Christianity practises or proposes them, men easily see them as a natural ideal and a desirable rule. Having received from Christianity the idea and at least a partial realisation of what is, after all, only a human quality and a reason fully conformed to their nature, the Christian can offer himself to those who do not share his Catholic or even Christian faith—

perhaps not even explicitly his faith in God—with a programme of humility and civilisation in which the others recognise their aspirations. He can share in activities and very largely in ideas, on this field of action, with all men who, though not positively sharing his faith, are on the side of a fully and truly human man. It may even happen (because Catholics are often not as good as their Church, and others are better than theirs) that others have seen or realised some aspect of the human ideal better than we have, and that we can learn from them certain treasures of our heritage. But setting aside accidental events, of which history is full, and sticking to what concerns our subject here, there exists a field—let us call it the *Field of the Decalogue*—which is, by the essential condition of creation, a field of Christ, of the Church, a possession of Catholicism; but it is also, by its intrinsic nature, a field common to all, and in which all can co-operate, in so far as they understand and respect that nature. It comprises essentially what Maritain pronounced on the subject of the implications of love, in which are expressed the fundamentally similar aspirations of human nature: the existence of God and the origin of all things in him, respect for truth, and the dignity of the human person.

This 'field of the Decalogue' also covers exactly that field in which, as we have seen from the facts, the Church accepts and indeed counsels co-operation.[49] We have therefore at least an approximation to our question: we know on what objective field Catholics can accept pluralism, that is, collaboration for the building up of the work of mankind, with men having different religious or philosophical positions from their own. It is the field of the natural law or the Decalogue. Let us now try to define in what subjective conditions Catholics can take part, as Catholics, in any wide measures of collaboration.

These conditions seem to me to consist chiefly in these two points: Catholics must always be themselves, and they must never equivocate.[50] If we are not always ourselves, the result will be, not co-operation, but absorption: we shall not be contributing a Catholic collaboration, we shall not be present as Catholics. This presumes, *on the part of our potential partners*, that they really respect in us our quality as Catholics, that they accept us with our

Catholicism, as it is, in its affirmations and demands. To take a modern instance, this is something which many political partners of the Catholics in France lose sight of, in connection with the Christian schools. Even among the best intentioned, many have refused to see in this matter anything but a question of personnel and economic conditions, whereas the essence, at least in theory, is the ideal of a complete and homogeneous education in the spirit of the faith. Catholics, too, must really be able to present their idea of the end and the means, it being understood that they make no claim to impose it on others. Finally, the partners with whom we are prepared to co-operate must beware of suppressing an essential element of the Catholicism whose support and co-operation they profess to desire, or of indirectly introducing, even without bad intentions, some conditions or considerations which would compromise some point of doctrine directly involving the Church herself.[51]

On the part of Catholics, the duty of being themselves, of avoiding watering-down, means that the more they leave the protection of their own group and cease to rub shoulders with other Catholics, the more they must try to strengthen their convictions and make their principles more intimately their own. The safeguarding of the Faith, mentioned in several of the documents I have quoted, can be carried out on two lines, neither of which should be developed to the exclusion of the other: from outside, by the 'cadres', which was the aim of many of the 'works' in the nineteenth century; or from within, by a stronger injection of Christian vitality and convictions, by a more 'vitaminised' Catholicism. It is a general law, often verified in the history of the Church, that the more expansion of life there is on the frontiers, in the missionary enterprise, the more must life be intensified and closely attached to its centres. It is not by accident but by organic necessity that Catholic Action, the new form of the Church's 'influence' without 'powers' over the world, is primarily a school for the formation of consciences. Nor is it by accident that several recent papal documents, addressed to those who advocate co-operation, put in the foreground new values of spirituality, in the direction of initiative and a bold and creative collaboration in the organisation of the world.[52]

These documents themselves can be our warrant that Catholics can be unconditionally loyal to their faith and their Church, and at the same time entirely loyal to the world. That condition is quite as necessary as the other, but this is not the place to develop a whole philosophy of the Christian's attitude to the things of the world.

Our other condition was, never to equivocate. This second condition will be fulfilled on the Catholic's side if he has fulfilled the first: to be himself, appearing and acting according to the honest demands of what he is. But he will have to try to discern very clearly the *idea* of the collaboration he is offered, and if it is a matter of supporting an institution, the idea of that institution; for an institution is animated and constituted by a ruling idea which is bigger and stronger than the men who belong to it. The real ideal may be disguised under externals more honourable than itself. We may be made use of, simply to swell the reputation or power of an undertaking in which we could really do nothing. We might serve as hostages, powerless to make our point of view heard. We must see at the outset, and reconsider as we go along, whether our freedom is respected and whether we can be sure of conditions for a collaboration which allows us to remain wholly ourselves.

In practice, moreover, both our independence and the effectiveness of our Catholic contribution will depend largely on the strength of our consciences and on our worth, not only religious, but human and even technical. It is not only an axiom accepted in Catholic Action circles, but a fact of experience, that the effect of our influence and spiritual independence is in direct proportion to our human worth, our competence, our honesty and frankness. Once again, the twofold loyalty to God and to men, to the Church and to the world, is the paradoxical law of our witness and its effectiveness.

It is obviously indispensable that our partners, whoever they may be, should show an equal respect for the truth. Unequivocal collaboration is impossible with men whose idea of truth is relative, changeable or dialectical. Such were the avowed supporters of Machiavellianism, such were the Nazis with their idea of a dynamic truth, determined by the interest or the instinct of the *Herrenvolk*. Such are the Marxists, with their criticism of the 'thing in itself' and their dialectical concept of truth, 'finalised' by the movement of history as interpreted by their doctrine. It is a fact of experience, acquired in Catholic thought and practice, that with the Marxists it is possible to co-operate for precise and limited objectives, such as help to strikers or revision of wage scales, but never totally and permanently for the realisation of a human and social order, on the ends, foundation and means of which we are too partially and insufficiently agreed.

To conclude this essay I shall say a few words about one condition of pluralism, which I should have treated at greater length, and even made it the centre of my theme, if the arrangement of the reports of these 'days' had not already led us to a sufficiently wide treatment of tolerance. That condition of pluralism is that we should renounce totalitarianism, that is, the claim made by the sovereign political authority to determine and therefore to form the whole personality of man.

The need for this renunciation is obvious on the part of the state, or the governing machinery of political society. Pluralism as a political doctrine has a duty to justify and illustrate this point, possibly also to criticise or revise the notion of sovereignty, not failing to reply to the objection which may be raised from the needs of the moral unity of the nation. This is not our business here.

On the other hand, we cannot avoid asking ourselves, in conclusion, how the totalitarianism of the faith can be reconciled with pluralism. For there is a totalitarianism of the faith, and even of the Church, since the faith claims to be a final and absolute truth, and the Church claims the duty and the right to form the whole man, to determine and fashion his whole personality.

That is true, but we must see on what conditions it is so. The faith—of which the Church regulates the formulation and communicates the grace by the sacraments—does indeed aim at fashioning the whole personality, but only on the basis of the free adherence of the person, a step in which that person realises itself in the most radical and decisive way: whether it is by a new and deliberate choice or by a deliberately renewed choice, ratifying a state of fact. If, as is natural, that personally interiorised faith becomes militant and tries to transform other lives, or even the states of things and institutions, this will only be by example and the spiritual communication of convictions. The Church's Magisterium itself has no *power* over unbelievers, but it can and does wield over them a real spiritual authority, by a testimony aided by the Holy Spirit, both in itself and in the consciences which it touches. According to the teaching of the Church, the freedom of the act of faith is such that it has been thought possible to find in its demands and implications a favourable basis for the idea of tolerance.[53]

There is indeed an intolerance of the Church which must not be questioned and which I, for one, defend in its integrity. It is that which is exercised by her *magisterium* and by the conscience of her members (each on his own account), in the actual order of faith. The Church, as an organism living in the truth of the faith by the grace of the Holy Spirit indwelling and guiding her, can only condemn error and cast it forth. But can she do so otherwise than by her own means, spiritual means, which of course do not exclude, towards her own members, the force of sanctions, but spiritual sanctions? The Church can never renounce the totalitarianism of faith, the intransigence and intolerance of the truth, but without denying anything of herself she can refuse to exercise them otherwise than by spiritual means and the way of conscience.

It is in this perspective that I would reply to an objection, the force of which has held me up for a moment. It is drawn from the similarity of bodily evils and spiritual evils, of which error in general, and religious error in particular, is far the worst. Would you allow, it is asked, alcoholism, tuberculosis, polygamy or prostitution the freedom to propagate, through a mistaken scruple against using constraint? Why, then, allow it to error, which is incomparably more harmful? The parallel applies in some respects, but not in all, because there is a change of order which must be taken into account. It was through ignoring this and treating as strictly homogeneous things which are not so, that in the Middle Ages the pope was so often accorded a temporal power (which he does not possess and which everyone, since then, denies him), on the strength of the following argument: he who has the higher power has also the lower: if the pope has the plenitude of power *in spiritualibus*, *a fortiori* he has it *in temporalibus*. This purely dialectical argument forgot only one thing:

that the spiritual is not a higher degree of the temporal, but a unique and positive order, positively defined and instituted by the word of God. Superior *a toto coelo* to the temporal, it may well be inferior to it in the proper order of the temporal and, for example, in the use of compulsion. There are even texts in the gospel which say so fairly explicitly. It is easy to understand that the temporal power, which wields the sword to constrain the wicked,[54] forbids by force certain things directly contrary to the natural law (and therefore to the law of the Decalogue). But *that form of constraint*, while it belongs to the natural power of princes, does not belong to the spiritual authority of the Church, which can wield only a spiritual authority and spiritual sanctions. It does not belong to her, because it has not been given to her. The dogmatic intolerance of the Church is a holy thing, but it has its own field of action, which it is important clearly to recognise.

The Church, moreover, as we know, admits *civil tolerance*.[55] On that point there is no question. In virtue of that *de facto* tolerance, religious and philosophical pluralism is allowed and co-operation on a wide scale can be practised in this field, and in the conditions we have tried to define.

The question reappears, however, from the existence of what is called the Catholic state, one which, officially acknowledging men's supernatural destiny, professes obedience to the Church's rules in matters of spiritual truth, and applies its state powers, and therefore the force of its laws and if necessary its sanctions, to obtain the application of the Church's rules.

At the end of an already lengthy study, this is an enormous debate opening before us. I shall not embark on it, and besides, I have already given an idea of the positions I should adopt in it. I would only say that it is conceivable, as a matter of fact, that in a society which is unanimously Catholic and means to be so, the spiritual law could take the form of a civil law, provided with sanctions appropriate to such a law. But I think it very doubtful whether we can make such a state of affairs a requirement, at least in theory, of the Church's mission and of the unchangeable deposit of revealed truth entrusted to her. I repeat: what that mission and that deposit demand in themselves is that we try to bring about the subordination of human works to the one and only last end, which is supernatural. That is precisely what the *thesis* demands: no less, but no more. That this should be effected by subordinating the State to the Church's *jurisdiction*, as of one power to another, is, I repeat, one of those hypotheses produced by history, one which has given much satisfaction to the Church, but to which she is not bound by any essential link or any statement of strictly dogmatic force. Doubtless, none of the theories so far proposed is fully adequate to the state of the facts, but I think that what is called the theory of directive power is nearer the truth than others, because it expresses, independently of any historical situation or pastoral convention, the demands of the bare essence of the Church.

In any case, it is on the theology of the Church's relations with the temporal power that the present question turns. That question, like many others, has no chance of being rightly approached and solved unless the theologian possesses, not only a strictly dogmatic training and knowledge, but also a good historical training and knowledge. The former enables him to accord the absolute its due place, but the latter is necessary to enable him to give its due place to the relative. This is indispensable if he is to avoid turning the relative into an absolute.

ADDENDUM. FURTHER TEXTS OF PIUS XII

That a unilateral supernaturalism should not adopt such an attitude (*sc.*, to rely on man, not on economic or nationalist systems, for building peace in truth) on the pretext that we live in the world of Redemption and are therefore withdrawn from the order of nature, or again to claim to recognise the collective character of that system as 'historical truth', in the sense that it too corresponds to the divine will, are errors to which no Catholic can in any circumstances subscribe. The right path is quite different. In both camps there are millions who have preserved, more or less genuinely, the imprint of Christ; they ought to be invited, on the same title as faithful and fervent believers, to work together to renew the basis of unity of the human family.[56]

Does this mean that there can be no collaboration in the service of the world community, in institutions where God is not expressly acknowledged as creator and lawgiver of the universe? Here it is necessary to distinguish the levels of co-operation. Not forgetting, in fact, that his ultimate aim is to contribute to the eternal salvation of his brethren, the Christian will remember that the coming of the Kingdom of God in men's hearts and social institutions nearly always requires a minimum of human development, the simple requirement of reason, to which every man normally submits, even if he has not the grace of faith. The Christian will therefore be ready to work for the relief of all material suffering, for the universal development of a basic education, in a word, for all kinds of undertakings aiming directly at bettering the lot of the poor and disinherited, being certain that he thus fulfils a duty of collective charity and is preparing for more and more men to attain a personal life worthy of the name, thus promoting their spontaneous entry into the great concert of efforts which will lead them to a better state, and will enable them to look upwards, to accept the light and adhere to the only truth which can make them truly free.[57]

... That is why the co-operation of Catholics is desirable in all institutions which respect, in theory and practice, the facts of the natural law. . . .

They will find, in the organisms which aim at a universal humanitarian goal, generous souls and noble minds, capable of rising above material cares and of understanding that a truly collective destiny of mankind presupposes the absolute value of every one of the persons who compose it and establish it until the age of the true society, which the earthly community can only faintly reflect and adumbrate.[58]

In conclusion we give you two directives: first, to collaborate with neutral and non-Catholic organisations, if and in so far as you thereby serve the common weal and the cause of God. Secondly, to participate more fully in international organisations.[59]

NOTES

1. Text of a report presented to the *Rencontres Doctrinales de La Sarte* (Huy), Belgium, Oct. 1951, and published in the official report of the session, in the volume *Tolérance et Communauté Humaine. Chrétiens dans un monde divisé*, (*Cahiers de l'Actualité relig.*), Tournai and Paris, 1952, pp. 191–223. I have here made some additions to the 1951 text.

On the same set of problems I would also refer to T. L. Bouscaren, 'Co-operation with Non-Catholics. Canonical Legislation', in *Theological Studies*, 3 (1942), pp. 475–512; J. C. Murray, 'Intercredal Co-operation: Some Further Views', *ibid.*, 4 (1943), pp. 100–11, 467–74; W. Parsons, 'Intercredal Co-operation in the Papal Documents', *ibid.*, pp. 159–82; C. d'Oultremont, 'L'engagement des catholiques dans les institutions non-chrétiennes', in *Évangéliser*, (Brussels), 12 (1957–8), pp. 536–53; 'Le sens chrétien de la Vie internationale', Rencontre d'Études, Assisi, 1958 (roneo, 57 pp.).

2. *AAS*, 1950, p. 841.

3. Encycl., *Il fermo proposito*, 11th June 1905; *Actes de S.S. Pie X*, vol. II, p. 93.

4. See *Sum. Theol.*, IIa IIae, qu. 11, art. 3; qu. 47, art. 13 (see qu. 55, art. 2); *Quodl.* X, art. 15.

5. These are the two cases studied by P. Rousset, 'Deux expériences pluralistes dans l'Europe du XIIe siècle' in *Zeitsch. f. schweizer Kirchengesch.*, 46 (1952), pp. 113–29. See also M. Pacaut, 'Tolérance et laicité au Moyen Age', in *Cahiers d'Histoire* (Lyons), 4 (1959), pp. 7–18.

6. See, for example, J. Lecler, 'Politique nationale et l'idéa chrétienne dans les temps modernes', in *Études*, 20th Feb., 5th and 20th March 1933; 'La laïcisation de l'État en France dans les temps modernes', in *Construire*, fasc. X (1943), pp. 178f; *L'Église et la souveraineté de l'État*, Paris, 1946, pp. 172f.

7. Lacordaire, Letter of 27th July 1859 to Falloux, published in *Le Correspondant*, 243 (1911–12), pp. 858f; for *Civiltà*, see the study by Canon Aubert, in the volume quoted above (n. 1), *Tolérance et communauté humaine.*

8. See *Doc. cath.*, 1954, col. 1291f, the text of the Letter of the Dutch episcopate, 1st May 1954 (with notes).

9. Leo XIII, Letter *Longinqua Oceani*, 6th Jan. 1895, Pius X, Letter *Singulari Quadam*, 24th Sept. 1913 to Cardinal Kopp, Archbishop of Breslau (*AAS*, 1912, pp. 657f); Letter of the Congregation of the Council to Cardinal Liénart, 5th June 1929. For *Quadrageismo Anno*, see the next note. Notice that the Letter to the French episcopate, in which Pius X condemned *Le Sillon*, criticised the idea of an association and general co-operation in the work of civilisation which is essentially moral, every man freely affirming his convictions: for Catholics this would involve a sort of promiscuity (see *Actes de Pie X*, vol. V, pp. 135–6).

10. It is well known that in England there are no Catholic trade unions, but Associations of Catholic Trade Unionists, in conformity with Pius XI's demands in *Quadragesimo Anno* (*Actes*, Bonne Presse, VII, p. 107) for cases in which the bishops approved joining neutral trade unions. With the English case we may compare that of the United States, where there are no Catholic trade unions, but an 'Association of Catholic Trade Unionists': see *Esprit*, Nov. 1952, p. 655, n.

We may see a parallel to the case of the syndicates in the directives given some years ago for the participation of French Catholics in conferences and action against contraception. The letters of Cardinal Merry del Val, then Secretary of the Congregation of the Holy Office, to Cardinal Andrieu, 25th April 1921, and to the Cardinal Secretary of State, 23rd July 1921, disapproved of Catholics taking part in interdenominational congresses, and instructed them to form separate commissions (see *Doc. cath.*, 18th June and 13th–20th Aug. 1921).

11. See a brief schema, with the essential references, in the article 'Église et État' in the encyclopedia *Catholicisme.*

12. See Eph 6:17.

13. See, for example, Döllinger, *L'Église et les Églises*, French trans., pp. 34f J. Lecler, *L'Église et la souveraineté de l'État*, pp. 91f; E. K. Winter, 'Kirche und Staat. Kritische Bemerkungen zu Jacques Maritains Lehre von der Potestas Indirecta', in *Zeits ch. f. öffentl. Recht*, 9 (1930), pp. 44–65; G. Saraceni, quoted below, n. 17.

14. Speech of 20th Feb. 1946 to the new cardinals: *Doc. cath.*, 1946, col. 176.

15. See J. Leclercq, *Jean de Paris et L'ecclésiologie du XIIIe siècle*, Paris, 1942. I have given some references to contemporary theologians in the article in *Catholicisme*, mentioned in n. 11.

16. See E. K. Winter, *art. cit.*, n. 1; J. Lecler, *L'Église* . . ., n. 11; G. Saraceni, *op. cit.* below, n. 17, ch. 3; Congar, art. in *Catholicisme*, above.

17. G. Saraceni, *La potestà della Chiesa in materia temporale e il pensiero degli ultimi cinque Pontefici* (*Il diretto ecclesiastico.* 2), Milan, 1951, especially ch. 2.

18. In this connection Pius XII's admirable Speech of 20th Feb. 1946, already quoted, should be read again. It forms one of the foundations of a theology of the laity, and I refer to it as such in *Lay People*, especially Part II, ch. V.

19. 'La théologie de la collaboration' in *Vie Int.*, 10th Oct. 1937, pp. 7 and 8. In the same review, 25th Dec. 1935, pp. 371–8, M. de Gandillac had already acquitted of 'a so-called liberalism' (the title of his article) Catholics who had joined with men of the left in a common defence of the human person against the rise of the totalitarian powers.

20. 1st Dec. 1935.

21. Encycl. *Caritate Christi*, 3rd May 1932: *AAS*, 1932, pp. 178 and 184; *Doc. cath.*, 27 (1932), col. 411 and 416–17.

22. *AAS*, 1937, p. 102; *Doc. cath.*, 37 (1937), col. 964.

23. Encycl. *Sertum Laetitiae*, 1st Nov. 1930, to the bishops of the United States: *AAS*, 1939, p. 644; *Doc. cath.*, 41 (1940–4), col. 120.

24. *AAS*, 1940, p. 11; *Doc. cath.*, 41 (1940–4), col. 105.

25. Text in G. K. A. Bell, *Documents on Christian Unity*, 3rd series, Oxford, 1948, pp. 138–9.

26. On this very interesting attempt at union between Christians in social action, see H. Fermat, 'Le Glaive de l'Esprit', in *Cité Nouvelle*, Dec. 1942, pp. 854–64 (reproduced in *L'Unité chrétienne*, ed. Catholicité, Dec. 1944, pp. 28–33); J. Murray, 'Le Glaive de l'Esprit' in *Études*, Feb. 1946, pp. 259–74 and Oct. 1946, pp. 98–111; G. K. A. Bell, *op. cit.*, pp. 138f; *Doc. cath.*, 43 (1946), col. 975f (text of the statutes); *Lumen Vitae*, 1946, pp. 145f; *Ami du clergé*, 3rd April 1947; etc.

27. *AAS*, 1942, p. 21; *Doc. cath.*, 43 (1946), col. 939.

28. Broadcast of 1st Sept. 1844: *AAS*, 1944, p. 251; *Doc. cath.*, 12th Nov. 1944, col. 2.

29. *AAS*, 1948, p. 252; *Doc. cath.*, 45 (1948), col. 774.

30. See, for example, the Christmas message of 1945, and these lines from one of the later encyclicals, *Sempiternus Rex*, 8th Sept. 1951 (I quote from the text

of *La Croix*, 21st Sept.): 'Who is not alarmed at the hate and cruelty with which the enemies of God, in many regions of the earth, threaten to abolish or try to remove all that is divine and Christian? Against the united battalions of these men, it is impossible for those who are marked with the sacred character of baptism, and so are bound to fight the good fight of Christ, to remain disunited and dispersed.

'The chains, the sufferings, the tortures, the groans, the blood of those who, known or unknown, in countless multitudes, have lately suffered and still suffer today for the constancy of their virtue and the profession of their Christian faith, are a voice, more powerful every day, urgently appealing to all to embrace the holy unity of the Church. . . .'

Pius X, Letter of 11th June 1911 to Mgr Fanconio, Apostolic Delegate to the United States, about the Carnegie Foundation for international peace: see *AAS*, 1911, p. 473; Leo XIII, Letter of 22nd June 1892 to Bishop Fava of Grenoble, after the Congress of the A.C.J.F.: text in *AAS*, 25 (1892–3), pp. 69f.

31. For example, the German bishops in their pastoral letter of 2nd Aug. 1890 (before *Rerum Novarum*), advocated co-operation between Catholics and non-Catholics in matters of social action: see J. Rovan, *Histoire de la Democratie chrétienne*, II, *Le Catholicisme politique en Allemagne*, Paris, 1956, p. 108. For France we may quote the Declaration of the cardinals and archbishops, 28th Feb. 1945: 'For the creation of this better social order, we ask Catholics to be ready to collaborate with all men of good will who, whatever their belief, desire it as we do.' (*Doc. cath.*, 42 (1945, col. 229); see the Declaration of the French episcopate on the human person, the family and society, 13th Nov. 1945 (*Doc. cath.*, 43 (1946) col. 8).

32. 10th Dec. 1948.

33. See, for example, the articles in *Osservatore Romano*, of 9th, 10th and 13th July 1951, and the speech on 11th July by Cardinal Roncalli, then Nuncio at Paris (later Pope John XXIII).

34. *Les deux sources de la moralité et de la religion*, Paris, 1912, p. 335. (English trans., *The Two Sources of Morality and Religion*, London, 1935.)

35. Speech of 2nd June 1948: *Doc. cath.*, 45 (1948), col. 771–2.

36. Yves de la Brière, in *L'Union des Églises du point de vue catholique*, Comité nat. d'Études Sociales et polit., session of 24th March 1930, p. 7. Pius XI himself noted in *Quadragesimo Anno* that the standards adopted in 1919 in the organisation of labour revealed such agreement with the directives of Leo XIII that they might have been drawn directly from them (*AAS*, 1931, p. 183).

37. See n. 30.

38. After quoting from his personal experience, he said: 'There exist, therefore, certain elementary principles of a moral and religious character which constitute the original patrimony of all peoples, and on which we presuppose an understanding, as it were, on an inevitable basis of common life, in order to bring about the construction of the true social and worldwide order of justice and peace.' Speech of 18th June 1951: *Osserv. Romano*, 29th June; *Doc. cath.*, 15th July 1951, col. 846. The whole speech could be quoted in this connection.

39. Here are some examples:

Defence of religion: Against the threat of a danger to evangelisation, Indian Catholics and Protestants combined, during the last war, first in a congress, then in an organisation, the 'Christian Community': see *Construire*, fasc. 1 (1941), pp. 250f. In Jan. 1948 the different Christian communities and the Israelites of Egypt formed a common front of action against a law on the courts of justice which would have abolished the religious jurisdictions.

Social action: Catholics (97 delegates) and Socialists (195 delegates), at a congress in Zurich in 1897, collaborated to work out a national and international code of labour (see E. Dolléans, *Histoire du Travail*, Paris, 1942, pp. 280f). Collaboration of Catholics in activities and efforts for peace: see M. Pribilla, *Um kirchliche Einheit*, Freiburg-i-B., 1929, p. 7, n. 5 (refer.) and pp. 240–64. Participation in action against contraception, alcoholism and tuberculosis, and in various leagues of public morality. Or again, in action in favour of the sanctification of Sunday, e.g., in Switzerland in 1950; etc.

For the case of action against contraception, see above, n. 10. The present practice appears to be much less rigid.

40. This answer was not yet in that book (pp. 220–1), but it is developed in the fine lecture given to the Fourth World Congress of Faiths for the defence of the human person, 'Qui est mon prochain?', published in *Vie Int.*, 65 (1st Aug. 1939), pp. 165–91. It was repeated more briefly in 'The Achievement of Co-operation among Men of different Creeds', in *The Journal of Religion*, 21 (1941), pp. 364–72; *L'éducation a la croisée des chemins*, Paris, 1947, p. 23; and finally in an address to UNESCO, 7th Nov. 1947; text in *Nova et Vetera*, Jan. 1948, pp. 1–14. The ideas are resumed in *Raison et raisons*, Paris, 1947, pp. 331f; *L'Homme et l'État*, Paris, 1953, ch. IV.

41. Article in *Vie Int.*, p. 190. It seems that in other categories the remarkable way in which A. Dondeyne has proved the obligation and the possibility of co-operation is very close to this position of Maritain. He showed, in fact, that in every man there exists, at the root of his action, an intention of universal bearing. The actual man reveals and realises that intention only in an objectification which always goes beyond the fundamentally universal intention which started and inspired it and, moreover, starts and inspires other objectifications as well. See his contribution to the volume from which the present report is taken, pp. 107–22: 'Tolérance et collaboration comme données philosophiques assumées par la foi.' See his report in *Foi Théologale et Phénoménologie*, Paris, 1951, especially pp. 35–6.

I mention here some other similar approaches, with the same conclusions: P. Ganne, 'Christianisme et valeurs communes', in *Équipes enseignantes*, work-programme, 3rd term, 1949–50, pp. 55–63; M. D. Chenu, 'Morale laïque et foi chrétienne', in *Cahiers Universit. Cathol.*, Dec. 1953, pp. 112–29: for us Christians, God and Christ are 'implied' in the imperative of conscience. But the transcendence of God means, precisely, that though he is within nature and its movement, he does not intervene *on its level*, and allows it autonomy at that level. Fr Chenu connects this state of things with 'profane Christianity' and the mode of action which must be employed in it, namely, witness. We need a faith strong enough to prompt our action without appearing in a narrowly denominational way, and to inspire that action and a real respect, on this level, for the values of human life which we share with others.

42. *Ibid.*, p. 191.

43. *Loc. cit.*, above, n. 38.

44. See my 'Note sur les mots "Confession", "Église" et "Communion" ' in *Irénikon*, Jan. 1950, pp. 3–36.

45. That is why the Church requires groups to be specifically Catholic wherever it is a question, not only of worship, but of religious instruction and education. See CIC, c. 923, sect. 1, 1258, 1374, 2259; *AAS*, 1920, pp. 595f; 1922, p. 8. For mixed schools in Orthodox countries, see the instruction of the Sacred Congregation of the Inquisition to the Greek Uniate bishops, 28th Aug. 1900.

46. *Lex nova, quae est lex libertatis . . . est contenta praeceptis moralibus naturalis*

legis et articulis fidei et sacramentis gratiae: Aquinas, *Quodl. IV*, art. 13; see Suarez, *De legibus*, lib. 10, c. 2, n. 5, 20 (we owe these references, and several in the preceding note, to Pribilla's work cited in n. 39, which on pp. 241f deals with the question of collaboration between Catholics and other Christians).

47. In this perspective a valid meaning could be given to the reply of Jules Ferry, when asked what morality should be taught in the schools: 'It is only necessary to show these young minds the true and pure light which, from the beginning of the world, according to a profound saying, is the light which enlightens all men.' (Speech of 10th Dec. 1880 to the Senate, quoted in G. Weill, *Hist. de l'Idée laïque en France au XIXe siècle*, Paris, 1925, p. 278).

48. Gen 1–3.

49. It is interesting to note here a very similar position of principle on the part of the Orthodox Churches, whose ecclesiological principles have so much in common with those of the Catholic Church. See, for example, V. Sesan, in *Procès-verbaux du Premier Congrès de Théol. orthod. à Athènes, 29 Nov.–6 Dec. 1936*, Athens, 1939, p. 294; C. Lialine, 'L'Action de l'Orthodoxie' in *Qu'est-ce que l'Orthodoxie?*, Brussels, 1945, pp. 212f; and the Orthodox reactions after the Amsterdam Conference of 1948.

50. On these subjects pp. 67f of Étienne Gilson's *Pour un ordre catholique* (Paris, 1924), should be read again. I have benefited from them here.

51. This point might be illustrated by the withdrawal in 1924 of the co-operation which English Catholics had at first given to the 'Conference on Christian Politics, Education and Citizenship': see the letter of the bishops of the Province of Birmingham, 12th Feb. 1924 (in *Doc cath.*, XI, 1924, col. 1246–8).

52. See particularly Pius XII, Speech of Pentecost 1941 (Ed. Action Populaire, n. 26); Allocution of Christmas 1942 (*ibid.*, n. 25–6). See in my *Lay People*, an anthology of utterances of the Church's pastoral *magisterium* in this sense (App. III, pp. 444f). I have since collected others.

53. See J. Leclercq, 'État chrétien et liberté dans l'Église', in *Vie Int.*, Feb. 1949, pp. 99–111. See also the report by Léonard in the collection from which this paper is taken.

54. Rom 13:1–7.

55. See, in the first place, Pius XII, Speech to the Rota, 6th Oct. 1946 (*Doc. cath.*, 1946, col. 1187); A. Vermeersch, *La tolérance*, Paris, 1912; Y. de la Brière, 'A propos de la tolérance civile. Le droit supérieur de la vraie religion et les nécessités de la paix publique', in *Miscellanea Vermeersch*, Rome, 1935, vol. II, pp. 171–86; M. Pribilla, 'Dogmatische Intoleranz und bürgerliche Toleranz', in *Stimmen der Zeit*, 144 (April 1949), pp. 27–40 (French trans. in *Unité chrétienne et tolérance religieuse*, Paris, 1950, pp. 147–72).

56. Christmas message, 1954, *Doc. cath.*, 1955, col. 76.

57. Jn 8:32.

58. Allocution to the members of the eleventh plenary week of *Pax Romana*, 25th April 1957, *Doc. cath.*, 54, 1957, col. 647–8.

59. Allocution to the Second World Congress of the Apostolate of the Laity, 5th Oct. 1957: *Doc. cath.*, 54, 1957, col. 1426.

CHAPTER NINE

The Christian's Attitude in a divided World

I. UNITY IN THE TRANSCENDENCE OF THE FAITH[1]

It has often been said that men are divided not so much by ideas as by mentality, by their way of thinking and approaching everything, including the ideas themselves. Sociologists like Hauriou and Delos have even introduced this idea of mentality into the definition of nationality, and those who have lived abroad are inclined to agree with them. But there is a case for considering the question from the point of view of Catholics themselves.

In France, until recent years, the religious question, latent or overt, was at the root of all our political divisions. What Poincaré said to Charles Benoît—'between you and me lies the whole question of religion'—illustrates the fact on which, under Leo XIII, all the 'rallies' came to grief and on which we have so often come to grief since: the fact that the words 'Republic' and 'republican' had an ideological and dogmatic sense far beyond the constitutional or even political sense, a sense which implied an anti-Catholic religious attitude. Protestants could be republicans, Catholics could not. It was a religious question which divided Frenchmen, at the very heart of politics.

We are now allowed the character of republicans, if we really wish to claim it sincerely. In French political life and even in the internal life of Catholicism, this is a new fact of great importance, a freedom and a victory which we must not allow to be taken from us. The fact is that after a century's delay the word 'republican' has undergone a development like that of the word 'patriot', which from 1789 to 1793 was a sort of equivalent to it. Now, however, nobody denies us that title. We should rather be induced to deserve it the better.

If the religious question used to divide Frenchmen at the heart of politics, it was no doubt because Catholics, with few exceptions, were politically unanimous. But indeed, the closer one examines the question, the clearer it becomes that the exceptions were many: the general picture, however, was homogeneous. If our situation has changed in the public life of the nation, it is because our political unanimity has been dissolved. That represents, there can be no doubt, a good thing, a lifting of the mortgage, a liberation, which the younger generation, to whom the name of Maurras is almost meaningless, cannot imagine. Once again, they reap what their elders have sown, just as their elders had in their day reaped the fruit of other labours.

But an opposite and correlative danger threatens to appear, precisely in proportion as the political homogeneity of Catholics is dissolved: the danger that instead of the religious question dividing Frenchmen within politics, the political question, by determining and inspiring different mentalities, will divide Catholics within religion.

It is no secret that in the whole Catholic body, thanks to a freedom of which non-Catholics cannot form a true idea, there is a great variety of tendencies and currents. It is legitimate, it is natural, it contributes to the beauty and richness of the Church, as the theologians like Aquinas and the popes have often proclaimed. Nobody, at least in principle, can object to that. From the political point of view, there will always be what we may call, despite the unpleasing character of that vocabulary, Catholics of the right and Catholics of the left. And as the right and the left are distinguished chiefly by different mentalities, there will always be, among Catholics, different tendencies whose influence will extend to the manner of approaching, considering, expounding and defending doctrine. The connection between certain doctrinal attitudes and a certain political position is something easy to justify by reason and still easier to establish inductively from facts.

From this, I think, we can draw the following conclusion: Catholics must be led, above all, to an effective cult of the transcendence of the Gospel and the faith. Above all mentalities, we share in truths and affirmations which are the very stuff of the Christian tradition: that which has been delivered to us that we may live by it. But that transcendence itself is only found if we grasp the Christian truths and affirmations at a sufficient height, as near as possible to their source. Here we are greatly indebted to St Thomas, to whom we owe all that is most essential and precious in our intellectual formation. But we know too that to make St Thomas himself the literal standard or the complete expression of the Christian affirmations would be to fail to go back to the source, which is older than Aquinas and on a higher level.

It is in a Christianity, a piety and above all a theology which are familiar with their sources that Catholics can recover and practise their unity. We know what these sources are: they are, chiefly, the actual fact of the Christian life, lived in common under the guidance of the *magisterium*, the bible, the liturgy and the fathers, then the most approved theologians, who are themselves not so much sources as, like us, users of the sources from which they derive all their worth. When we all daily resort to these sources, when we all really live in these 'places', when the bible is once again the matrix of the thought of every one of us, then we shall know that Christian faith and truths far transcend the particular attitudes, often more human than Christian, which are the grounds of our oppositions. The diversities will remain among us, but they will no longer be oppositions, because they will be realised and willed as relative, in comparison with a deeper, vividly experienced unity.

Happily, such a return to the sources, already sanctioned by Pius X, is the common characteristic of all that counts, all that really contributes anything to the present Catholic activity, whether apostolic, pastoral or theological. Thus we are advancing naturally towards a greater unity, by advancing farther and—according to whether we imagine the spring as gushing from the ground or coming down from the mountains—going deeper or higher into the pastures of Christ, whose sheep we all are.

II. UNIVERSAL BROTHERHOOD[2]

A Christian ideal, but also secular

We often hear quoted, with a little alteration, Chesterton's saying that the modern world is full of Christian truths run mad. And indeed it certainly seems that the modern world is marked by a sort of explosion of the truth which the Middle Ages aspired to contain in a single body, the truth of the 'Christian republic' or 'Christendom'. The Middle Ages ended in a sort of dislocation or dismemberment. Its great dream of unity, which to its glory it realised for a moment, at least within the bounds of the West, was as it were effaced, in the century which our history-books have taught us since childhood to call that of the Renaissance, the Reformation and the great discoveries. These discoveries are many and well known: printing, America, etc. But the greatest, without any doubt, was man's discovery of himself.

Man's frontiers and potentialities were found to be wider than had been thought. The Christian spiritual forces which had inspired and filled the ancient Catholic unity were swamped, as it were, by the tasks of a new world, for which there opened out gigantic spaces, where loomed, like immense caverns, problems hitherto unknown. The new world, which emerged from the irruption of new demands and the sudden widening of horizons, carried over from the old Catholic home all sorts of ideas and values, and it is by them that it has lived, not without distorting them, but also not without sometimes considerably developing them. The idea of universal brotherhood, as we shall see, is one of them.

It needed time to explore the enlarged domain of the new mankind, to raise to the level of these new ideas the truth, always possessed by Christians, that all men are brothers. That knowledge was certainly very deep. But it is just the very deep ideas or feelings which sometimes lack the means or the intermediaries to be produced on the surface, which is the level of history and practical life. Indeed it is not sublime ideas or sentiments which we lack, but the imagination, the daring, and the decided will to translate them into action on the level of ordinary life, lived by men in the concrete. That is why Christians have sometimes been outdistanced, in putting into practice the ideas drawn from their treasure, by those who live by those ideas, but outside the ranks of the Church.

It is not that Christians have done nothing: far from it. By her supernatural character, by her missions, by the fundamental egalitarianism of her prayer and sacraments, by her dogmas of the fatherhood of God, the universal redemption, the mystical body and the communion of saints, the Church has always been the first witness to the universal brotherhood of man. That is beyond dispute.

But it is also a fact that on the practical level, that idea of brotherhood has been propagated, and certain action has been initiated for it, by secularists, I mean by men to whom the Church was an alien and even, they thought, an enemy. The idea of brotherhood comes indeed from the Gospel, and the Gospel has been brought to men by the Church. Yet no one can deny that in the idea of fraternity by which our contemporaries are animated, the revolutionary theorists, the freemasons and the eighteenth-century philosophers count for something, and also the great 'secularists' whom we have had to fight, indeed, because they attacked us: P. Bert, Lavisse, F. Buisson, F. Pecaut, not to mention politicians who were not exactly Christians: L. Bourgeois, Viviani, Jaurés, and authors who are certainly not to be commended in all respects, such as Victor Hugo, Zola and even Voltaire.

The truth is that the great Christian idea of universal brotherhood, realised as far as it then could be in the restricted and closed society of the Middle Ages, was planted out, at the dismemberment of the sixteenth century, in a soil which wanted nothing to do with the blessing of the Church, and there grew up and bore fruit. It has been the secret inspiration of a world which sprang from Christian seeds, but wished to know only man; a world which, turning away from God, was passionately concerned with man, with the lot of man *in this* world. Was it not the Revolution of 1848 which corrected and completed the motto of 1789 to '*Liberty, Equality and Fraternity*'? Thus the ideal of the universal brotherhood, which now occupies men's minds, though it comes originally from our Master Jesus Christ, also proceeds partly, and directly, from a world which has broken with

Christianity and is often at even open war with the Church of Jesus Christ.

In this there is a tragic fact, which we can only suffer as a scandal, and which also exists, unhappily, in other fields as well. It forms part of that great tragedy of the lost unity, of the breaking-up of the truth, which I have described. How could we have reached a situation in which it fell to men in opposition and war against the Church to vindicate and put into practice a fundamentally Christian ideal? But also, how can we witness these efforts, we who know whence they came and whither they really lead, without wanting to take part in them, and to take part in them according to what we are and what we bear in us, that is, in our capacity as 'salt of the earth'? Not, of course, in order to take charge of them by way of authority, which would savour of a clericalism we ourselves declare to be outmoded, but in order to play our part in the work of men and to contribute to the world that 'reinforcement of soul' which Henri Bergson said in 1932 was the need of the world's 'overgrown body'.

The special rôle of Christians

For if the brotherhood of man has always been an ideal and a duty, today it is more urgent than ever, especially in its character of *universal* brotherhood, for we have entered on an age in which human problems can afford to be considered only on the scale of the worldwide, the cosmic, the ecumenical, the universal. It may be a truism, but it has not sufficiently penetrated our living consciousness, that air travel has begun to abolish the obstacle of distance. The time is near when it will take less time to go from Paris to London than many people spend every morning travelling to their offices or factories. Brazil or the Argentine are within hours of us, and you can get the Paris or London papers there almost as quickly as in a provincial town.

We should not be too ready to answer that this only concerns a very small number of people, for it already changes the conditions of the relations between men in a way which really affects us all, and will affect us increasingly, in ever faster rhythm. Without any doubt, the unity of the world is in process of attainment. The idea proposed by Garry Davis, of a single world citizenship, can no longer be called Utopian, for the process of its achievement is already begun. Very probably this will come about in forms quite different from anything we can now imagine, but come about it will. It will need many experiments, many attempts and also setbacks. In the sphere of achievements we cannot deduce the application of even a right idea by the mind alone. No one, however much of a genius, could have deduced from the first 'aeroplane' the aircraft of today: we have had to go through the indispensable trials and delays of experience. It will be the same with the unity of the world and universal brotherhood, but they will be achieved. Our rôle, once again, is to take our share in the efforts leading to them, and to bring them a soul. These two points are both necessary. Without concrete participation in the efforts, our spiritual contribution will be somewhat unreal and probably ineffective. Without the spiritual contribution—supernatural we dare to say—we should not take our part in the effort according to what we really are, according to what we cannot be asked to renounce, but to which we may rightly be asked to be faithful: our character as Christians.

To take our part in the efforts of men means entering with them into the chain of suffering, co-operating actively in all the initiatives of brotherhood which correspond both to our powers and to our convictions: it means really doing something, something real, by which human brotherhood may be achieved in some degree. We all have something we can do: enter into relations with foreigners, for example, welcome them, help them to make contact with our society; make contact ourselves with other countries, learn and read their language; support movements for promoting brotherhood, and in the first place, of course, our Catholic works, missionary, charitable, educational, etc. Finally, it is within everyone's capacity to develop in himself fraternal dispositions, and to influence opinion, for his small part, by propagating these ideas in his own circle.

Contributing a soul to men's efforts for universal brotherhood means bringing it back, as far as possible, to its source, which is the fatherhood of God. It means developing those aspects of Christian dogma, taken really from its heart, which are the basis of that brotherhood, and doing so without shrinking from exacting applications, such as the fathers drew, for example, about the propriety of every kind of 'having'. It means formulating ourselves a more truly 'catholic' soul: less provincial, less stay-at-home, less inclined to see error in what is merely unaccustomed: a soul eager to broaden itself, to the best of its powers, to the utmost bounds of the truth, of the good, of life, of mankind and God's plan for it. It means having a real spirit of brotherhood towards everything which can be an object of communion for us. It means, finally, directing our prayer along the lines of that great intention which in our association the Apostleship of Prayer is the special intention for this month of August.

Here we must not be content with words or with what amounts to the same thing, beautiful but empty sentiments. One shudders at the thought of all the sublime things we think and say, but which result in—what? In filling programmes, covering paper; and then? To accept an intention for prayer, especially when, as here, it concerns the hunger and the hope of men, is not simply to obey a rubric, to observe a rite. If, in forming that intention of prayer, we do no more than that, we had better do nothing at all. We may deceive ourselves, but we do not deceive God, or men.

On the other hand, if we truly take it to heart to pray, really to pray, to intercede for the world in the burning manner of Catherine of Sienna, imploring: 'Mercy for Catherine! mercy for the Church! mercy for the world!', if we do that as we do something we really care about, something really indispensable in which our hearts and our human lives are involved, then indeed let us pray, and by praying help to contribute a soul to the efforts of men who are groping towards the light. Our prayers will meet with God's plan, which is to unite all men in one family, even in one single body, the body of Christ. Our prayer will move God to raise up the men we need, to frustrate the men of violence and pride, to support and guide the men of peace and unity. In any case it will have the result obtained by all sincere prayer; it will do good to ourselves, it will develop and strengthen in us a brave and true spirit of brotherhood. And to that extent, already, it will create universal brotherhood in that kingdom of which each of us is king, the kingdom of our own heart.

III. SIMPLE NOTES ON THE CATHOLIC NOTION OF FREEDOM[3]

The subject of freedom is on the programme of several societies for the 1945–6 session. It has more than one aspect and includes more than one problem. Sometimes the subject in question is free will, the freedom of choice: sometimes it is the world of political, social or economic liberties: sometimes it is the inner freedom of conscience, that Christian freedom of which Paul and the gospels speak.

These different problems are not unconnected, and the use of the same word for them all suggests that there is a common fundamental idea which it may be useful to all to have elucidated. That is why I shall consider here the notion of freedom in general, with the object of providing a starting-point for those who will have a more limited problem to study.

The Rousseauist concept of freedom

It is certainly not because I enjoy thinking in opposition that I shall first oppose a notion of freedom which might be called revolutionary, Rousseauist or liberal, and is rejected by the Church. It is rather because this notion saturates our intellectual atmosphere, we meet it everywhere, it is at the back of many historical positions and many attacks on the Church, moreover it will serve to set my own position in clearer relief.

This is the notion underlying the *Declaration of the Rights of Man*:

'Freedom consists in being able to do whatever does not harm others: thus the exercise of every man's natural rights has no limit except those which assure the enjoyment of the same rights to other members of society. Those limits can be determined only by the law' (Art. 4). It would be a hard problem to find out the historical origins of this idea of an absolute freedom, stated without conditions as supreme value. But we can find an expression of it as early as Rousseau, who wrote: 'What man loses by the Social Contract is his natural freedom and an unlimited right to whatever attracts him and can be attained by him: what he gains is civil freedom and the property of all he possesses. To make no mistake about these compensations, natural liberty, which is limited only by the powers of the individual, must be clearly distinguished from civil liberty, which is limited by the general will.'[4]

The characteristic of this revolutionary or Rousseauist concept is that freedom is not defined by reference to anything other than itself, but is stated by itself, for itself. As an unlimited right of a man to whatever attracts him and can be obtained by him, it has no limits but the similar rights of every other man (*Declaration*) or the powers of the individual (Rousseau). It is conceived simply as a value of enfranchisement with regard to everything which might limit man's spontaneity, an absence of bonds, constraint or obligation.[5] It is stated unconditionally and desired for its own sake, without limits. It is obtained only in so far as man is freed from all that might claim to impose itself on him.

This idea was shared to some extent by those Catholics who, in the nineteenth century, conceived the noble ambition of reconciling their age with the Church, and particularly by the group led by Lamennais, with their organ, *L'Avenir*. Their aim was generous and we still profit by the movement they began. But they had not sufficiently tried out and purified their ideas, they had not sufficiently examined the tradition and thought of the Church. Thus they did not wholly avoid the danger of accepting notions and positions which were not those of Catholicism. They also wanted to go too fast, without waiting till the mysterious processes of history had sifted the theories, allowed the movements to reveal by development what they really had in them, and finally made possible certain *rapprochements* which in the beginning were not ripe. Having a very vivid and pure feeling that their age was the age of freedom—perhaps because of Lamennais's excesses and the discredit these brought on his ideas, these young Catholics did not see clearly enough how much their age also wished to be the age of justice,—they sincerely took up the revolutionary hymn of liberty. They too stated it for itself, as an absolute: 'That freedom, absolute in its essence, has no limits but itself and stops only where its exercise would become a violation of the liberties of others.'[6] They desired it in all its consequences and, for example, in a régime of absolute freedom for the Press:

'We desire complete freedom for the Press', wrote de Coux in *L'Avenir*.[7]

On this basis and in this line was developed a liberalism which in the nineteenth century encountered the condemnation of the Church.[8] The word 'liberalism' must be clearly understood, for it covers some very diverse things. There is a liberalism which is on the level of the 'thesis' and the very principles of thought: it is simply an adaptation of the principles of modern rationalism in its non-aggressive form. That is essentially the liberalism the Church has condemned. But there is another liberalism, on the level of the 'hypothesis'; it is that which, taking account of an historical situation, honestly professes an attitude of tolerance in the midst of a now divided world, in which believers are not even a majority. This liberalism, which I hope we all profess, is not condemned by the Church, and even forms an increasing element in her practice. These distinctions in vocabulary are easy to make now: we profit by perceptions which were only reached after many crises and misunderstandings. In the period of *L'Avenir* (in which title our present day was briefly anticipated) these distinctions were not sufficiently drawn. Doctrines incompletely worked out or sifted were promoted from hypothesis to thesis, mingling tolerance of practice with a certain indifferentism of principle, which the Church could not allow. That was one of the motives for Lamennais's condemnation.[9]

It is in the context of the opposition between, on the one hand, these two still imperfectly distinguished liberalisms and, on the other, a Catholic tradition which likewise was incompletely detached from certain historical modalities, that the famous *Syllabus* of Pius IX (1846) must be understood. This document, which sums up many previous fragmentary pronouncements, must be understood *historically*, that is, in its context, apart from which many of its expressions lose their real meaning. It condemns indifferentism or latitudinarianism, as well as a 'liberalism' in which freedom would include, in its very definition, the right to profess error as freely as the truth,[10] and the acceptance, in the same indifferent tolerance, of any form of worship and any opinion.[11]

In reality, the grand debate of that age on freedom must be seen in the larger context of the gigantic conflict which, ever since the Renaissance, has raged between the Catholic dogma of a positive revelation and an immanentist philosophy of the perfect autonomy and sufficiency of man.[12] Beneath the Rousseauist and revolutionary notion of freedom, stated as an absolute value, without reference to any objective standard, there was affirmed a rationalist notion of man, conceived as an absolute autonomy.[13] There was rejection of an authority which dominated, chained and limited his freedom. The famous formula, 'Neither God nor master', sometimes seems to be a hyperbole of parliamentary rhetoric, but it is the rigorous formula of a whole *mystique*, of which the *mystique* of absolute freedom is but one application.[14]

Without pretending to a logical series or a complete enumeration, here are some other of its applications, connected with the above, in history as in doctrine:

1. The total independence of reason with relation to faith, reason being answerable to no 'authority', even God's, with the parallel affirmation, *as a matter of principle and ideal*, that civil society is totally independent of the Church.

2. 'Laicism', or secularism which it is now common practice to distinguish from 'laicity' (meaning the effective neutrality of public education), and which involves an aggressive attitude towards religion, precisely because this, claiming to be revealed, implies the affirmation of the authority of God. When the advocates of the laws against the religious congregations justified the proscription of the teaching orders by a basic argument, it was to the philosophy of freedom that they appealed, and to the principle according to which men who had restricted or forfeited their freedom by vows, were disqualified as educators of the French people.

3. The all too common manner of stating the problem of freedom *versus* authority, representing these values as contradictory, treating them as realities only existing in inverse proportion, so that freedom only asserts itself in proportion as authority yields it place, and authority only exists by reducing or crushing freedom; a manner of stating the problem which is inevitable, in fact, if freedom has been made an absolute value, posited without reference to any other. Whereas authority and freedom cease to be incompatible if both are referred to God.

4. Finally, in large areas of contemporary literature, the reign

of 'sincerity'. Not so much sincerity regarding the true, which is reverence for objects and represents a very noble form of submission; but sincerity to oneself, regarded as another absolute value, a sort of innocence and holiness. It matters little what is said, or what the consequences are, provided that it comes out from us, that it has the accent of a lived experience, of a sincerity; provided that it has 'tone'. Predominance of that experience and that sincerity over the quest of the absolute or the objective truth: the desire to taste *everything*, experience *everything*. The only sin is not to be sincere (is that not the expression of Guehenne?). Everybody knows André Gide's position: 'I have lived too cautiously till now! One must be without law to hear the new law. Oh deliverance! Oh freedom! Wherever my desire can reach, there will I go!'[15] And Michel Vieuchange, on the threshold of a life full of promises, which were to be broken too soon by an adventure in which he met God, had written these significant words: 'Not to seek the absolute, but simply life'.[16]

The Catholic notion of freedom

Freedom is a very great thing. The Catholic Church has defended and asserted it throughout the ages. She did so, for example, at a time when parents married off their children against their wills; she maintained, even against the civil laws, the validity of the marriage of minors without their parents' consent. Again, against immoderate Augustinians, against the Protestant reformers, and their Catholic imitators, Baianist or Jansenist, finally against the fideists, she affirmed the existence of free-will, even in fallen man.[17] And more recently she stood firm against every totalitarian claim by the dictatorships to subordinate the individual wholly to the state.[18]

Yet freedom is not the supreme value: it is not an absolute value, independent of everything else. It is a derived value, because it is a value *founded* on something else. *Above freedom, there is the good.*

The traditional philosophy[19] connects freedom with a certain quality of human knowledge, and therefore of human nature.[20] The animal is bound by the sensation of the immediate, which presents itself and releases its instinct. Seeing a piece of meat, the dog feels an imperious 'That's good!' and cannot help pouncing on it, unless some equally imperious and more immediate sensation (like sickness or the blow of a stick) keeps the former instinct in check. Man, on the other hand, is not drawn only by the immediate good offered by sensation: he knows other goods: he attains by his intelligence to the idea of the good in general, the idea of the absolute Good, to the distinction between what is the end and what are the means. He has the idea of end and means. He can realise the relative order of goods, including the absolute and the totality of good. Faced with that absolute, he would be entirely subjugated. But so long as he is faced, or believes himself faced, with relative goods which, though ends in relation to lesser goods, are still means in relation to a greater good, he can always hold himself back. Because he has the idea of good in general, and the ideas of end and means, he himself judges his choice and is not under compulsion to an immediate good. Because he conceives the absolute good as his end, he can always, beyond a particular good, desire a greater. Because he is spiritual, he can reflect on himself, judge and criticise his action. He is not compelled by attraction: he is free.

That is why men are seen not only to refuse a piece of meat, though they may be hungry, in order to obey a higher call,[21] but willingly to sacrifice their lives out of loyalty, for example, or in the service of their country. Sacrifice is the infallible mark of freedom: it is also its best school.

For it is plain to see that freedom thus conceived is a point of arrival and something conquered, at least as much as a point of departure and something given. Whether, with Jacques Maritain, we speak of 'freedom of choice' and freedom 'of autonomy', or with Abbé Mouroux of 'free will' or the power of choosing, and the 'freedom' of self-realisation and fulfilment of the person, we always presume a progress from an elementary freedom to one that is truly full. One truly possesses only what one has conquered. Starting with free choice, we must strive by education and discipline to achieve a royal self-mastery. Catholic freedom is not enfranchisement from every bond, it is not absolute independence, it is a freedom of self-mastery, founded on the consecration of ourselves to the absolute of the Good. It is because we are bound to the absolute Good that we are free as regards relative and partial goods. Freedom is contrasted with the animal's slavery to the attraction, only because it is founded on an attachment, attachment to the good. It exists as freedom *with regard to* something, only because it is, at bottom, freedom *for* something, freedom for a service.[22]

From these principles flows a very important principle: *freedom does not consist in absolute independence*: it is not defined by the possibility of choosing good or evil. That possibility is part of the condition of *human* freedom, which is elementary and precarious, but it is not required by the very notion of freedom. To be free does not *consist* in being independent with regard to the good. In its higher degree, even with us men, freedom is bound up with an extremely strong attachment to the good. It consists rather in being so consecrated to the good and the true that we dominate error and evil, and even relative truths and goods, which in themselves are limited.

That is why God is free, at least in his will which bears on creatures and the order of his providence, although he cannot sin. That is why Jesus Christ is free in his human will, although he too is impeccable. He could not disobey his Father, yet it was freely that he obeyed him, because it was in his act of obedience that he merited salvation for us. He himself speaks of this obedience in terms which clearly show how free he was in it. '. . . I lay down my life that I may take it again. No one takes it from me, but I lay it down of my own accord. I have power to lay it down, and I have power to take it again; this charge I have received from my Father. . . . I do as the Father has commanded me, so that the world may know that I love the Father. Rise, let us go hence.'[23]

Our Lord himself teaches us that freedom does not consist in being able to do evil as well as good, but that, on the contrary, evil is a slavery, and the service of the good is liberation: 'If you continue in my word, you are truly my disciples, and you will know the truth, and the truth will make you free. . . . Every one who commits sin is a slave to sin. The slave does not continue in the house for ever, the son continues for ever. So if the Son makes you free, you will be free indeed.'[24] It would be easy to develop this doctrine from other passages of the gospel or from the writings of St Paul. Study of the parable of the Prodigal Son[25] will specially help us to understand the slavery of sin.

Perhaps it is in the line of what has just been expounded that we should understand the passages in Genesis[26] on the tree of the knowledge of good and evil, passages which usually raise a question without an answer. Man created in the image of God was set by God in a state of freedom. But freedom according to God does not mean being able to choose good or evil; it means being able to attach oneself to the good represented by God, or made known to us by him. The act of tasting the tree of knowledge of good and evil represents the possibility for man of also knowing evil of determining for himself, apart from God and his word, what would be good for him.[27]

Perhaps it would be useful to conclude by sketching at least one application of this Catholic point of view to the delicate question of education. Freedom does not consist in 'an unlimited right (of man) to all that attracts him and can be attained by him'. Therefore its standard is not the choice or experience of evil as well as good. Man is sociable by nature. That means that it is in his nature to learn and be educated. It is good, and even no doubt necessary, that the child should experience by himself the consequences of certain ways of acting, but it would be against his well-being and against the very intention of his freedom, to refuse to guard him, by education or teaching, from the experience of evil, or the doubts and questionings which he is unable to bear.

More often than some people realise, one comes across parents who say of their children: 'He is free; he will do what he wants; he will choose his religion freely when he grows up.'[28] This idea is no doubt inspired by a very noble and vivid idea of the freedom of the human person, but it ignores the real and complete nature of things. Furthermore it involves a manner of acting which, without offending the rights of truth or sacrificing the good of the child, entirely respects a freedom which God himself honours so much that for its sake he permits sin and all its consequences. Certainly we can never meditate too often on the warning of Lacordaire, who devoted all his latter years to the education of the young: 'We must never have cause to remember that even *once* in our life we performed our religious duties under the force of compulsion or in obedience to mere conventions.'[29]

Certain people have taught that out of respect for the child we should allow absolute freedom to the play of spontaneity and never let his life be influenced by authority or law or any adult points of view. Such, for example, is the theory of A. S. Neill, who has founded a school on these principles: Summerhill, in Suffolk.[30] Not everything in Neill's observations and reactions is false. But a discussion of his views would raise the whole debate on the limits and precise nature of natural goodness. In these simple notes I have merely meant to raise the problem by connecting it with the principles expounded above.

In the same line of thought, it would remain to consider, finally, the concrete relationship of authority to freedom, the principles and methods of an education for freedom by pedagogic discipline, in the school, in the home, and among the youth movements.[31]

IV. THE TEMPORAL ORDER AND RELIGIOUS TRUTH[32]

It is a great honour to be asked to inaugurate the debate which Abbé Berrar has just declared open. We are concerned with a debate, and therefore with a question proposed: with a discussion, and therefore with an open question. There is to be dialogue between men qualified for a profitable discussion, whose intellectual eminence guarantees that they will deal with the questions objectively and fairly. Personally I agree with the vast majority that tolerance is a debatable question. It must be admitted that the word 'tolerance' is vague (Gabriel Marcel has criticised it minutely); it does not correspond to any really satisfactory theological category. It has rather a descriptive value, and suggests something psychological rather than theological. I should prefer to say that we are going to study tonight the question of religious freedom, as defined in the Charter of the United Nations in the following terms, proposed and accepted in December 1947:

> Individual freedom of thought and conscience, freedom to profess a faith or to change it, are sacred and absolute rights. Further, every individual, alone or in association with others who agree with him, has the right to profess his belief by the exercise of private or public worship, the observance of rites, the teaching and practice of his religion. Every individual therefore has the right to freedom of religion, conscience and

belief. He has the right to change his belief and to practice any form of worship or religious rite. No act contrary to this belief may be imposed on him. Every individual of full age and sound mind, alone or in association with others who agree with him, has the right to receive or to give all religious instruction. These rights and liberties shall not be subject to any restriction other than those prescribed by the law and necessary to protect public order, and the well-being, morality, rights and liberties of others.[33]

Religious freedom is thus defined in all its fullness. In our present debate we shall be specially concerned with religious freedom in a social order in which the public authority is at the service of a doctrine. I choose a purposely very wide formula, so as to include, for example, the case of the modern totalitarian states, but also the Christian state, and more particularly the Catholic state, or let us call it, if you like, the state whose government is in the hands of Catholics, who intend to act as Catholics in their governmental capacity. This debate has accordingly been announced under the title: 'Temporal order and religious truth.'

Thus we clearly define the field within which we raise our question. It is not the field of the Church herself, for she as such cannot but reject the errors which in her language she calls heresies. We all reject unambiguously that tolerance or doctrinal liberism which is really indifferentism. The very existence of the Church is here at stake. But we add that while the Church cannot but reject errors and cast them out from her bosom, she does so in her own order: in so acting, the Church must respect the freedom of the act of faith, and use only her own means, which are spiritual. All theologians agree in saying that the Church cannot by herself use the death penalty. That to me seems obvious. The Church must therefore exclude error from her own body, but by her own means which are spiritual: excommunication and spiritual sanctions, but also prayer, penance, everything by which the Church can further the conversion of men to the truth. The question is therefore raised, not at all in the order of the Church herself, but in the temporal order, the order of the relations of the temporal power with religious truth on the one hand and with men on the other.

Here it is necessary to recall the Catholic principles in all their force. It is very dangerous, and a wrong method of action, to propose a theory of fact before proposing a theory of right, or to propose a theory of life before that of the structure. Life exists and must be respected, but in the framework of the structure. The fact exists, but must be written into the framework of the right. Such are the general and practically classical principles received in Catholic theology (I say theology because they are not dogmas).

First principle:

There is a religious truth, there is a revelation proceeding from God, a religious truth or positive revelation of which the Church has charge, with the charismata or graces appropriate to that charge of teaching; graces of truth.

Second principle:

The chief end of men, and of the world too, is in fact supernatural, positively supernatural. God has created the world for himself, for communion in his own innermost life. Further, temporal society has no other end but that of individuals, and their last end is supernatural.

Conclusion:

The temporal authority must so arrange the social order as to favour that supernatural end, with which the Church is essentially concerned. Now the temporal authority cannot succeed in this unless it obeys the Church. The ideal is therefore a temporal society directed by the Church. I remark that in my opinion this does not prejudge the manner in which we conceive the relations of the Church with temporal society. This in no way implies the idea of what has been called a jurisdiction of the Church over the city, a thesis which I for one do not support. I believe that the requirements of Catholic doctrine are satisfied if the relations of the Church with temporal society are conceived, not as relations of jurisdiction, but as those of a *magisterium*. This position has been called in theology a 'directive power'.

We thus reach the 'thesis' which may be called classical in theology, of a temporal society directed by the Church, one to which the Church prescribes the ends and all the chief means, one in whose legislation the Church has a say, a temporal society which would thus be harnessed to the regulations of the Church, to the directives and rules imposed by the Church herself, and would be a kind of temporal extension of the Church.

This is the thesis which existed in our western countries under the régime of Christendom, the Christian republic, when the Church and temporal society lived in symbiosis. That thesis was worked out when there was practical unanimity from a religious point of view, an unanimity infinitely superior, in any case, to the majority which in our democratic countries enables a fraction of the citizens to impose their will on the rest.

But in modern times we can say that in practically all countries we have entered a state of things in which religious unanimity no longer exists. Men are divided in their convictions. Especially since the Reformation there have been, in the same country, citizens sharing the same culture, the same earthly common goods, the same national loyalty, but having different religious convictions.

This fact has led in practice to the secularisation of the State, and its first great agent among us was Cardinal Richelieu. While striving to refashion the religious unity of France, he accepted the consequences of the fact that it no longer existed. He was the first to ally with the German Protestant princes against the Spanish Catholic power, and followed a policy which was national, not denominational. It is from him that we can date political secularism, as Lecler does in his articles in *Etudes*. This was next developed in a wide movement of ideas, especially after the French revolution, which completed the process of the secularisation of the state.

It thus became necessary to find a formula for this new state of affairs, which was becoming almost universal. On the one hand, this was done by distinguishing between the thesis and the hypothesis (the thesis is the ideal I have outlined above, the hypothesis is the line of conduct demanded by the actual situation). On the other hand, the distinction, already expressed from the beginning in the Church, was made between dogmatic intolerance, which is the act of the Church herself, and civil tolerance, which is the act of the rulers, in States where the citizens are of diverse religions, Catholics and non-Catholics, or Christians and non-Christians.

In our days there are very few countries where there is sufficient religious unanimity to allow of a situation of thesis for a State, that is, of a sort of identification of the State with a clearly determined religious doctrine, and the use of public force for the purposes of that doctrine. From the Christian aspect there only remain Spain and certain countries of Latin America. The Spaniard's great argument is that catholicity, the profession of Catholic faith, forms part of 'Hispanity', the national character itself. I do not know enough about Spain, its history and culture, to give a judgement. But a friend of mine assures me that the statement rests partly on a fiction, and that the thesis could not be supported without ignoring half of the history of Spain in the nineteenth century. I quote this opinion only in order to invite experts on Spanish questions to offer their evidence.

There are obviously other cases besides Christian cases, of symbiosis between a state and a religion. Though I scarcely dare presume to do so in the presence of Professor Massignon, one could mention the situation in certain Moslem lands: the Sudan, Turkey or Persia, where the condition of Islam, ideologically and sociologically, is wholly comparable.

But in the overall situation of the modern world we have a state of affairs in which religious unanimity does not exist, one in which the state is therefore obliged to be structurally neutral from the denominational point of view. A denominationally neutral state will no longer place itself, as things are, in the situation of thesis, under the direction of the Church, letting itself be modelled by her doctrinal and canonical rules. In nearly all cases the state finds itself obliged to define a plane of neutrality. I shall return to this point later.

This duality of the situation explains a fact which often seems extremely scandalous, and particularly shocks Protestants. That is the fact that while in a country like Spain the Catholic Church is intransigent to the point of reducing the freedom of Protestants to what I think is an inadequate level, that same Church, in other countries, pleads freedom of conscience in order to gain the freedom she does not always enjoy in such democratic countries as Switzerland or Sweden. At this moment it is being debated in

Sweden whether the religious orders, and particularly the Jesuits, should be granted authorisation. In those countries the Church pleads freedom of conscience. In Spain she pleads the positive right of revelation, of which she has the charge. This causes scandal. Where you are in a minority, people say, you plead freedom of conscience: where you are in a majority you use power. There could be an odious aspect to this, but I think we must try to understand the question. It is natural, from the point of view of the principle I have explained, that the Church should have different methods of action according to whether she finds herself in a country which is unanimously Catholic (or supposed to be so), or in one where the Catholics are only one in a thousand. In the former case, practical unanimity allows the demands of the Church to be followed even on the level of public life: in the second case the question does not even arise.

It is a fact that many of the best minds among Catholics now feel a profound dissatisfaction with what may be called the classical position. This dissatisfaction has been caused and fostered by a certain number of facts on which I cannot enlarge, but I want to consider here the motives behind it. There are three which I think are the chief:

The indirect power (meaning, as you know, a certain manner of conceiving the relations of the Church and the temporal power) is really only a limited direct power. Similarly, the theory of the hypothesis is scarcely anything but a thesis, a limited intolerance. At bottom, that theory, which is the 'classical' position, leaves in us a germ of intolerance. Here is a great difficulty. Do we Catholics feel able to dispel the enormous suspicion which hangs over us, that we would be ready, if we could, to restore the Inquisition and to persecute? This suspicion exists in every Protestant conscience. It is not often expressed in France, but it is expressed in countries with a Protestant majority; the Scandinavian countries, the United States. In these consciences it constitutes an unsurmountable barrier. My ecumenical experience convinces me that the great obstacle, the supreme obstacle, is distrust. That distrust is fed by the suspicion that if we were to become the masters again, we could be persecutors.

In this connection I should like to quote a paper by Professor Franz Leenhardt of Geneva, who says: 'If the Catholics became the masters and applied their theories, we Protestants would have nothing left but to disappear.' Paul Blanshard's book, recently published in America, repeats the same theme even more violently. It could be summed up thus: 'If the Catholics rewrote the American Constitution, what should we find?' I could answer that question easily enough: the American Constitution derives in reality, through the English Nonconformists, themselves inspired by Hooker, from the Catholic theologians of the Middle Ages. But we are still faced with this enormous difficulty, this suspicion of intolerance which hangs over us, and cannot be dissolved by the classical position of the thesis and the hypothesis.

A second very important motive is that 'tolerance' is indivisible. This is a term used by the League of Nations before 1939 about peace. How can we plead freedom of conscience in the Ukraine, where three million Catholics are forced to join the Orthodox Church, or in the Scandinavian countries, where Catholic freedom is still subject to some restrictions, when we ourselves, concretely and historically, do not practise it in Spain or, to a lesser extent, in Italy and the Catholic countries of South America?

It is a very great difficulty. I am going to present it by recourse to a literary document which may surprise some of you. You know that in France, in our claims for the Christian schools, we plead the right of the parents to choose the teaching they desire for their children, a right which we say is part of the natural law. That principle figures in many pronouncements of our bishops. But lately J. V. Simcox, an unrepresentative English Catholic, has published a pamphlet with the title: 'Is the Roman Catholic Church a secret society?' It is, he says, and the English Catholic bishops who plead the natural law have no right to claim it, because, according to the teaching of Catholic theologians, that law is suspended or overruled by the higher positive law of the faith, and the benefit of it is not guaranteed to heretical or schismatical parents. This example is perhaps accessible only to priests and to such laymen as are familiar with theological or canonical ideas, but I quote it because it presents our problem very forcibly. Abbé Berrar alluded just now to the chronicle of Robert Rouquette, who noted recently that the World Council of Churches, in a protest against the persecution in Hungary, abstained from interceding for the Catholic Church. Rouquette thought that the motive for this abstention was this: the Catholic Church cannot be given the benefit of the principle of freedom of conscience, which she herself denies in Spain. Let her fend for herself with her principles! It is very hard. It is perhaps not even a very generous sort of Christianity, but it presents the question under consideration in an inescapable form. For my part, in 1946 I had written an article in *Témoignage Chrétien*, protesting against the violence with which Catholics in the Ukraine were compelled to join the Orthodox Church. I could write it, and had the right to write it, because in 1938 I had protested in *La Vie Intellectuelle* against the fact that the Polish authorities and the army itself had taken part in the destruction of two hundred Orthodox churches in the Ukraine. I could only protest in the one case because I had protested in the other.

A third motive. There is grave dissatisfaction among Catholic consciences, at least in France, about the generally accepted position. It seems that this does not allow for what might well be called the positive values of 'laicity'. This can only be understood in the French situation. I defy any but an exceptional Spaniard to understand it! Just as no doubt I could not understand his point of view. . . . The question has been specially explained in an article by Vialatoux and Latreille,[34] to which I shall allude in a moment. Moreover, in our Catholic university circles, a great effort is now being made for a positive understanding of laicity. Living as Catholics, in the Church, and as university men or women in a public organism whose constitution is that of laicity, they owe it to themselves to harmonise their two loyalties and so to understand and practise their duty of laicity in a Christian manner. This leads them to give value to other principles than those so far expounded. Dogmatic intolerance and civil tolerance; thesis and hypothesis: they do not want to deny these principles but to give value to others which will perhaps transcend them, because they will have brought to light other aspects of the truth; and that is not the work of a day. We have to overcome a great illusion, the illusion of thinking that the social doctrine of the Church (the doctrine of the Church in matters which concern the historical situation) is a doctrine all ready-made, as monolithic, if you like, as dogma itself. What is called the Church's social doctrine consists of principles which develop in a situation, and as the situation changes, because the world is developing and evolving, so the Church's social doctrine develops in the course of time and in space. It develops under aspects it had not formerly known.

That is very important, but often forgotten, so much so that the question now before some of our best minds is how to give value to a certain number of positive aspects of the truth besides those considered in the position called classical.[35]

In particular I see three new elements which some of us are trying to evaluate. They do not deny the former elements, but they may perhaps transcend them. I wish to put them forward and hope they may provide material for our debate.

1. Tolerance seen as a form of respect for the freedom of the act of faith;

2. Tolerance seen as a form of respect for the transcendance of the Church;

3. Tolerance seen as a form of respect for the truth.

From the titles alone you can see that these are no trifles.

Tolerance as a form of respect for the freedom of the act of faith

This is the point emphasised by Rouquette, Vialatoux and Latreille. The Church's teaching on this point is formal. The act of faith, which is a man's supreme act, the act by which he chooses his destiny, is an eminently free act. Freedom is something we claim eagerly enough in connection with the free schools. But freedom is not something abstract, it has concrete implications. There is freedom, and there are the conditions of freedom, just as there is history and there are the means of history. This is something that we Catholics easily forget because, being chiefly anxious about moral rectification in the order of intention, we always tend to forget the order of concrete means. Well, in the modern states there is the freedom of the act, and the concrete means of the freedom of the act of faith. Now, in a Catholic state such as Spain, for example, which intends to be Catholic even as a state, a religious examination is required for every post approved by the State. To be a pharmacist you have to pass an examination in religion. Practically and concretely, does this not pose a question for the freedom of the act of faith? It is a well-known fact that when the government is ideological in a certain direction, all those who are followers by temperament, or are obliged to follow by necessity, will go in the same direction.

Here comes in a very important element, which I have explained in my article in *La Revue Nouvelle*, and which I think is a principle of explanation for many problems. The old world of Christendom which, as Péguy remarks, lasted till the Revolution, was an objective world. They had only one idea: the rights of tradition and authority, to follow the accepted ideas. They had no thought for anything but the object. Aquinas said: 'It matters little by whom something was said, or how: what matters is to know whether it is true or false.' Now the moderns tend rather to say the opposite: 'What matters is to know by whom a thing was said and how it was arrived at. It matters little whether it is true or false.' The modern world is characterised by what I should call the discovery of the subject.[36] The snag lies in putting sincerity above truth. The great reaction of the *Syllabus*, of the pontificates of Pius VIII, Gregory XVI and Pius IX, aimed precisely at vindicating the primacy of the good over freedom and of the truth over sincerity. There is, however, a real value in the point of view of the subject: the concrete conditions of his access to the truth must also be considered. In this respect the subject, a spiritual, free person, has rights which in practice imply a certain freedom of error. To adhere to the truth with the spiritual quality required by the act of faith, a man must have certain conditions of freedom, which in the concrete involve the subject's right to be mistaken.

Tolerance as a form of respect for the transcendence of the Church

This has been illuminated by Jacques Leclercq. In a Christian state, the state serves as a support to the Church, which guides it and subjects it to herself. Ideally this is fine, but it is only an ideal. In practice, in that symbiosis which medieval theologians compared to a single body with two sides, actions are reciprocal. There is action, but also reaction. If the State is in a way harnessed to the rules of the Church, the Church risks being harnessed to the state's methods of action. The State serves as support to the Church, but it sometimes demands compensations, or takes them without asking, if they are not given. We know that one of the Church's dearest principles is that of independence and transcendence. This moves her to avoid that excessive symbiosis with a state, always apt to drag her into political adventures from which she has nothing to gain. Thus we arrive at that denunciation of the mixture between the Church and what Maritain calls the Christian world. We have suffered in France from that excessive symbiosis between the Church and the Christian world, and now we seek a Church set free from those bonds, but not disembodied. The Church is rather like Aristotle's God: *Segregatus ut imperet*. When she climbs high, she emphasises her transcendence and her prestige increases. When the Church loses her temporal weight, she gains in spiritual weight. Just as there are concrete implications of the act of faith, so there are concrete implications of the Church's independence.

Tolerance as a form of respect and service for the truth

Here I refer you, with no need to add anything of my own, to an article by H. Sternberger in the review *Die Wandlung*, 1943: 'Toleranz als Leidenschaft für die Wahrheit.' Tolerance is something indispensable for anyone who has the passion for truth. It is in fact a question of a complete conquest of the truth. I am afraid my allotted time has nearly expired, and I cannot develop, as I should have liked, the personal aspect, the individual applications of that idea. But at least let me briefly sum up the application which I have myself made on the level of collective research and the general movement of minds. The modern world seems to me to be marked by a sort of explosion of truth. Now, the splinters of that truth have remained active where they have fallen. The Christian idea of human brotherhood, for example, or of human justice, has issued from Christianity, it has animated a whole world where it has been fertile, it has not remained moribund (for example, it inspired movements like socialism), to such an extent —and this is the crucial point of my argument—that the fragments of all these splinters of truth must be picked up wherever they are to be found, along with whatever of value they have been able to bring forth. Obviously, these fragments of truth have often been spoiled. We shall only be able to collect them in order to purify them before integrating them: but we must first collect them where they are and where they have brought forth fruit, which is not to be despised. So we shall not really be able to attain to an integral truth without respect for these fragments of itself. The problem of Catholicism is the same as that of ecumenism. Tolerance is only one form of the passion for truth. We must respect those delays in maturation which God imposes on us, respect the plan of God, who 'writes straight with crooked lines', in the words of the Portuguese proverb which Claudel put on the title-page of *The Satin Slipper*. We must not anticipate the last judgement. There is such a thing as respect for the bad seed which, after a fashion, works for the Kingdom of God and the Church. I readily admit that my point of view will not be accepted by everyone. I believe that in the Church there are different functions, and that we have not all in the same degree the vocation to work for integration. But it seems to me that this is the peculiar mission of our age: to reunite in the Catholic body all the fragments which belong to it as of right and which, separated from it, are scattered throughout the world. Such is my conviction. So you can guess how pleased I was, when I was teaching apologetics to my students last year, to hear one of them say to me: 'After all, Father, the real apologetic is ecumenism.'

I know these considerations are bound to leave room for difficulties which will be formulated in objections. For my part I believe that it is the same with the theories about the relations of Church and state. It is certain that the different theories and viewpoints concerning the relation of the temporal power with religious truth are inadequate. That is why I think that a debate like this ought to be inaugurated, in order to give opportunity of expression to what we may call the complementariness of minds and positions.

NOTES

1. *Vie Int.*, Feb. 1948, pp. 368.
2. *Messager du Sacré-Coeur*, July–Aug. 1949, pp. 249–53.
3. Paper read to the 'Days' of the University Parish of Paris, on 28th Oct. 1945. Published in *Des journées dispersées de 1945 aux Journées de Paris, 1946.* Supplement to *Cahiers de la Paroisse Universitaire*, pp. 43–54.
4. *Social Contract*, Bk I, ch. 8. When the individual has entered society, the sort of absolute freedom he had before, marked by 'an unlimited right to all that tempts him and can be attained by him', is transferred to society itself: ch. 7.
5. I realise that Rousseau is not only the theorist of a new society, but also a man who has fundamentally traditional sentiments and speaks a different language. The same ch. 8 which we have quoted ends thus: 'On what precedes we could add that man acquires not only the civil state, but also moral freedom, which alone makes man truly master of himself; for the impulse of appetite alone is slavery, and obedience to the law one has prescribed to oneself is freedom.'
6. *L'Avenir*, 27th Jan. 1831; quoted in Trannoy, *Le romantisme politique de Montalembert avant 1843*, p. 148.
7. *L'Avenir*, 21st March 1831, quoted in Trannoy, *ibid.*
8. Encycl. *Mirari vos*, against Lamennais (Denz. Bann., n. 1613f); Letter of Pius IX against Frohschammer (Denz. Bann. 1666f, 1674); Letter of Pius IX to the archbishop of Munich (Denz. Bann. 1679); Encycl. *Quanta cura* (Denz. Bann. 1779); Encycl. *Libertas* of Leo XIII (Denz. Bann. 1932). But the same doctrine is formulated by Gregory XVI in 1832 and by Leo XIII in 1888, in quite another tone and in a different climate of thought: compare the texts in Denz. Bann., n. 1613–14 and n. 1932.
9. Encycl. *Mirari vos* (Denz. Bann., n. 1614).
10. Denz. Bann., n. 1715–18.
11. Denz. Bann., n. 1777–80.
12. See, for example, my *Conclusion* to the enquiry of *Vie Int.* into the causes of modern unbelief, *Vie Int.*, 25th July 1935.
13. This is the meaning Newman gives to the word 'Liberalism' in Note A of the Appendix to the *Apologia*, and that is why he refuses to call himself a Liberal, although he professes himself in profound sympathy with Montalembert and Lacordaire.
14. This could easily be illustrated from the works quoted, for example, by Capéran for political ideologies in *L'invasion laïque* and for scientist ideology, *L'Avenir de la Science* (Coll. *Présences*), pp. 128f.
15. André Gide, *Nouvelles nourritures*, p. 22. Rousseau had spoken of 'an unlimited right (of man) to all that attracts him and which he can attain'.
16. *Smara*, Plon. 1932, p. viii.
17. Countless texts; here are a few: *Indiculus* on grace (Denz. Bann., n. 120f); Council of Orange (Denz. Bann., 174, 181, 186); Council of Quierzy against Gottschalk (Denz. Bann., 316f); Council of Valence against Scotus Erigena (Denz. Bann., 325); Leo IX (Denz. Bann., 348); Bull *Exsurge* against Luther (Denz. Bann., 793 and 797); Pius V against Baius (Denz. Bann., 1027, 1039,

1041, 1065f); Condemnation of Jansenius (Denz. Bann., 1093f); of Quesnel (Denz. Bann., 1388) of Bonnetty and his fideism (Denz. Bann., 1650); etc.

18. Encycl. *Mit Brennender Sorge* against Nazism; Pius XII's Christmas message, 1942; etc.

19. Somewhat technical expositions of the Thomist idea of freedom will be found in Sertillanges, *Thomist Philosophy*, Springfield, Mo., 1956; Garrigou-Lagrange, in *RSPT*, 1907 and 1908; Maritain, 'L'idée thomiste de la liberté' in *Revue Thomiste*, 1939, p. 440. It will also be useful to refer to J. Maritain, *Du régime temporel et de la liberté* (Paris) and J. Mouroux, *Sens chrétien de l'homme* (Paris), ch. vii and viii. This book outlines, on the philosophical plane, the notes of a very fine Christian humanism.

20. *Tota ratio libertatis ex modo cognitionis dependet*: Aquinas, *Verit.*, 24, 2.

21. See, in the persecution of Antiochus Epiphanes against the faithful Jews, the death of the old man Eleazar and of the Seven Brothers and their mother: 2 Macc 6:18f and 7.

22. May I here quote a German and an English author? *Frei werden nicht* von, *sondern* für *etwas*; 'Freedom so far as it is a treasure must be freedom *for* something as well as freedom *from* something' (William Temple, *Christianity and Social Order*, p. 45, London, 1942).

23. Jn 10:17–18; 14:31. Speaking of her abandonment to the will of God in the matter of her entry into religion, Marie de l'Incarnation said: 'And thus my spirit was free and abandoned, so that it could neither wish nor choose anything': Relation of 1654, XXIX, (*Écrits spirituels et histor.*, vol. II, Paris and Quebec, 1930, p. 271). See also R. Garrigou-Lagrange, 'La liberté impeccable du Christ et celle des enfants de Dieu', in *Vie Sp.*, April 1924, pp. 5–20. See also 'L'Église et la liberté' (*Semaine des Intellectuels catholiques*, 1952), pp. 248, 255 and 256.

24. Jn 8:31–6.

25. Lk 15.

26. 2:9–17; 3:5.

27. See W. Vischer, *Das Christuszeugnis des Alten Testaments*, vol. I, pp. 69, 75.

28. On this subject I should like to quote this little story by La Fouchardière, told by L. Brunschvig (*Les ages de l'intelligence*, pp. 131–2): 'A long time ago, I knew an old townsman in the country who was very avaricious and not without a knowledge of psychology, if he must be judged on this account. On one New Year's Day or a birthday, he found himself obliged to give a present to a young nephew, three years old. Before the eyes of his family, who were aghast at such generosity, he smilingly produced from his wallet a fifty-franc note and offered it to the child. But at the same time, with the other hand, he drew from his pocket a superb orange, a fruit then rather rare in that region. "Choose!", said he to the nephew. The child did not hesitate . . . and the old miser, with a sigh of satisfaction, put the note back in his wallet.'

29. Quoted in J. Lacointe, *Le Père Lacordaire à Sorèze*, Paris, 1881, pp. 202–3.

30. A. S. Neill, *That Dreadful School*, London, 1937.

31. There are some excellent things in W. Foerster, *Pour former le caractère* (Paris): in *Autorité et liberté*, by the same. See also O. Leroy, 'Autorité et liberté en éducation', in *Vie Int.*, 25th March 1937; etc.

32. From a shorthand report of a speech in the debate on tolerance, arranged by the *Centre catholique des Intellectuels Français*, 20th March 1950. Published in the Supplement 'Sciences religieuses' of *Recherches et Débats*, no. 10, July 1950; reproduced in *Doc. cath.*, no. 1123 (15th June 1952), col. 729–38.

33. Compare this text with articles 18 and 19 of the *Universal Declaration of the Rights of Man*, in *Doc. cath.*, no. 1039, 27th March 1949, col. 408.

34. *Esprit*, Oct. 1949.
35. I have myself written recently on this question, particularly in *La Revue Nouvelle* of 15th May 1948. There was a short but very interesting article by Leclercq in *La Vie Intellectuelle* for Feb. 1949; then the chronicle of Rouquette in *Etudes* for Sept. 1949, and finally the well-known article by Vialatoux and Latreille in *Esprit*, in Oct. 1949. That is our main documentation. There are some other texts too, notably in Germany, an article by Pribilla. A French translation of this appeared, subsequently to this debate, in the collection *Unité chrétienne et tolerance religieuse*, Editions du Temps Present.
36. See Congar, 'Mentalité de droite et intégrisme', in *Vie Int.*, June 1950.

CHAPTER TEN

Racial Questions and Theology[1]

NOWADAYS FEW CHRISTIANS AWARE OF THE demands of their faith are content to live out the religious relationship it creates, alone with God, as it were outside time. Fundamentally, of course, this relationship is above time; it belongs to eternal life, which is social in essence (*socialis vita sanctorum*, says Augustine), but not necessarily historical. The purely contemplative life is an undeniably legitimate form of it. It does not isolate from men, but it releases from time. But what is dominant among Christians of today is the desire, we might say the need, to assume the burden of their time in a Christian manner, to accept its appeals and challenges to give them an answer drawn from faith. Appeals and challenges are not far to seek. They follow one another like the waves of the sea, scarcely giving us time to draw breath.

Among these problems of time there is the problem of race. This is only one particular section of the enormous problem of the relations between human groups. Peace is the tranquillity of order. Order presupposes justice, which is violated by any attempt at domination, any trampling upon the field of security and the life of another group. Now, we inherit historical situations in which some human groups, having as their principle of cohesion not only common interests, but a shared culture, historical destiny and racial origin, dominate other human groups whose principle of cohesion is likewise a shared culture, historical destiny, racial origin, religion: in short, in so far as this is a reality, a shared race. The storm-centres, the zones of conflict are well known. The Negro problem in the United States, the situation in South

Africa, the crisis of decolonisation, as we see it in the former Belgian Congo and finally, with religious aspects of the highest importance, the problem of antisemitism. A. Schwartz-Bart's *Le dernier des Justes* posed this question lately in such a way that (in spite of serious exaggerations) no Christian can evade questioning himself on his attitudes and responsibility, and that, too, at the very time when deplorable incidents were recalling in disturbing fashion the bad days of the Nazis.

We have to assume the burden of this problem of interracial relations whenever we are required to do so. Now we are required to do so not only if we live in South Africa or if we have Jewish relations. There is now a worldwide solidarity of opinion: at least the evidence of it is now forced on us all. It is by my reactions to distant events that I build up in myself the true man I ought to become, and the opinion of French Catholics is not without influence on the attitude of other men, far away from us, who are faced with the problems to which we react. That solidarity is extremely real. It makes us, to some extent, jointly responsible.

It is important to know what faith (or theology, which interprets and elaborates the indications of faith) has to say on problems of this sort, and in what conditions it can speak. The reflections we shall make on this subject are valid by analogy for other problems in which faith and theology equally have a say. For they have a say wherever human conduct is involved. The words of Alberic Gentil, in reply to the theologians who intervened in questions raised by the colonisation of the New World: 'Silence to the theologians in a domain which is not theirs!'[2], stand self-condemned, and cover their author with ridicule, just as the words of Las Casas or Francis de Vittoria covered them with glory. Theology lays down principles. It therefore also excludes, rejects and condemns maxims or courses of conduct contrary to the principles it lays down. From those principles it draws a certain number of conclusions.

But between these principles and their most general conclusions must be located the intermediate effect of facts and situations. Moral theology has always known them under the name of circumstances. It has generally analysed them within the setting of individual life and personal action, not of collective life and the infinitely complex web of history. But when questions are raised on this level, as is the case today with many problems of relations between races, we must remember that between the most transcendent principles and the solution lies the mediation of facts, situations, political, economic and cultural structures, of certain conditions of life and certain representations which are at the same time, and equally, very stable and very mobile: stable on the short view and in times of calm, but developing on the long term and more rapidly in times of crisis and instability.[3]

When we speak of the mediation of historical situations, representations and structures, this must be understood in two directions: what proceeds from the transcendent idea to the solutions and what proceeds from the facts to the ideas, considered in their process of application. On the one hand, the solutions (which in any case are not obtained once for all but are perfectible) pass through representations and structures, they form them and become part of them. On the other hand, the principles find their way to the solutions by taking account, as a relative but sometimes practically imperative fact, of the historical situations, representations and structures existing at the time.

There is the direct, abrupt way, which spurns the situations of fact and immediately projects the absolute demands of the transcendent ideal into a future which is hurried on by some convulsion and heroic action. It is the way, not of the reformers but of revolutionaries; it is also the way of the prophets. It was followed in an exceptionally pure and brilliant way, in the field which concerns us, by Mahatma Gandhi. He met his death in the end from the bullet of a Hindu, who accused him of betraying Hinduism by practising and preaching brotherhood between Hindus and Moslems. He died a witness to brotherly love, a victim of religious and racial strife. It is a fact that several of those who in late years have been actively and clearly engaged in racial conflicts, trying to bear the burden of them and to overcome their intolerable evil, refer their action to Gandhi and advocate a programme of non-violence.[4]

But one cannot be a prophet just for the asking. It needs a vocation and heroic fidelity. If there is one lesson which Gandhi teaches us it is this, that non-violence is not to be practised simply by joining in a non-violent demonstration or signing a manifesto, or even by fasting in a good cause. The ideal of non-violence involves a total reform of oneself, which is exacting, painful to the flesh, penetrating the whole of one's being, even the most elementary and intimate dispositions: one's judgement, heart and desires, nerves and body, imagination and interior speech, rule of life, etc.

The world needs prophets: it is they who advance things most decisively. But they do not solve all the questions, and history does not always obey them. It is not even certain that their spurning of the intermediaries and the situations is always in place. It must come at its proper time. It is not certain that in a given situation the greatest truth and the greatest love are on the side of the intrepid application of a pure ideal principle, without consideration or compromise of any sort. Think, for example, of a sudden abolition of slavery by the apostles, or of an immediate proclamation of a single liberal code of law for all men, without distinction of race, culture, historical heritage or nationality.

It is well known that all who are alarmed at the proposal of a demanding, more or less revolutionary ideal, are relieved when they are told that we must take account of the circumstances. For then they can recover, and find their feet and breathe again. But they risk merely recovering and no more: that is, denying in practice the ideal they were so alarmed to hear proposed. The demands of the absolute, pure principles must not be watered down in passing through the historical structures, respecting the delays, compounding with the arduous and complex conditions of reality. They must be kept alive and reaffirmed in the solution, and beyond their present limits. The spirit is neither enclosed in the forms in which it strives to be expressed, nor exhausted by them. It insists on going beyond. Thus, for example, the demands of human brotherhood which flow from the gospel do not abolish the legitimacy of national structures, but they are not wholly satisfied by them. Over and above his military service, which may be combatant service, the Christian faithful to the gospel must try to assert love and brotherhood:[5] he must even try to promote their diffusion in structures better than those we have. This much is certain, that if Christians can be blamed for anything, it is for having often been too timid and conformist.

The application of theology to such a question as that of interracial relations involves, therefore, these three stages: first, stating the principles and their consequences in their absolute truth. Second, applying them in practice in the conditions of the historical circumstances. Third, in this stage itself and beyond, actively searching for a greater fidelity to the absolute nature of the principles and their demands, to the point of having to act as witness or prophet, even at the risk of bodily harm. We propose to examine the racial question from the point of view of Christian doctrine, according to these three stages in turn.[6]

Christianity absolutely rejects racialism

Racialism means distinguishing between human groups, and placing them in an order of importance, discriminating against certain of them, asserting that their human qualities and characteristics are genetically determined and fixed.

Certain racialists argue from the bible; on the one hand, from the very idea of the election of a *people* as such, along with the order to exterminate others (Amalekites, Philistines, etc.); on the other hand, from the biblical story about the descendants of Noah, and particularly Ham, cursed for his lack of filial piety. Some English writers in the eighteenth and nineteenth centuries defended the slave trade on these grounds. Quite recently, a Calvinist pastor in South Africa justified *apartheid* from the bible.[7] This is an example of what results from the tendency, so dear to upholders of theocracy, to claim that they know from the bible what God thinks of the history of their time. But the abominable legend of 'the accursed sons of Ham' has no foundation in theological tradition.[8]

In point of fact, the bible is not racialist.[9] The election of a people as such, which is at the heart of the old dispensation,[10] is not based on blood nor on genetically determined human qualities, but on the will of God, *in spite of* the lack—or rather we should say, *because of* the lack—of human greatness in that people.

It is true that Israel always set a high value on her position compared with that of other peoples, but it was from a religious point of view, that of her own election, and the ignorance of the other nations as to the place of the true God.[11] It is religion, not race, which admits a man to Israel.[12] Besides, even the election of a people as such is superseded since the coming of the Son of God and the sending of the Holy Spirit. The universalist proclamations, already numerous in the Old Testament, especially in the prophets,[13] become a reality in the Church. Her catholicity, proclaimed from the moment of her birth on the day of Pentecost in the sign of the tongues, shows that the Church, *by her very existence*, is the negation of racialism. In the religious relationship with the Father, by the Son, in the Holy Spirit, which is the very substance of Christianity, there is absolutely *no* discrimination based on any racial particularity. There is a priority of divine economy in favour of the Jews, for everything began in Jerusalem.[14] There is a historical priority of the east, then of the Greco-Roman world, then of the white peoples of the west, including America, in the propagation of the gospel. But this providentially willed priority is only historical, so much so that it is not unreasonable to suppose that one day our paganised continent might be re-evangelised by coloured men, the pagans of yesterday, the Christians of today and tomorrow. However that may be, in the Church as she has been in the past and as she is today, there is absolute equality in the order of faith, of love, of prayer, of salvation and of the communion of saints. On this plane, there is really neither Jew nor Greek, neither slave nor free, but one and the same life in Jesus Christ.[15]

A racialist assertion, with the consequences of segregation which it entails, would strike at the very heart of Christianity and even of biblical Judaism. For this is its heart, that there is one God, and he is the Father of all; all good proceeds from him; men, his children, are brothers; they are called to imitate God, their Father, by loving as he loves, excluding nothing except evil. In particular, to exclude anyone on the pretext of fixed genetically determined characteristics, which would make human groups radically unequal, is, biblically and Christianly speaking, atheism. For it is to deny that God is God. How could we say 'Our Father', if we excluded some men from the quality of brothers, and therefore of children of God? We might still, indeed, invoke 'Providence' or 'Destiny', and do so under the name of 'God': even Hitler allowed himself this. It would be a lie and a blasphemy, for we should be denying him whom we thus invoked.

In a general way, one of the biblical truths most urgently needing to be meditated, proclaimed and put into practice, is the union of anthropology and theology; the fact that the former is based on the latter, but also the impossibility of framing a true statement on the true God which is not pregnant with decisive statements on man himself. The bible is not a textbook of science, it is not even a history textbook in the ordinary and secular sense of the word. It tells us about God and ourselves: about God first, and about ourselves in the close relation which unites us to God and is such that man loses his true nature if he does not maintain that relation; but it is also such that we misunderstand God if we misunderstand the image of God which is in man. Thus the universal and brotherly love of men is a direct consequence of monotheism.

Now on the plane of ideas racialism is the radical negation of brotherly love: it destroys it on the plane of psychological dispositions. For if charity is ever to advance from a purely general profession to effective, concrete attitudes, it must presuppose certain dispositions of heart and mind, which may be summed up as the brotherly sense of the other. Just as religious sentiment rests on a certain moral structure of respect, so Christian love of our neighbour rests on a certain sense of the other, consisting of an absence of contempt and mistrust and the presence of an *a priori* openness and sympathy, a desire to understand and share. Racial prejudice and, still more, racialism raised to a theory, implies not love but contempt and mistrust of the other. The colonial, in his unfavourable aspect, has been characterised by a lack of the sense of the other.[16] The racialist carries about with him a 'colonial' mentality and takes it to extremes: moreover he is, as we shall see, a twin brother of the colonial. And as nothing is more impassioned, more unreflecting, than a prejudice of one group against another, the racialist becomes the slave of a real complex, which saps the very roots of his charity.

St John, the apostle of love, says: 'He who hates his brother is a murderer.'[17] It is true. It is impossible to hate a man, or even to despise him, without at some time having a thought like this: creatures like that should not be allowed to live! But Dostioevsky has shown us, in his character Smerdiakov, in *The Brothers Karamazov*, that such a thought is the very principle of murder.

As I grow in age and experience, I am increasingly struck by the fact that the reality of moral attitudes begins at the level of knowledge, of representations and understanding. We too often forget this, and that is why so many good intentions, though perfectly sincere, remain sterile and useless. Many think that morality begins with feelings and that the field of knowledge or the use of the intelligence have nothing to do with it. Nothing could be less true. There is a duty of knowledge: ignorance can be a sin, and in this connection so can stupidity. There is a duty to be informed, to have true representations. There is obviously a duty to express an accurate thought truly. In many very important spheres, inability to respond to the demands of Love and the Spirit of God springs from grave failings, by deed and omission, on the level of knowledge and representations. *Esprit de corps*, first cousin of the spirit of pride and self-justification, is one of the greatest obstacles to the establishment of healthy and Christian relations between human groups. It plays a great part in those 'non-theological factors' of opposition, which in turn have such a decisive part in maintaining, to say the least, our Christian divisions.[18] The field of interracial relationships is obviously its favourite ground. Nothing is easier than to connect a certain number of faults, which displease or annoy me, with the colour of a skin, the shape of a face, the use of a language, the images of a style of life different from my own and perhaps very poor. Propaganda and caricature readily make use of certain real elements (which are easy to grasp but should have been criticised), in order to create complexes of feeling, often all the more powerful because they are neither tested nor kept under control. Nazi racialism learned to carry this art to a high degree of perfection, to the special detriment of the Jews.

Thus the first duty of the Christian, and indeed of every man who wants to preserve a genuine brotherly sense of the other, is to criticise his representations, to keep up a vigilant resistance to propaganda and images which foster and express *esprit de corps*: then to build up in himself, by true information and, if possible, by personal contacts (for which there is no adequate substitute), a psychological structure of potential brotherly communion. We can never insist too strongly on these questions of representations and images, of information and contact, nor on the harm caused by distortions and propaganda.

Racialism is a recent phenomenon. As a theory it dates from

the nineteenth century (the romantic nordic myth: Gobineau; H. S. Chamberlain, the source of the mediocre Alfred Rosenberg). Even the idea of 'race' was not recognised till the eighteenth century. In the first half of the nineteenth it was still not widespread in France, and the word only had the sense of stock, line or family, considered in their origin and physical unity.[19] As an attitude, racialism is the twin brother of colonialism. The anti-semitism of antiquity and, deplorably, of Christians (some traces in the Fathers, many events in the Middle Ages, mingled with an attitude of tolerance and respect), was not racialist in origin.[20] The notorious phrase *perfidia judaica* belongs to an entirely theological category, even sometimes canonical-theological: it stands for the refusal or the absence (possibly culpable) of faith in Jesus Christ, in members of the people whom God had loved and chosen.[21] It is well known that John XXIII removed these words from the prayers of Good Friday.

The first manifestation of racialism, and those very marked, are found in certain Spanish conquerors of the New World; though even these men were not without a certain missionary viewpoint, unenlightened but subjectively sincere.[22]

Solorzano tells us in his *De Indiarum Iure* that many denied that the Indians were truly human, in spite of their human appearance, because they lacked intelligence. Peter Martyr Anghiera, Francis Lopez de Gomara, Peter de Cieza of Leon, Girolamo Benzoni (of Milan), Simon Majolus, Gregory Garcia (although a colleague of the admirable Las Casas), repeated, all through the sixteenth century, a slogan which enabled them to keep the Indians in *encomienda*, that is, in a condition of near slavery. It was then that Pope Paul III, at the instigation of the Dominican Julius Garcez, Bishop of Tlascala, published a series of bulls in May and June 1537 which no doubt represent the first pronouncements of the Roman *magisterium* on racial questions:

> It has come to our ears that our beloved son in Christ, Charles, Emperor of the Romans and also King of Castile and Leon, has published an edict against those who, inflamed with greed, were displaying an inhuman spirit towards the human race: an edict forbidding his subjects to reduce the Indians of the West and South to slavery or to deprive them of their

goods. Considering the Indians themselves who, though outside the fold of the Church, are not deprived and must not be deprived of their freedom or their goods, since they are men, and therefore capable of faith and salvation, and must not be reduced to slavery, but invited to life by preaching and example . . . (here follows an excommunication reserved to the Holy See, against all who may reduce the Indians to slavery or deprive them of their goods).[23]

The enemy of the human race has suggested to some of his minions the idea of spreading in the world the opinion that the inhabitants of the West Indies and the southern continents, of whose existence we have only lately learned, should be treated as animals without reason and used exclusively for our profit and service, on the pretext that they did not share the Catholic Faith and were incapable of adopting it.

We, unworthy Vicar of our Lord, have to direct all our efforts to guarding the flock entrusted to us, and also to bringing the scattered sheep to safety. We see the Indians as real men, who are not only capable of adopting the Christian faith, but aspire to it.

And with the desire of remedying the evil that has been done, we decide and declare by this present letter (of which every priest must sanction the translation by his seal) that the said Indians, together with all other tribes whom Christendom may yet in the future come to know, must not be deprived of their freedom or their goods—allegations to the contrary notwithstanding—even if they are not Christians, but on the contrary they must be left in the enjoyment of their freedom and their goods.

The Indians and the other nations who may still be discovered later must be converted only by the word of God and the example of a good and holy life.[24]

Next year[25] the Dominican Francis de Vittoria, in his lectures on temperance, and then in 1539 in his *De Indis*, established that, the Indians being men, the same law applied to them and in Spain. In a world of enlarged horizons, before the new fact of Europeans and men of colour living together, and faced with the first pretensions of a bitter and violent colonialism, the Church's position was clearly defined: the Indians—and equally black and yellow races—are men *like Europeans*. Neither natural law, nor faith, nor salvation know the barrier of race.

Christianity therefore absolutely rejects all discrimination in principle which claims to justify itself by the idea of race. However, it gives the facts of race a positive sense and accepts their value on its own grounds for existence and expansion. To tell the truth, it is wrong to speak here of the facts of race, isolating them from the much more complex fact of the existence of peoples and nations: the Catholic liturgy speaks of 'peoples', and so do the Fathers. They see the entry of the different peoples—each with its genius, expressed in its culture and language—into the great Catholic unity of the Church, as a realisation of the Church's catholicity and the grace of Christ, who wills to be 'fulfilled in all'.[26] The fullness potentially contained in Adam became explicit in the course of human history: it is in fact the foundation of that history. It is called to enter into the body of the Second Adam, the sole final object of God's good pleasure, and to deploy the infinite riches of his grace. The Church is thus built from above and from below, from heaven and from earth, from Christ and from Adam.

Clearly, this idea of catholicity is an ideal. It is real, certainly, but it has hardly been granted us to perceive, in detail, all its positive and beneficial reality. *In history*, the entry of peoples and the contributions of races has often given rise to crises, for whenever the human asserts itself, particularism appears. When we come in contact with some culture, remote from its own proper world, perhaps rather rough, alien, ill-balanced, uncreative, we realise that the ideal of catholicity I have described requires more faith and less carnal spirit than is usually ours.

The rôle of the historical structures

In a speech delivered on the first of January 1891, for the anniversary of the 1863 Emancipation Act, Archbishop Ireland of St Paul celebrated the abolition of slavery and then, on the question of Negroes in the United States, took up a position condemning all segregation.[27] He broke all barriers, swept aside all arguments pleaded in favour of maintaining or erecting it. But in conclusion he added:

> Must the homes of the Whites be opened to the Negroes? Must I meet them in my drawing-room, in perfect social equality? I answer that every man is master in his own house: our homes are privileged places where each of us follows his own tastes and desires, and no one, White or Black, rich or poor, can cross its threshold without the owner's invitation, and no one has the right to censure the owner's conduct.

By giving his answer on the plane of personal freedom and the sacredness of the domestic hearth, Archbishop Ireland placed it on unassailable ground. The question, however, goes far beyond that of whether I must receive men of another colour in my home. For that is not difficult, and happens often enough in our country. The real question is whether social life as such should be carried on regardless of the existence of different ethnic or racial groups, doing away with every difference, not only of behaviour—that concerns everyone—but of treatment.

The problem is not too difficult in a country like France: or rather, the number of men of other races—Negroes or North African Moslems—who live among us is so small that it is possible not to see the problem. It remains a matter of individual cases. But in a country like South Africa the material facts present an extremely difficult problem, and world opinion has been informed about it in a great many publications, some documentary and sociological, others literary.[27] About nine million Africans, belonging to several peoples, and three hundred thousand Indians, live alongside two and a half million whites and one million coloured. The whites, descendants of the Dutch colonists and French Huguenot or English emigrants, possess 83 per cent of the land and all the political power: scarcely five per cent of the Africans can read or write, although considerable efforts and large sums have been devoted to providing schools for their use. A draconian code of law maintains a total separation, and prevents even physical contact between whites and coloured (*apartheid*); the latter provide a labour force, miserably poor and uprooted from its original surroundings, for the industries managed by the whites for their own benefit.

It is evident that in the religious sphere the law of human equality and fraternity is of force directly and absolutely. For the last ten years scarcely a week has passed without Christians and ecclesiastics of different communions speaking and acting in their support. Catholics are far from being the last in this.[29] But the Pastoral Letter of the Catholic archbishops and bishops of South Africa, dealing with the general question in May 1952, made the following statement:

> If the attitude of the Europeans were the only reason for the racial problem in South Africa, it would be easy to condemn it as unjust and unchristian, and to try to eliminate it by suitable and gradual education. But the problem is more complex than that. It arises because the majority of non-Europeans, and especially the Africans, have not yet reached the degree of development which would permit their integration with the Europeans in a homogeneous society. Any attempt to induce them, all at once and by force, to adopt the European customs and usages would be an illusion. . . .

The bishops then listed four areas of difficulty. The third was the existence of a group of non-Europeans, divided and at odds with one another, the majority of whom were still incapable, as a whole, of taking part in a social and political life of a western level and style. There lies the problem. The gospel excludes *absolutely* any discrimination based on race. But when we proceed from the principle of fraternity and equality to the practice of an egalitarian and fraternal social life, other elements besides race have to be considered. They belong to that mediation of certain representations, historical situations and social (and economic) structures of which we have spoken. How can men form a society together if they have nothing in common in the order of culture, hygiene, the representation and idea of life, their most spontaneous customs and reactions? A certain amount of 'every man in his own home' is obviously justifiable. It must never, however, be justified by a *racial* principle as such, and therefore never by the criterion of colour. We must never allow or seek protection in a situation in which one group, considered inferior, is oppressed by another, considered superior, nor yet in a situation in which the law, or custom with the force of law, sanctions inequality in what concerns the rights of the person. Finally, social justice in the realm of law, and charity in the supernatural order, imposes strictly on the different groups, each in proportion to its means, the duty of working for the promotion of relations of trust, understanding and esteem, justice, friendship and brotherhood.

On the subject of South Africa, where these problems today are at their most acute, another consideration is sometimes mentioned. It concerns a challenge to the white race and to the assured primacy which in fact it holds at present in the world, as the bearer of cultural values of priceless worth. It certainly looks as if the achievement of mankind's highest values were in effect bound up with the white race.

Personally I am far from deaf to this consideration, provided it is understood that the highest human value upheld by the white race is that of respect for the person. This is a part of the truth, but a relative part, which must be carefully weighed. Certainly the values of rationality, of personalisation, of freedom, which have been developed by the white race, and also owe so much to Christianity, are no small things! All the same, the balance is far from being entirely on one side. Analytic genius is not the whole, nor perhaps the last word, of the life of the spirit. Whites (and Christians too, unhappily) have not avoided, they have even carried everywhere, the love of profit, of purely material comfort, and the abominable reign of money. They will perish of it. We may wonder, in fact, from the Christian point of view, whether a challenge to the white race and its historical primacy is not a condition for the gospel and the design of Pentecost to be more effectively carried out. The Church and the gospel are themselves independent of that primacy. No doubt they must become so more effectively, by the coming of new historical conditions. This cannot come about without crisis, like any great historico-social change, and it is inevitable that the crisis will involve shocks, disintegrations and wounds. Should we not face them positively, in faith, hope and charity? Is not that an element in that Christ-assumption of time, about which I was speaking earlier?

Let us hear the lesson of one of our predecessors. Writing about the year 417, just when the arrival of the Barbarians was challenging the order of the Roman Empire, in which Christianity had taken form and developed (an order quite as good as that of the west in the nineteenth century), Orosius, a disciple of

Augustine, thus expressed his thoughts in a little book called (nonetheless) 'Against the Pagans':

> If the Barbarians have been sent on to Roman soil for this one end that the Christian Churches of East and West should be filled with Huns, Swabians, Vandals and Burgundians, and countless other races of Christians, we ought to praise and exalt the mercy of God because, *though it be through our destruction*, so many nations have seen the truth of Revelation, which without doubt they could only discover by this means.[30]

Above all compromises, the mind of Christ is supreme.

'Fundamental equality', I wrote in 1953,[31] 'does not necessarily involve all factual equalities on the level of cultural, social or political life. The transcendent principle of human equality is expressed in that of the primary natural rights, those which are summed up in the words: "the dignity of the human person". But there are men who cannot read, and there are men who do not wash. Others, who do wash and can read, are not bound, at all costs and in everything, to associate with them.' Upon which a Swiss official of *Pax Romana* pointed out to me, alluding also to the words of Archbishop Ireland quoted above: 'When we talk with educated negroes or with the poor, or with any of those who are repulsed by "good society", they often say that equality of civic and political rights matter little to them so long as people will not receive them or marry them.'

Here, in fact, is a pretty good test of our freedom from all racialist attitudes: would we marry a negro or negress? Would we let our daughter marry a negro? But the full practice of the spirit of the gospel goes far beyond such questions, which can only be individual. In reality it is the whole complex of the relations between human groups, and especially racial groups, which beyond all the political, economic, social and cultural conditions, must be traversed, animated and if necessary overthrown, by the gospel imperatives of brotherhood and love.

On many occasions popes have exhorted Christians to make charity a principle of social and political action, and not merely a purely personal and inner motive or dynamic principle of inspiration, but a standard determining the actual content of the action. 'The political domain concerns the whole of society and in that respect is the field of the widest sort of charity, political charity.'[32] That means that charity, the love which proceeds from God himself, which loves all that God loves and as he loves it, is not only a principle of personal life, but seeks to animate all the human behaviour of Christians, including the plane of social and public relations. It means that in the matter of interracial relations the Christian must not only *endure* the delays and compromises imposed by the historical structures: for these are human and relative, susceptible of being evolved and fashioned by men. The love with which God loves men, which in us is charity, must be applied to loving them *as* God loves them[33] and be affirmed *in* those historical situations as a moving, inspiring and normative element, so as to introduce into them elements which are living and dynamic, generating new situations. Today, within the framework of their desires to embrace as Christians the unhappy and tragic world in which they live, many Christians have heard that call to be a sort of firstfruits, in that direction, of a world more conformed to the gospel. In North and South Africa, in the United States, here in France, everywhere in short, some Christians are creating relations of love and brotherly service, between groups which are opposed but have already risen above unjust, cruel or conflict-laden social situations.[34] That is their vocation. Like the roots of a tree, which find their way through the almost invisible interstices of a mass of rock or a cement wall, and end by cracking or splitting them, those acts of love and brotherhood work with the irrepressible dynamism of truth and life.

Life is not analytic but synthetic. For the sake of clear argument we have distinguished three stages, but in actual life they must be put together again. It is in one single activity that Christians live the absoluteness of the Gospel imperatives, the adaptation to factual circumstances, the slow maturing of the human situations, the call to supercede them, the possibly prophetic testimonies to love, *as* God loves. The Christian's attitude to the facts of race is composed of all these together.

NOTES

1. Published in *Revue de l'Action Populaire*, no. 142, Nov. 1960, pp. 1031–40.
2. *De Jure Belli*, 1588.
3. To give some examples, it is obvious that the gospel required, and was bound some day to bring about, the abolition of slavery, just as it requires today, as always, the abolition of the proletarian condition and of war, for all these things are contrary to its affirmation of human brotherhood, founded on the affirmation of monotheism and the fatherhood of God. But for slavery to be eliminated, many representations had to evolve and new structures of economy and work had to be created. It will be the same for the elimination of war and the proletarian condition. We may regret that the evolution has been so slow, and Christians so timid, often in fact so little Christian, so little anxious to honour the demands and appeals of the gospel. It is also a fact that we usually exaggerate the obstacles which delay the creation of new structures. In 1936 there were those who said that paid holidays would ruin our economy. When a crisis or a revolution obliges us to make haste, we find solutions, all the same. We say that charity constrains us, but it hardly looks like it!
4. For example, Michael Scott (*A Time to Speak*, New York, 1958), who has worked among the Herreros of South West Africa; Martin Luther King (*Stride towards Freedom*, New York, 1958), who tells the story of the negroes of Montgomery, Alabama.
5. The state, the supreme public authority in the national order, certainly has the right to impose military service on those citizens who are capable of performing it. The French state has the right to send young Frenchmen to Algeria. It can commit them to the act of war and demand the sacrifice of their lives. It has these rights because national communities are legitimate and valid structures of earthly human life. But their legitimacy does not derive from any eternal, divine law, nor even from an absolutely essential condition of human nature. There exists a human community above and beyond national communities. If some day human life were to be effectively organised on the level of the universal community of men (as it has begun to be in some particular sectors and has always been the case with the Church), it is clear that the conditions of validity of the national communities, in so far as they claim and exercise the attributes of sovereignty (and especially the right to make their interests prevail by force), would be correspondingly modified. *Absolute* conscientious objection ignores what is *at present* a legitimate structure of human society. That is the decisive reason why I, personally, reject it, while recognising its possibility as a prophetic affirmation or a personal vocation, and wishing that we could have a law to guarantee the rights of objectors. But it is clear that the structures of human community which legitimise national state sovereignty, with national armies and national military service, have not the absolute, sacred character which they would have if they had a divine, eternal origin, flowing from the timeless nature of things. One day, no doubt, the present state of affairs will be left behind. There are already many signs of this. But the structures now in existence, and legitimate, would have to evolve. Once again, I cannot proceed immediately from

the affirmation of brotherhood and the law of Christian charity to deduce a line of conduct which would express them all at once and just as they are. Between the transcendent principles and the actual conclusions there lies an intermediate influence of national or historical structures, which conditions the application of those principles. But, though some of these structures belong to the essential nature of things, there are some which are merely historical, which can be changed and in fact are being changed.

6. Several of the points following are developed in my pamphlet *L'Église catholique devant la question raciale*, published by UNESCO in 1953.

7. Thus H. J. C. Snijders; see SOEPI, 16th May 1958, p. 2.

8. See P. Charles, 'Les Noirs, fils de Cham maudit', in *NRT*, 1928, pp. 721–39.

9. See *L'Église catholique* . . ., pp. 29f; Everett Tilson (Prot.), *Segregation and the Bible*, New York, 1958.

10. See Deut 7:7; 10:14–15; Ezk 16:3–15; 1 Cor 1:27.

11. See E. Weber, art. 'Laos' in *TWB z. NT*, vol. IV, pp. 45f.

12. See Judith 14:10; J. Bonsirven, *Le Judaïsme palestinien au temps de Jésus-Christ*, Paris, 1935; vol. I, p. 19. The conversion of the Khazars of the southern Volga to Judaism (ninth–tenth centuries).

13. See *L'Église catholique* . . ., p. 32.

14. See Jn 4:22; Rom 1:16; 2:10; Lk 24:27.

15. See Gal 3:28; Col 3:11.

16. See O. Mannoni, *Psychologie de la Colonisation*, Paris, 1950.

17. 1 Jn 3:15.

18. This subject of the 'non-theological factors' of division has been much studied in the ecumenical movement, at the 1937 Conferences, then at the Ecumenical Institute at Bossey in Nov. 1951, then at the Lund Conference in Aug. 1952. See M. Villain, *Introduction à l'Œcuménisme*, Paris, 1958, pp. 72–5;

19. Thus still found in Chateaubriand. No doubt it was Kant who gave the first precise definition of the concept of race: *Bestimmung des Begriffs einer Menschenrasse*, 1785: Werke, vol. IV, p. 225.

20. For antiquity and early Christianity, see M. Simon, *Verus Israel*, Paris, 1948, p. 239.

21. On this subject we had the scientific studies of E. Peterson, ('Perfidia judaica' in *EL*, 1936, pp. 296–311), of J. M. Oesterreicher ('Pro perfidis judaeis' in *Theological Studies*, March 1947, pp. 80f), of B. Blumenkranz ('Perfidia' in *Arch. Latinitatis Medii Aevi*, 1952, pp. 157–70). Even before the suppression of the troublesome words by John XXIII, the Congregation of Rites had approved the translations 'unbelief', 'refusal to believe' (*AAS*, 1948, p. 342).

22. We have two excellent studies on ideas which operated in various senses in the Spanish colonisation of the sixteenth century: J. Hoefner, *Christentum und Menschenwürde. Das Anliegen der Spanische Kolonialethik im Goldenen Zeitalter*, Trier, 1947; Lewis Hanke, *Colonisation et conscience chrétienne au XVIe siècle*, Paris, 1957.

23. Bull (or Brief) *Pastorale officium*, addressed to Cardinal John of Tavera, Archbishop of Toledo, 29th May 1538.

24. Bull *Sublimis Deus*, 2nd June 1537 (some date it 19th June). On the same day, another Bull, *Veritas ipsa*, to the Discalced Religious, expressed the same ideas.

25. Madrid, 1934.

26. Eph 1:23. For this theology of catholicity, see my *Divided Christendom*, London and New York, 1938, ch. III; the art. 'Catholicité' in *Catholicisme*, vol. II, col. 722–5; 'Unité de l'humanité et vocation des peoples', in *Vie Sp.*,

Suppl. no. 44 (1958–1), pp. 70–87; H. de Lubac, *Catholicisme. Les aspects sociaux du dogme* (*Unam Sanctam*, 3), Paris, 1938. (English trans., *Catholicism*, London and New York, 1950.)

The encyclical *Evangelii Praecones* emphasises respect for the cultures of every people and the contribution which these cultures can make to Catholicity.

27. Text in my *L'Église catholique . . .*, pp. 46f.

28. Besides Gandhi's autobiography, there is Alan Paton's *Cry, the beloved Country*, London and New York, 1948, and the story of Peter Abrahams, *I am not a free Man*. Among recent reports are E. H. Brookes and J. B. Macaulay, *Civil Liberty in South Africa*, London, 1958; Archbishop Hurley, 'La legislation raciale en Afrique du Sud', in *Doc. cath.*, 56 (1959), col. 857–61; *Informations Catholiques Internationales*, no. 122 (15th June 1960), pp. 11–23.

29. Various manifestations can be followed in *Inform. Cath. Intern.* (for example, for U.S.A., no. 62 of 15th Dec. 1957); from the Protestant or Anglican side, in SOEPI (Geneva).

30. VII, 41:4. On this 'passons aux barbares' (Ozanam) of the early Church, see J. R. Palanque, etc., *Le Christianisme et l'Occident barbare*, Paris, 1945; A. Mandouze, 'The Church and the Collapse of Roman Civilisation', in *History's Lessons for Tomorrow's Mission*, Geneva, 1960, pp. 39–50.

31. See *L'Église catholique . . .*, p. 58.

32. Pius XI. See also the letter signed by Cardinal Dell'Acqua, addressed to M. Raoul Delgrange, president of the Conference of international Catholic organisations, 8th April 1957, *Doc. cath.*, 54 (1957), col. 603–5. See also A. Liégé in *Équipes enseignantes*, 2nd term, 1957.

33. See Mt 5:43–8.

34. Many facts will be found, for example, in *Missi*; in the *Bulletin du Cercle St-Jean Baptiste*; in the *Inf. Cath. Int.* (see above, n. 29). Also, with a mainly Protestant documentation, Harriet Hamon Dexter, *What's Right with Race Relations*, New York, 1958.

CHAPTER ELEVEN

The Question of Interracial Marriages[1]

I SHALL NOT HERE CONSIDER MARRIAGES contracted in countries inhabited by people of different race or colour, by Europeans who have lived there for some time. In those cases it is usually the man who is European. I shall consider marriages between Europeans and persons of another race or colour who have come to work or study in the west. In such cases it is nearly always the girl who is the European.

These marriages take place. They seem to be rare in Germany and Switzerland, where the social and family background does its best to prevent the parties meeting, even when the girls might desire it. They are found in England and even more often in France. The United States are a case apart, and I shall not deal with them here.

In France we are chiefly concerned either with North African Moslems who have come to work in the towns or, mainly, with Indo-Chinese or negroes who have come to study in the universities. There are no statistics that I know of, but at a guess about ten per cent of Christian negro students end by marrying French girls. There are many reasons for this. They are often very handsome, attractive boys and the winning of a white girl no doubt seems something desirable in their eyes. Finally, and this is a serious motive, they can scarcely find any African women at their level of culture, because of their education and their contact with the west. The difficulties facing such unions are easily imagined.

The first occurs at the outset, especially in bourgeois families, which are usually the ones concerned. The negro student may be received very kindly, as a friend of the children, but as soon as the girl speaks of him as her fiancé, there is very often opposition. Often the family absolutely refuses, perhaps for reasons I shall develop later, perhaps owing to a general, unreflecting reflex. If the girl persists, the parents may break with her and repudiate her. Generally the break does not last and a reconciliation takes place after two or three years.

The second difficulty is the situation which awaits the girl. It is obviously necessary that she and her future husband should share a really common outlook on life. This is a condition, in my opinion the most important, of every union if it is to have any chance, humanly speaking, of success. The question of religion is here of such decisive importance that it can scarcely be exaggerated, because it is bound up not only with moral judgements and the scale of values, but with fundamental psychological attitudes, with social frameworks, even, it may be, with the rules and laws of the community. Personally, I should be strongly opposed on principle to marriages with Moslems, and indeed, they are much frowned on in Moslem countries.[2] Islam has so formed the mentality of the peoples it has conquered that there is little hope of any real community of outlook on life. The difficulties may perhaps not be so acute as long as the couple remain in the west. But what if they had to settle in a Moslem country? Islam is solidly and indissolubly a religion, a canon law, a form of life, a legal code, a policy and a culture, all at once. Even apart from divorce or polygamy, which are always possible, Islam allots a much lower position to women than that known by European women. And what would become of their Christianity?

With a negro boy, things do not necessarily go any better. From the material point of view, everything depends on the post he obtains. The most delicate point is connected with the close cohesion of the African family and the inviolable nature of its customs. It is a difficulty not only for the white girls but for the negro family. The family wonders whether the girl will accept their customs; the girl must wonder if she will be accepted by the family. If the family has accepted the marriage and the girl, there will be no difficulty in the second generation about the integration of the children.

For all these reasons, and also so that she may know what she will find, it is a good thing for the European girl, before entering on a definite engagement, to go for a visit and spend a year, for example, in Africa.

Such marriages belong *par excellence* to the sphere in which my former distinction, between the question of race or colour, and that of social or cultural milieu, can and must be applied. Christianity, and even human truth, on a lower level, make it a duty for us to exclude from our hearts all feelings or expressions of segregation motivated by reasons of race or colour as such. That leaves some *real* and reasonable questions (not intact, of course, but at least asked) as to the community life or union made possible by the cultural state, differences of mentality, diversity of language or social inequality. Such problems sometimes exist already between members of the same country, Christians of the same religion, enjoying the same level of culture and comfort, and so on, for example, in Belgium, between Flemings and Walloons. Clearly, these problems may become so acute, and present such insoluble difficulties, when it is a case of Europeans on one side and native Africans on the other, that not only is one excused from the duty of living a common life, but it is completely mistaken (except in some extraordinary case) to want to unite two lives in marriage. Difficulties which do not exist in Europe, or in a Europeanised milieu in another continent, can be insuperable if a young man takes his wife to the Far East or to Africa, where he risks being caught up by a milieu which is really too different. But for *him*, life in a European or Europeanised milieu must also present difficult problems.

The obvious danger, when we dwell on these difficulties, is that we may glide from one motive to another: either we carry over social or cultural disparity to the plane of *strictly* racial disparity or discrimination, and ascribe to the colour of the skin our repulsion for manners of behaviour or life which are alien to our own, or we allow an irrational racial prejudice, more or less masked and more or less violent, to colour our appreciation of the social, cultural or religious disparity. We think we are absolutely free from racialism, and then one day, if we are at all perceptive about ourselves, we see that we have just had a reaction secretly caused by a racialist attitude. To purify one's heart of racial prejudice requires much self-mastery and self-control, clear perception, watchfulness and self-criticism, not to mention a sense of humour. To be Christians we need to be intelligent and use our intelligence. This is increasingly true, as the world becomes more complicated and men more demanding, having learned from history and revolution. If there is one truth I have learned from life, it is this, that truth is not unilinear, but dialectic: I mean that we must always hold to two poles, between which there is a certain tension or opposition, though both are necessary. If ever deliberately or actually, though legitimately, I turn aside a gesture of concrete community of life with the Other, I must question my heart, which God tests as he tests the heart and reins.[3] We must ask ourselves whether our profoundest attitudes are those of the Gospel.

Our relations with the other are in the foreground of our present-day problems. On the one hand, modern psychology has rediscovered, with fresh precision, that man's health depends on the truth of this relation with others, and that the secret of that truth lies in knowing that the other is a person too, that is, an original centre of consciousness, of representation and construction of the world, an original centre of consciousness with its own projects, joys, ambitions and disappointments, its lawful space for self-expression and self-affirmation.[4] Human health consists in respecting the other as being a person equally with oneself, and if possible communicating with him in love and inner freedom.

On the other hand, it seems that today the susceptibility of persons, their vivid awareness of being original subjects of consciousness and projects, has increased. And at the same time, the world has become smaller: we have become physically nearer to one another, we touch one another more often and more closely. It is just when the world is becoming unified that national feelings are being expressed with terrible virulence, especially among peoples who have hitherto been more or less oppressed or held in tutelage. The peace of the world is at stake. That peace, like peace in the family and with its neighbours, depends on each one recognising the other for what he is and respecting the legitimate plan of life he has formed as a person. Yes, that is the secret of peace. It is one of the elements of that order, of which peace is simply the tranquillity.[5]

When it is a question of the different Churches, that truth of the relations with the others is called ecumenism. Other factors of course, special to this domain, come in to complicate the question. But this one, in an initial and decisive moment, is present on the plane of our relations with the others. On that plane, there is an analogy, a profound relationship, a solidarity, between the attitudes we adopt in the different fields of relations between human groups in the same country, of interracial relations, of interdenominational relations and of peace. In these different domains a man's fundamental attitude will be much the same. If one has it, one naturally has it in all the fields where it applies.

NOTES

1. A note prepared for my book published in German, *Die katholische Kirche und die Rassenfrage*, Recklinghausen, 1961, pp. 101–8. On this question I recommend *Le Problème racial*, by J. Poirier and others, Lyons, *Soc. Public. Mission.*, 1961 (published after this note was written).
2. See the periodical *Nord-Africains en France. Comprendre*, no. 10 (10th Sept. 1957).
3. Ps 7:10; 25:2, Vulg.
4. I recommend the reading of F. Künkel, *Die Arbeit am Charakter*, Schwerin, 1929. Also, M. Oraison, *Devant l'illusion et l'angoisse*, Paris, 1958, esp. p. 47.
5. This is the famous definition by Augustine, '*tranquillitas ordinis*': *De Civ. Dei*, XIX, 13; see *Sum. Theol.*, IIa IIae, qu. 29, art. 1, ad 1.

INDEX OF NAMES

INDEX OF SUBJECTS